LOS ANGELES TIMES
MODERN CALIFORNIA COOKING

Los Angeles Times

Publisher: John P. Puerner
Editor: John S. Carroll

Los Angeles Times
BOOKS

Book Development General Manager: Carla Lazzareschi

Food Section Editor: Russ Parsons

Design: Tom Trapnell

Nutritional Analysis: Bruce Henstell

ISBN 1-883792-59-2

Copyright © Los Angeles Times 2000

Published by the Los Angeles Times
202 W. 1st St., Los Angeles, CA 90012

First printing September 2000

Printed in the U.S.A.

Table of Contents

Key to Recipe Symbols

★   One of the Los Angeles Times'
Best Recipes of the Year

♥   Health-conscious recipe

🕐   Time-saving recipe

INTRODUCTION

I am a born-again Californian.

They say that there are none who believe so strongly as the convert, and I am certainly in no position to dispute that argument. In fact, I offer myself as evidence in its favor. Though I was born in Sacramento, it was to a military family, and the state was just one of many we briefly called home before moving on. It wasn't until I was in my 30s, established in my career and with a family of my own, that I moved back. And though I had lived many places and done many things, in many ways I count that return as the real beginning of my life.

It's all because of food. One thing you learn moving around and living in different places is that food is what sociologists call a "signifier." It is one of the ways that we differentiate ourselves from other people. As important as what we choose to wear or where we choose to live, what we choose to eat is a statement about how we see ourselves. As the French philosopher Brillat-Savarin said: "Tell me what you eat and I will tell you who you are."

Though that might seem a common enough attitude today, it was far from always that way. Before, food was more of a cult. You might meet someone at a party and talk about the things most people talked about—work, sports, family, books, politics—and then a hint would drop. You might say something about eating or cooking and her eyes would light in a particular way. You would respond in kind, and if that first impression turned out to be true, you would sneak off to talk alone, about sautes and barbecues, apples and herbs. You would compare notes on favorite restaurants and exchange tips on wine stores and places to buy cheese. Happy in your secret conversation, the rest of the crowd would fade away and you could talk for hours about cooking. Of course, the party always ended and then you'd skulk back to join the real world. Food was just not something serious people spent much time thinking about.

But when I moved to Los Angeles in 1986, I found a city full of people like me. Food was the common obsession. It seemed that everywhere you went, that was what people were talking about. My aberration was no longer something to be hidden; it was actually encouraged. It was even—dare I say it—considered cool. In California, I learned, sharing food was something that everyone did. Workplace potlucks might hop from Korean noodles to carne asada to Boston baked beans and nobody really thought that much about it. Everyone gardened or knew someone who did, so fresh herbs were not considered the exotic ingredient they were elsewhere. On top of that, with our moderate, Mediterranean climate, they were available all year around. Basil in February, just imagine.

Of course, to a newcomer in the 1980s, the most obvious thing was the restaurants. Los Angeles was just in the process of transforming itself from a graveyard of culinary dinosaurs into one of the most exciting dining cities in the country—and maybe the world. Encouraged by a population flush with boomtown money, chefs played a dizzying game of one-upsmanship, vying to top each other in the lavishness of their restaurants, the exclusiveness of their ingredients, the inventiveness of their technique. The stars came to Patrick Terrail's and Wolfgang Puck's Ma Maison and pretty soon, everyone else wanted to, too. True foodies—in those days that meant the French kind—preferred Jean Bertranou's L'Ermitage. From those wellsprings emerged Spago, Patina, L'Orangerie, Citrus, Michael's, Trumps, Valentino, St. Estephe, Campanile. We had classic French restaurants, a few upscale Italian places (just a hint of the flood that was to come) and even those places called—for want of a better term—New American. Chefs became as popular as ballplayers or actors. Puck, Joachim Splichal, Michael Roberts, Mary Sue Milliken and Susan Feniger, John Sedlar, Michel Richard, Michael McCarty, Mark Peel and Nancy Silverton—the list seemed endless.

All of this high-end dining had a broad trickle-down effect—a few chefs and some of the more adventurous foodies began venturing beyond what had been the acceptable boundaries of fine dining and started exploring the city's rich assortment of ethnic restaurants. Los Angeles became known as the place trends came from. Thai cooking was the first big thing and the common question soon was "What's the next hot cuisine?" (ignoring, of course, that every cuisine is hot at home). Regional Chinese restaurants in Chinatown and Monterey Park soon found that their popularity was no longer limited to their neighborhoods. The same happened with Mexican restaurants. And then it was off to the races. Caribbean, Cambodian, Peruvian, Persian, Lebanese, Indonesian, Indian — even Uzbekistani. If you could find a country on a map (and even if you couldn't), odds are there was a restaurant of that type in Southern California. This interest in ethnic dining had two big effects. It introduced eaters to tastes that were outside their experience, erasing many preconceptions of what good cooking was all about. It also democratized restaurant dining. Because these ethnic restaurants were almost always much cheaper than the usual run of big-deal restaurants, you no longer had to be a member of the platinum card set to eat well.

And then, of course, there was home cooking, again and always. Having been exposed to the subtleties of fine dining, newly fluent in a half-dozen menu languages, an army of ardent amateurs moved back to reinvigorate the home kitchen. No longer was a good home cook someone who had a half-dozen great dishes in his repertoire with which to satisfy both family desires and the demands of entertaining. The new cook was expected to be a version of Puck, et al, writ small. He was expected to be able to turn out a nearly endless repertoire of dishes, and not only those he'd learned from cookbooks. Spontaneity and innovation were no longer regarded as the sole purview of the professional chef. It became common for people to talk about the Indian dinner they had prepared last weekend and the Sichuan menu they were thinking about for the coming one. Or maybe they'd just go with some things they'd been thinking about lately, inventions of their own.

This was accompanied by a boom in shopping for food, shared not only by gourmet stores and high-end groceries, but also by ethnic markets—which began to notice the same crossover phenomenon the restaurants had—and by farmers markets. From 1985 to 1995, the number of farmers markets in Southern California nearly tripled. You no longer had to drive miles to find a farmers market; odds were there was one in your neighborhood at least once a week. Again, there was a significant trickle-down effect. The neighborhood grocery, which had been cruising along selling much the same inventory since the

1950s, began adopting many of the same ingredients found in other markets. Not only could you find baby mixed greens for salads, but also organic produce as well. Ethnic selections began to expand, not only in terms of pantry ingredients like soy sauce or tortillas, but also in more sophisticated offerings of meat and produce—smoked pork and collards for black customers, thin-sliced beef and cleaned cactus paddles for Mexican ones.

The recession of the '90s, which was felt long and hard in Southern California, stunted the growth of fine dining, but fueled a wave of Italophilia quite unlike anything the city had seen before. For several years, it seemed, every other restaurant that opened was called Trattoria Something or the Other. While most of them focused on food cost—a plate of pasta makes a hefty return to a restaurant's bottom line—there were always cooks focusing on the simple, elegant perfection of great Italian cooking. Even ingredients that can be hard to find in most of Italy—lacinato kale, cavolo nero cabbage and locally made buffalo milk mozzarella—started showing up in Southern California supermarkets. At the same time, the farmers market movement continued to boom, tripling again from 1990 to 2000. No longer was it a matter of finding a market in every neighborhood, in some neighborhoods you could find a farmers market almost every day of the week! It became a commonplace that California home cooking meant the simple art of eating seasonal fresh food prepared with top-quality ingredients and a minimum of fuss.

What strikes me looking back over the last 15 years worth of food sections is just how much the Los Angeles Times has accurately reflected the way the cooking has changed, meeting the extremely varied needs of all of our Southern California readers. Beginning with food editors Betsy Balsley (from 1973 to 1990), then Ruth Reichl (from 1990 to 1993) and Laurie Ochoa (from 1993 to 1998), they have created quite a legacy of incisive, creative reporting on matters concerning cooking. Of course, they did not do it alone. Dozens of talented writers, editors and cooks have contributed: Dan Berger, Minnie Bernardino, Mayi Brady, Donna Deane, Cindy Dorn, Rose Dosti, Tracy Crowe, Nick Cuccia, Joan Drake, Emily Green, Barbara Hansen, Kathie Jenkins, Jennifer Lowe, Charles Perry, Marge Powers, Judy Pryor, Dan Puzo, Margaret Sheridan, Janis Sih, Greg Sokolowski, and Toni Tipton are only the ones who were full-time members of the food staff. Countless other freelance writers, columnists and photographers have also made inestimable contributions. A debt is also owed to all of those chefs, cookbook authors and readers whose recipes we have adapted over the years for use in the newspaper and in this book.

While this collection is in no way intended to be a cooking encyclopedia, I hope that you'll find a little bit of everything here, from the basic to the complicated, from Korean and Croatian to Midwestern. For those of you who have grown up with the Southern California food scene, I hope this book will bring back some happy memories. For those who are newly arrived, or are enjoying this book out of state, I can only say give it a try—and welcome to the cult.

RUSS PARSONS
Los Angeles Times Food Section Editor
Los Angeles
June 28, 2000

ETHNIC CUISINE IN SOUTHERN CALIFORNIA

One of the reasons Los Angeles is such an exciting place to cook is because it is so diverse culturally. A separate book would be needed to explore fully all the ethnic pockets in Los Angeles, so the following list merely touches the highlights. In most cases, these groups are the largest settlements anywhere outside the borders of their homelands. In addition, there are sizable communities of Cubans, Nicaraguans, Indonesians, Jamaicans, Lebanese, Sri Lankans, Burmese, Nepalis, Tibetans and many more as well as British, Scandinavians, Italians and others of European origin. One can never lack inspiration with such a wide range of enticing dishes and ingredients to draw on.

ARMENIA

Southern California has the largest Armenian community outside of Armenia itself. In Los Angeles alone, approximately 350,000 Armenians live in Hollywood, Pasadena, North Hollywood and nearby Glendale.

Armenian markets are rich sources of specialty meats such as basturma (seasoned, dried beef), string cheeses, rice-stuffed grape leaves and the cracked wheat needed for pilaf and kufta, which are meatballs made with an outer coating of wheat and meat kneaded together. Bakeries produce luscious pastries, including nut-stuffed baklava, twisted choreg and, at Easter, ring breads embedded with hard-boiled eggs, their shells tinted with onion skins.

Armenian restaurants and kebab shops abound in areas where Armenians congregate, but some of the best food appears at church festivals. For these events, church women make their finest pastries, showing off skills passed down through generations. Dinners of lamb kebabs, pilaf, salad and pita bread are seasoned with the enthusiasm of volunteers who cook to raise funds for charity. Cookbooks compiled by church members and sold at the festivals serve as valuable archives of Armenian cuisine and customs.

BANGLADESH

Bangladeshis add yet another spicy nuance to the Los Angeles food scene. Their cuisine is basically north Indian with a strong Islamic influence because the inhabitants of Bangladesh are almost 90% Muslim. The area of greatest concentration is in central Los Angeles near the Islamic Center of Southern California at 434 S. Vermont Ave. Shops in this area sell the same lentils, rice and spices found in Indian markets as well as fish and other products exported from Bangladesh. They also serve as cultural centers where people meet and catch up on news from home. And they are good places to sample Bangladeshi cooking because all sell prepared food to eat on the premises or take home.

Along with fish, Bangladeshis are fond of goat, lamb and the rice and meat combination known as biryani. The meat must be halal, which means slaughtered according to Muslim precepts. Pork is never consumed. Typical desserts include sweetened yogurt, rice pudding and caramel custard. A legacy of the British, the custard is known simply as pudding, and often appears at Bangladeshi parties along with rasogullas, a typical Bengali sweet of milk balls in syrup.

CHINA

Once, Chinatown in downtown Los Angeles was the place to go for inexpensive combination dinners centered around such dishes as almond duck, sweet and sour pork, chop suey, egg fu yung, fried rice and fortune cookies. In those days, Cantonese food dominated. Then, slowly, foods from other regions appeared as chefs fled Communist China. Another wave of immigrants, from Vietnam, again changed the character of Chinatown, and Chinese entrepreneurs looked for new sites, spreading into the San Gabriel Valley.

Only a short drive from downtown Los Angeles, the communities of Monterey Park, Alhambra and San Gabriel are crammed with Chinese eating places, ranging from fancy seafood palaces to Hong Kong-style coffee shops with Asian-western menus. In a single shopping center, one might find a Chinese barbecue restaurant, a place that serves Chinese-Islamic dishes, a shop that specializes in Chinese jerky and restaurants that offer specialties from Taiwan, Beijing, Sichuan and Shanghai. A few blocks away might be a Taiwanese bakery, Shanghainese snack shop and a restaurant serving Chinese-Burmese food. Lines form on weekends at restaurants renowned for dim sum, which are small snacks served from carts that roll past the tables. Competition is intense, so prices are reasonable and quality is high.

Chinese markets have changed, too, expanding from corner groceries into pan-Asian supermarkets that stock not only Chinese staples but ingredients required for Thai, Indonesian, Vietnamese and Japanese cuisines. Some sell prepared dishes too, along with wines, teas, pastries and, of course, the woks, chopsticks and steamers that are essential to the Asian kitchen.

CROATIA

Tuna canneries and fishing fleets once dominated the economy of San Pedro, a coastal community that overlooks Los Angeles Harbor. Those industries have faded, but the people who manned them remain. Many are Croatians, originally from the Dalmatian coast, where fishing, winemaking and olive groves are major resources. It was natural for them to settle in a hilly area that overlooks the sea, in a state that also produces wine and olives.

There was a time when only Croatian was spoken in some San Pedro neighborhoods. Today, two Croatian clubs keep the old ways alive. They host barbecues, fish lunches and Christmas parties that center around traditional foods. Barbecued lamb is a must at any outdoor party, along with sausages known as cevapcici, sauerkraut, stuffed cabbage rolls and a wide assortment of baked goods such as apple strudel, nut cakes and cookies. The town has one Croatian-owned restaurant, Ante's, that still serves these dishes.

Croatian cuisine shows the influence of Austria, Hungary, Germany, Greece and Italy.

The Italian touch is so strong that risotto and pot roast with mostaccioli pasta are staples, and Croatians shop in Italian delis as well as in markets that carry Croatian imports, ready made cevapcici and marinated lamb for barbecuing. Not all Croatians live in San Pedro. They've spread to other communities as well, and there is a Croatian church in downtown Los Angeles.

EL SALVADOR

Pupuserias are as prevalent as taco stands in Los Angeles. They're relatively recent, arriving with the refugees who fled civil war in El Salvador in the 1980s. The Salvadoran community is widespread, with an especially large concentration in the mid-Wilshire area.

Pupusas are made from the same corn dough as tortillas, but a filling is stuffed into the dough before it is flattened and cooked on a griddle. The filling might be pork, beans, a combination of these two, or cheese and loroco, a green vegetable that is sold fresh in season. Pupusas are always accompanied by tomato sauce and curtido, which is a sort of slightly spicy coleslaw seasoned with vinegar rather than mayonnaise. The Salvadoran population of Los Angeles is so large-more than half a million-and pupusas are so popular that some Mexican restaurants serve them too.

Salvadorans also make meat and chicken tamales wrapped in banana leaves. Tamales called pisques are stuffed only with black beans. The Salvadoran quesadilla is a sweet cake that contains cheese. This may be confusing to those accustomed to the Mexican quesadilla, which is a tortilla filled with melted cheese. Salvadoran panaderias display a variety of tempting cakes and pastries, which are quite different from Mexican pan dulce. Among them are biscuit-like salpores, made with corn flour, rice flour or cornstarch. The bakeries usually sell tamales too and sometimes Salvadoran cheeses, sausages and other food products.

GREECE

Greek immigrants began settling in Los Angeles at the end of the 19th century. Most came from the south, where the climate is mild like that of Southern California. Their social life revolved around the Church of the Annunciation, which they established on San Julian Street downtown. World War II brought still more immigrants, and today the community is widespread rather than concentrated in a single neighborhood.

St. Sophia Greek Orthodox Cathedral at 1324 S. Normandie Ave., in the center of Los Angeles, draws worshippers from all parts of the city. This imposing structure, which has been designated a historic-cultural monument, today stands in the midst of a Latino neighborhood with Pico Boulevard as its central street. The area's multicultural character has earned it the name the Byzantine Latino Quarter.

Greek churches—and there are several in outlying areas—are not only social centers but disseminators of Greek cooking. Annual festivals draw crowds to feast on roast lamb, shish kebab, pilaf, moussaka and appetizers such as the spinach and cheese turnovers called spanakopita. Greek women take pride in their skill at making intricate desserts, and so the selection of sweets is always large. The most popular include the nut-stuffed layered filo dough pastry called baklava and kourambiedes, which are tender, rich cookies sprinkled with powdered sugar. Like other communities intent on preserving their culture, the Greeks collect their recipes in cookbooks published as church fund-raisers.

GUATEMALA

Chapin is a slang word for a person from Guatemala, so the word chapin attached to the name of a bakery or restaurant probably means that it sells Guatemalan food. The Guatemalan population of Los Angeles is large, although not nearly as numerous as the Salvadoran community which lives alongside of it. The food is distinctive: enchiladas that are layered like a tostada; hot dogs in a style that was introduced to Guatemala by German immigrants; rellenitos, which are plantain fritters stuffed with sweetened black beans and topped with thick cream. Tamales made with fresh corn are sometimes dotted with chipilin, a green sold in the herb section of Latino markets. Like other Central Americans and southern Mexicans, Guatemalans tend to steam their tamales in banana leaves rather than corn husks. Grilled meats and big soupy dishes of meat, chicken or turkey are well liked, and some Guatemalan restaurants serenade their customers on weekends in traditional style, with marimba music.

INDIA

If you're hungry for a masala dosa, the place to go is Little India, a conglomeration of groceries, restaurants, sari shops and jewelry emporiums in Artesia that serves as a gathering spot for Southern California's sizable Indian community. The greatest concentration of shops is along Pioneer Boulevard, roughly between 183rd and 187th streets. You can go there for lunch and afterward stock up on lentils, basmati rice, garam masala and other staples.

The masala dosa is a crisp rice and lentil pancake, often stuffed with spiced potatoes and served with coconut chutney and lentil soup. It is typical of south India, but food from other regions is available, not just in Artesia but at Indian restaurants scattered throughout Southern California. Punjabi curries, tandoori-grilled meats and Bombay-style snacks are especially popular. Sweet shops sell rich milk fudge, syrup soaked jalebis, which resemble pretzels, and spicy fried snacks.

Most restaurants concentrate on northern Indian dishes such as tandoori chicken, curries made with lamb or chicken, basmati rice pilaf and naan breads. Because so many Indians are vegetarians, there is always a good selection of non-meat dishes including dal (lentil) curries, aromatically seasoned vegetables and curries based on the mild Indian cheese called paneer. The most common desserts are khir (rice pudding) and kulfi, ice cream that might be flavored with mango, or pistachios and cardamom. And the most popular drink is chai, a bracing cup of tea combined with milk, sugar and spices.

IRAN

The 600,000 or so Iranians who live in the Los Angeles area comprise the largest group outside Tehran. In Westwood, Iranian restaurants, markets and other businesses are so prevalent that the area of Westwood Boulevard north of Santa Monica Boulevard has been called, informally, Little Tehran.

Shops sell everything from ornate furniture and recordings of Persian music to the elegant small glasses in which tea is served to visitors. Restaurants offer kebabs, rice pilaf and stews of meat or poultry called koresh. Markets are well stocked with Iranian specialty products such as yogurt combined with minced shallots, and breads such as barbari, an oval, ridged loaf that is long, like a baguette. Iranians are fond of fresh and dried fruits and nuts, and these are stocked in abundance. Traditional seasonings include dried lime powder, ground dried angelica, rosewater and zereshke, or barberries, which appear in some meat and rice dishes. The dark red powder called sumac is sprinkled onto kebabs and rice, and in Iranian homes may appear as a table seasoning, along with salt and pepper.

Lamb is the most common meat, but the availability of good beef in the United States has made that popular too. White fish accompanied by rice with herbs is traditional for Norouz, the Iranian new year, which heralds the start of spring. With kebabs and stews, Iranians eat chelo, rice cooked so that the grains remain fluffy and separate and a golden crisp crust forms on the bottom of the pot. This is only one of many rice dishes, some of them very elaborate. Stuffed grape leaves, cabbage leaves and vegetables, called dolmeh, are popular. And desserts range from delicate cookies, some made with rice or garbanzo bean flour, to baklava filled with almonds and pistachios and soaked with rosewater syrup.

JAPAN

An annual Nisei Week celebration attracts many visitors to Little Tokyo in downtown Los Angeles, which clusters around First Street. Japanese museums, a cultural center, shops and restaurants provide activities throughout the year. The calendar even includes an annual tofu festival. But the Japanese community, which began around the turn of the century, is not limited to downtown. The community of Gardena supplies still more Japanese shops, and an old Japanese district along Sawtelle Boulevard in West Los Angeles offers nurseries, markets, sushi bars and restaurants serving East-West fusion dishes as well as tempura, sukiyaki, miso soup and other conventional Japanese food.

Sushi bars are everywhere, and usually packed. They range from expensive places where sushi making is practiced as high art to modest neighborhood all-you-can-eat spots. Even supermarkets sell sushi packaged for takeout. Noodle and teriyaki bowls provide quick lunches in fast food shops, but serious diners can find restaurants with private rooms where customers sit on tatami mats spread on the floor and are served by kneeling hostesses. Teppan bars specialize in steaks that are sliced and cooked while the diners watch, and tempura bars offer succulent seafood and fresh vegetables fried in crisp, lacy batter.

In an interesting cultural exchange, most large Korean restaurants contain sushi bars and offer a Japanese menu, while a small number of Japanese restaurants specialize in Korean dishes that are prepared to the Japanese taste.

KOREA

The largest Korean community outside of Korea is in Los Angeles. An estimated 650,000 people of Korean origin live in or close by the city. Koreatown, just west of downtown, is jammed with markets, restaurants, cafes, bakeries, shops that sell Korean cookware, bookstores and other Korean-owned businesses. The main street is Olympic Boulevard from Crenshaw Boulevard east to Vermont Avenue. In this area, it is possible to eat as if one were in Seoul. Restaurants are so heavily patronized by Koreans that the food has not been changed to suit Western tastes.

Barbecued meats are especially popular. Topping the list are bulgogi-beef in a sweet soy sauce marinade-and kalbi-marinated beef rib meat. Sliced pork in a red chile mixture appeals to those who like spicy foods. Barbecue dinners include soup, rice and an assortment of side dishes such as marinated bean sprouts, marinated spinach, sticky-sweet beans, and one or more versions of kimchi, the spicy pickle that Koreans dote on. Along with barbecue dinners, restaurants offer casseroles brimming with seafood, chicken cooked with ginseng, hot pots based on tofu, noodles and many other dishes. Beverages include Korean beer, barley tea and, occasionally, Korean wine ladled out of rustic crocks.

Along with the makings of kimchi and other dishes, Korean supermarkets sell hot food to go, savory side dishes like those served in restaurants and marinated meats for grilling so that one can stage a full-scale Korean dinner at home with a minimum of effort.

MEXICO

Los Angeles might still be part of Mexico if California had not been ceded to the United States in 1848. Today, an estimated 4 million people of Mexican heritage live within the city's sprawling boundaries or nearby. Spanish is spoken widely, and holidays such as Mexican Independence Day and Cinco de Mayo call for major celebrations. The city has several Spanish-language radio stations and television channels as well as a Spanish-language newspaper, La Opinion.

Mexican neighborhoods are sprinkled with mercados (markets) that can supply almost any ingredient required for Mexican cooking. Look for achiote paste from Yucatan, the dried flowers soaked to make a sweet pink drink called jamaica, banana leaves for wrapping tamales, special cuts of meat for carne asada and an astonishing variety of fresh and dried chiles. Exotic herbs such as epazote and papalo quelite are stocked in nurseries, and an occasional market will offer such rare herbs as acuyo (hoja santa), a large anise-scented leaf that is widely used in southern Mexico.

Restaurants concentrate on sturdy northern Mexican chile stews, burritos, tamales, enchiladas and chiles rellenos. But it is also possible to find Oaxacan moles, the panuchos of Yucatan, Jalisco-style birria (stewed goat), and huge seafood cocktails like those of coastal Mexico. Taco stands dispense delicious snacks, and on any weekend it is possible to find menudo, the tripe stew that serves as a restorative after a night of partying.

THAILAND

Driving along the Hollywood freeway through North Hollywood, one glimpses an astonishing sight—a Buddhist temple so authentically Thai that it could have come straight from Bangkok. This is the Wat Thai at 8225 Coldwater Canyon Ave., a gathering spot for the large Thai community that has settled in and around Los Angeles. Early arrivals took up residence in Hollywood, and the eastern portion of Hollywood Boulevard, roughly east of Western Avenue, has been named Thai Town, the first official Thai community in the United States. An annual Thai cultural day parade and festival take place there.

Once considered exotic, Thai food is now as basic as hamburgers and tacos. Almost every neighborhood has a Thai restaurant. These are often labeled Thai-Chinese, because many Thais are of Chinese ancestry, and Chinese cuisine has strongly influenced their cooking. The most popular Thai dishes include satay (kebabs) with peanut sauce, barbecued chicken, the stir-fried noodles called pad thai, hot and sour shrimp soup and chicken-coconut soup.

Thai markets supply curry pastes, fish sauce, aromatic jasmine rice and other essentials, while some shops specialize only in delicate Thai desserts such as fine strands of egg yolk cooked in syrup. Pots for curry making, baskets in which to steam glutinous rice and woven containers in which to serve rice are also on hand.

Thais use a great variety of fresh herbs and vegetables. Among these are kaffir lime leaves, lemon grass, several varieties of basil, eggplants the size of golf balls, pea-sized green eggplants, and intensely hot small chiles. These plants thrive in Southern California's mild climate, providing the fresh ingredients necessary to produce dishes with authentic flavor.

THE PHILIPPINES

Filipino Americans are the largest Asian group in California and the second largest in the United States. Still, their presence is scarcely visible, food-wise. The few bakeries, restaurants and markets that exist are not concentrated in any one area. Their scarcity might seem to reflect a lack of interest in food, but this is not the case. Filipinos love to cook and entertain, but they are family-centered people who enjoy staging lavish parties at home. Often dinners are potluck so friends can exchange their specialties.

Filipino food combines Asian and European influences. Many dishes and customs, such as the afternoon snack called merienda, were acquired from Spain, which ruled the Philippines for more than 300 years. The Chinese contributed steamed dumplings, noodles and spring rolls, which Filipinos call lumpia. Other influences came from neighboring Indonesia and Malaysia.

The classic Filipino dish, adobo, is braised pork or chicken seasoned with soy sauce, vinegar and garlic. Barbecued chicken and pork are popular, and any fiesta demands lechon, a whole suckling pig. Filipinos also like variety meats. Accompaniments might be pancit, which is Filipino-style chow mein; garlic-fried rice or plain steamed rice. The food is mildly seasoned, except for dishes from Bicol Province in southern Luzon, where hot chiles are esteemed. Pungent in another way is bagoong, a fermented shrimp paste used as a condiment and seasoning. The fish sauce patis supplies salty flavor.

Filipino cooks excel in desserts, which range from European style cakes and ice cream with flaming mango sauce to sweet rice cakes flavored with coconut milk. A striking concoction that most restaurants serve is halo halo, which combines assorted beans, fruit, cubes of coconut or pineapple gel, purple yam paste, flan and ice cream with milk and crushed ice. And few cakes can surpass the meringue torte called sans rival, which sandwiches layers of cashew-dotted meringue with rich buttercream frosting.

VIETNAM

Pho, the Vietnamese rice noodle soup, has become a favorite quick meal in Los Angeles. A relative newcomer, it arrived with the refugees who flocked to Los Angeles after the fall of Saigon to Communist North Vietnam in 1975. Looking for new opportunities, immigrant Vietnamese set up pho shops and other businesses in Chinatown. Still more settled in Westminster and Garden Grove in Orange County, where Little Saigon has become the largest Vietnamese American community in the nation. The shopping malls, markets and restaurants along Bolsa Avenue in Westminster will provide a good introduction to this area.

Like the Thais, Vietnamese have dispersed throughout Los Angeles, opening shops in many neighborhoods. Along with pho, restaurants offer such dishes as soft fresh spring rolls, char-grilled beef and pork, ground shrimp molded onto a sugar cane stick and a tour de force meal of beef prepared seven different ways.

Bakeries sell baguettes and pastries that reflect the French colonial period in Vietnam. A potential rival to the hamburger and hot dog is the Vietnamese sandwich, banh mi, an arrangement of cold cuts with crisp sweet and sour vegetables and an optional touch of hot chile in a French roll.

Vietnamese food is fresh and light. An order of pho comes with a plateful of herbs such as Asian basil and mint, bean sprouts and green chiles which diners add to taste. Grilled meats are folded with lettuce and other fresh greens in large translucent wrappers made from rice. Crisp fried spring rolls are wrapped in lettuce and then dipped in a mixture of sugar, vinegar, fish sauce and red chiles. And to end a meal, or just to enjoy by itself, there is fragrant strong filter coffee poured into a glass and mixed with condensed milk-a Vietnamese version of cafe au lait.

BARBARA HANSEN
Los Angeles Times Staff Writer

O N E

Soups

VIETNAMESE BEEF NOODLE SOUP
(*Pho Bo*)

1998

♥

PHO IS THE NATIONAL FOOD OF VIETNAM, roughly equivalent to pasta in Italy. This recipe comes from a story done by Sacramento writer and restaurateur Mai Pham. You can prepare the broth early in the day and assemble the dish just before serving. Vietnamese cooks are very particular about making sure the broth comes out as clear as possible. This is why the roast and bones are brought to a boil, then transferred to a new pot of boiling water: The solids released from the initial boil are discarded with the first batch of water. If the onion begins to break up and muddy the broth before the recipe calls for it to be removed, take it out of the pot. And be sure to remove the spice bag before it starts to darken the broth or overpower the flavor. Fish sauce, star anise, rice stick noodles, Asian basil, culantro and Thai chiles are all available at Asian groceries. Culantro is a Southeast Asian cousin to cilantro.

■ BEEF BROTH

Water
1 (2-pound) chuck roast
5 pounds beef marrow bones
2 (4-inch) pieces ginger root, unpeeled
1 large onion
1/3 cup fish sauce
5 tablespoons sugar
6 star anise
3 cloves
1 cinnamon stick
1 tablespoon salt

• Bring 6 quarts water to boil in large stockpot.

• Put roast and bones in separate pot with water to cover and boil 5 minutes. Using metal tongs, remove roast and bones and add to first pot of boiling water. When water returns to boil, reduce heat and bring to simmer.

• Char ginger and onion. Rinse and add to broth. Add fish sauce and sugar. (Smell will initially be pungent but will subside.)

• Simmer, skimming surface often to remove foam and fat, until roast is tender, about 1 1/2 hours. Remove meat from broth, submerge in bowl of water 15 minutes to prevent meat from darkening and drying out, then wrap in plastic and set aside until ready to serve. (Refrigerate if soup is not being eaten immediately after cooking.)

CONTINUED☞

• Add water to pot if needed to bring to 5 quarts liquid. Put anise, cloves and cinnamon in dampened spice bag or wrap in damp cheesecloth and tie with string and add to broth. Let spices infuse about 1 hour in simmering broth, skimming surface often, then remove and discard spices and onion. (Note: Cooking spices too long makes broth dark and pungent; begin tasting broth after 45 minutes of simmering to check flavor.)

• Add salt and keep on low simmer while preparing noodles and condiments. Broth should be rich enough to serve after 2 1/2 hours total cooking time but can simmer longer; don't turn heat on and off if eating soup same day. (Note: Broth may taste salty but will balance out once noodles and accompaniments are added.)

■ NOODLES AND ASSEMBLY

1/2 pound beef sirloin steak, slightly frozen
Water
1 1/2 pounds (1/8-inch-wide) fresh or dried flat rice stick noodles (banh pho)
1 onion, sliced paper thin
4 green onions, chopped
1/2 cup chopped cilantro
Black pepper
1 pound bean sprouts
20 sprigs Asian basil (rau que)
12 leaves culantro (saw-leaf herb, ngo gai), optional
1/4 cup chopped Thai bird chiles or 1/4 cup thinly sliced serrano chiles
2 limes, cut into thin wedges

• Cut half of reserved roast from Beef Broth into thin slices and reserve remainder for another use. Cut partially frozen sirloin into paper-thin slices. Put roast and sirloin on separate plates and set aside.

• Bring large pot water to boil. Place handful of fresh noodles (enough for 1 serving) in sieve and lower into boiling water. Using fork or chopsticks, stir 15 seconds, then lift and shake off water. Transfer to large heated bowl. Repeat for 5 more bowls. (Note: If using dried noodles, soak in water to cover 20 minutes. Cook all at once until al dente, 2 to 3 minutes. Rinse well in warm water, then divide among heated bowls.)

• Place few slices roast and sirloin on noodles in each bowl. Bring Beef Broth up from low simmer to rolling boil and ladle 3 cups broth on each serving.

• Sprinkle 1 tablespoon sliced brown onion, 1 tablespoon green onions and 1 tablespoon cilantro on top of each bowl. Season with pepper to taste.

• Garnish with bean sprouts, Asian basil, culantro, chiles and squeeze of lime juice as desired at table.

6 main-course servings. Each serving with 3 cups broth: 649 calories; 1,873 mg sodium; 56 mg cholesterol; 8 grams fat; 118 grams carbohydrates; 29 grams protein; 7.07 grams fiber.

CRAB BISQUE

THIS RECIPE WAS CULLED IN 1987 from the recipe collection of the Neiman Marcus luxury department store for Rose Dosti's Culinary SOS column.

3/4 pound snow crab legs
1 carrot, diced
1 onion, diced
4 cloves garlic, minced
1 stalk celery, diced
1 leek, diced
2 ripe tomatoes, diced
2 tablespoons oil
Brandy or dry Sherry
Salt, pepper
2 cups fish stock or canned clam juice
6 tablespoons butter
1 tablespoon flour
1 teaspoon tomato paste
1 cup half-and-half
Cayenne pepper
Chopped parsley

• Split crab legs down middle and remove meat. Reserve large pieces of crab shell. Set meat aside for garnish.

• Saute carrot, onion, garlic, celery, leek and tomatoes in oil until vegetables are tender. Stir in 3 tablespoons brandy and salt and pepper to taste. Cook over high heat until deglazed. Add stock and crab shells and bring to rolling boil. Reduce to simmering and continue to cook 1 hour. Strain and discard crab shells and vegetables.

• Melt butter in small saucepan. Stir in flour until pale golden in color. Add to soup and stir until soup begins to thicken. Simmer over low heat 20 minutes. Add tomato paste, half-and-half, dash cayenne, salt and pepper to taste and additional brandy, if desired. Simmer 5 minutes and strain. Garnish with crab meat and parsley.

4 servings. Each serving: 424 calories; 1,127 mg sodium; 101 mg cholesterol; 32 grams fat; 16 grams carbohydrates; 17 grams protein; 1.14 grams fiber.

ROASTED EGGPLANT
and RED BELL PEPPER SOUP

★
1990

♥

YOU DON'T TASTE THE EGGPLANT in this soup Patrick Healy developed for his now-departed restaurant Champagne. Its silky texture is what you notice. But despite that, this rich, creamy soup contains only 150 calories per serving.

3 large Japanese eggplants
Salt, pepper
Extra-virgin olive oil
2 red bell peppers
1 large onion, sliced
4 cloves garlic, crushed
4 cups chicken stock
1 bunch fresh basil

• Wash eggplants and split lengthwise in halves. Lightly season with salt and pepper and sprinkle with olive oil to taste.

• Roast eggplants at 400 degrees 45 minutes or until tender and golden brown. Puree flesh with skin in blender or food processor. Set aside.

• Place peppers under broiler until skins are scorched on all sides.

• Place in plastic bag 10 minutes to soften, then peel and remove seeds.

• Puree flesh in food processor until smooth. Set aside.

• Heat 1 tablespoon olive oil in skillet. Saute onion and garlic until tender. Cover to sweat over very low heat 5 minutes. Add roasted eggplant puree and chicken stock to onion-garlic mixture. Cook over low heat 15 minutes until flavors blend and mixture is heated through. Puree mixture in blender or food processor until smooth, then strain into clean bowl.

• Season to taste with salt and pepper.

• Cut basil leaves into tiny cubes, resembling confetti.

• To serve, place serving of soup in deep bowl. Spoon red pepper puree in center and swirl into soup. Drizzle lightly with olive oil, if desired. Sprinkle with basil.

6 servings. Each serving: 89 calories; 569 mg sodium; 1 mg cholesterol; 6 grams fat; 6 grams carbohydrates; 4 grams protein; 0.43 gram fiber.

KAO SOI

THIS SOUP WAS DEVELOPED by Times Test Kitchen intern May Parich's mother, Surapee Parich, a quite talented Thai cook. May watched while she prepared it and took down the measurements. Kao soi garnishes are placed in dishes on the table so each diner can dress the soup to taste. Lime wedges and vinegared chile sauce are added if you like sour elements in your food; sugar and black soy sauce (thicker than regular soy sauce) are for sweetness. Fish sauce is added for saltiness, and chile oil adds heat. Cilantro and green onions are almost always added; fried shallots and pickled bok choy are less common but tasty additions. Unlike canned coconut milk, which is coconut milk and water, coconut cream is the thick cream that rises to the top of the milk. It is far richer than coconut milk and has a stronger flavor. It is sold in a can, usually in the same section of the market as coconut milk. It may also be purchased frozen. Asian egg noodles, coconut cream and fish sauce are available at Asian markets.

■ GARNISH

1/4 cup oil
3 tablespoons dried red pepper flakes
1/4 cup Thai chile sauce
1/4 cup vinegar
1/2 cup fish sauce
1/2 cup chopped green onions
1/2 cup chopped cilantro
1/4 cup sugar
2 limes cut in wedges
1/2 cup chopped shallots
1 cup fresh Asian egg noodles set aside from curry recipe, fried until crisp

• Heat oil in small saute pan over medium heat. Add red pepper flakes and saute 1 minute. Pour chile oil into small bowl. Mix together Thai chile sauce and vinegar and put in another small bowl.

• Put fish sauce, green onions, cilantro, sugar, lime wedges, shallots and fried noodles in individual small bowls.

CONTINUED ☛

■ CURRY

6 dried New Mexico red chiles, stems removed
1/2 cup shallots, peeled
1/2 cup cloves garlic, peeled
1/3 cup coriander seeds
1/4 cup cumin seeds
3/4 tablespoon curry powder
3/4 cup water
5 cups coconut cream
6 cups water
2 cinnamon sticks
3 pounds chicken thighs and chicken legs with skin
2 (1-pound) packages fresh Asian egg noodles, less 1 cup for garnish
1/3 cup fish sauce
3 tablespoons sugar

• Roast chiles, shallots and garlic on baking sheet at 300 degrees 10 minutes.

• Combine roasted chiles, shallots and garlic with coriander seeds, cumin seeds, curry powder and water in food processor and puree until smooth.

• Pour into large pot and cook over medium-high heat, stirring constantly, 1 minute. Add coconut cream, water, cinnamon sticks and chicken. Bring to boil, lower heat and simmer uncovered 30 minutes. Stir in fish sauce and sugar.

• Bring water to boil in medium pot. Add egg noodles and cook until tender, 2 to 3 minutes. Drain and divide among 6 large bowls. Divide chicken pieces and curry among bowls. Garnish as desired.

———————

8 servings. Each serving: 1,239 calories; 1,116 mg sodium; 198 mg cholesterol; 62 grams fat; 132 grams carbohydrates; 43 grams protein; 6.94 grams fiber.

ESCAROLE CHICKEN SOUP

IN THIS LOW-FAT RECIPE developed by Times Test Kitchen Director Donna Deane, the slightly bitter flavor of the escarole and the tartness of the lemon juice give the chicken broth a light, clean taste. You get more flavor when you poach the chicken in chicken broth instead of water. Be sure to skim excess fat off the broth before adding the escarole.

1 (1 1/2- to 2-pound) chicken
2 (49 1/2-ounce) cans nonfat chicken broth
1 celery top
1 small onion, quartered
Nonstick cooking spray
3 cloves garlic, minced
1 head escarole, cut into 1-inch crosswise slices
2 tablespoons lemon juice
Lime slices
Sprigs of cilantro

• Wash chicken well and remove giblets. Save liver for another use and set aside remaining giblets.

• Place whole chicken in soup pot along with chicken broth, celery top and onion. Add remaining giblets. Bring to boil. Reduce heat, cover and simmer until chicken is tender, 35 to 45 minutes.

• Remove chicken from broth and let cool. Chill chicken broth overnight along with chicken or let broth stand until fat rises to top. Skim off excess fat and strain.

• Discard skin or reserve for another use. Cover meat and set aside.

• Lightly spray wok or skillet with nonstick cooking spray. Add garlic and saute lightly.

• Add escarole and cook, stirring, until tender, about 10 minutes. Add escarole to broth and heat to boiling. Stir in lemon juice.

• Arrange several slices of chicken breast in bottom of large soup plate. Spoon broth over top. Garnish each with lime slice and cilantro sprig.

6 to 8 servings. Each of 8 servings: 137 calories; 136 mg sodium; 33 mg cholesterol; 8 grams fat; 4 grams carbohydrates; 12 grams protein; 0.17 grams fiber.

KATHLEEN'S HEARTY LENTIL SOUP

STAFF WRITER KATHY JENKINS developed this recipe for a story on winter soups

♥

1 pound dried lentils
1/2 cup dried split peas
3/4 cup brown rice
1 ham bone
2 large onions, chopped
2 cloves garlic, mashed
2 bay leaves
8 whole peppercorns
1 teaspoon whole coriander seeds
3 teaspoons ground coriander
4 teaspoons ground ginger
1 teaspoon cumin seeds
1 1/2 teaspoons lemon pepper
3 tablespoons dry chicken soup base
10 cups water
1 pound Italian sausage
4 small limes, quartered
6 large carrots, peeled and sliced
5 stalks celery, sliced

- Place lentils and peas in large stockpot. Cover with water and soak overnight.
- Drain lentils and peas. Return to stockpot with rice, ham bone, onions, garlic, bay leaves, peppercorns, coriander seeds, ground coriander, ginger, cumin seeds, lemon pepper, soup base and water. Bring to boil, reduce heat and simmer, covered, 1 hour.
- Partially cook sausage, then slice. Add to stockpot along with limes, carrots and celery. Simmer, uncovered, 1 1/2 hours or until lentils are tender.
- Remove limes and ham bone and discard. Taste to adjust for seasonings and add more water if necessary. Let stand several hours to blend flavors. Reheat to serve.

14 to 16 servings. Each of 16 servings: 280 calories; 437 mg sodium; 16 mg cholesterol; 8 grams fat; 39 grams carbohydrates; 15 grams protein; 2.49 grams fiber.

MUSSEL BISQUE

TURMERIC HEIGHTENS THE WARM COLOR of this sophisticated soup, which Times Staff Writer Barbara Hansen turned up at the venerable El Rey Sol restaurant in Ensenada. To make the crouton rounds, fry baguette slices in butter until golden brown.

1 tablespoon butter
2 cloves garlic, finely chopped
2 tablespoons minced carrot
1 tablespoon chopped green onions
1 tablespoon finely chopped white onion
2 tablespoons finely chopped tomato
1 dozen mussels in their shells
1 tablespoon flour
1/2 cup plus 2 tablespoons fruity white wine
2 cups chicken stock
1/4 teaspoon turmeric
6 tablespoons heavy whipping cream
White pepper
5 drops Pernod or sherry
Finely chopped parsley
4 crouton rounds

• Melt butter in saucepan. Add garlic, carrot, green and white onions and tomato and cook 2 minutes over low heat, stirring constantly.

• Increase heat and add mussels. Stir until mussels begin to open and give off juices. Stir in flour and wine. Cover and boil 4 minutes. Add chicken stock and turmeric. Cover and boil gently 7 minutes. Remove mussels.

• Set aside 2 mussels in shells for garnish. Remove remaining mussels from shells. Continue boiling soup base. Add cream and white pepper to taste, stirring constantly. Add shelled mussels and Pernod and continue to stir 2 to 3 minutes.

• Ladle bisque into 2 soup plates. Garnish with parsley. Open mussels in shells and place one in each soup plate. Garnish each with 2 croutons.

2 servings. Each serving: 408 calories; 1,107 mg sodium; 102 mg cholesterol; 26 grams fat; 12 grams carbohydrates; 17 grams protein; 0.28 gram fiber.

ROASTED RED PEPPER *with* PEAR SOUP

PEARS AND SWEET RED PEPPERS might seem like an odd combination for a soup, but it works surprisingly well. The sweetness of the pears seems to balance the acid of the peppers in this recipe, developed by Test Kitchen assistant Mayi Brady.

3 large red bell peppers
1 tablespoon olive oil
1 large leek, white part only, chopped
3 cloves garlic, chopped
1 pear, peeled, cored and chopped
1/2 teaspoon dried thyme
2 (14-ounce) cans vegetable broth
Salt, pepper

• Roast red bell peppers over open flame or under broiler until charred black. Allow to cool several minutes inside paper bag or under covered bowl. Rub off charred skin, remove core and seeds and chop.

• Heat oil in 2-quart pot, add leek and garlic and saute over medium-low heat about 5 minutes. Add pear and cook another 5 minutes. Add roasted peppers and thyme. Cook until vegetables are very tender, another 10 to 15 minutes. Add vegetable broth and salt and pepper to taste. Simmer another 15 to 20 minutes.

• Transfer soup to blender and puree until very smooth. Adjust seasonings to taste.

2 servings. Each serving: 359 calories; 2,166 mg sodium; 0 cholesterol; 12 grams fat; 59 grams carbohydrates; 8 grams protein; 3.92 grams fiber.

TUSCAN-STYLE MINESTRONE
(*Ribollita*)

TIMES RESTAURANT CRITIC S. IRENE VIRBILA contributed this recipe from the Cantinetta Antinori in Tuscany. Don't feel too bound by the specifics, Ribollita is an improvised soup that changes ingredients with the seasons.

1/2 pound dried white Tuscan beans
Water
1 ham hock or prosciutto bone
3/4 cup olive oil
1/2 cup chopped onion
1 carrot, chopped
1 stalk celery, chopped
1 small bunch kale, shredded
1 unpeeled boiling potato, cut into small chunks
1 small bunch Swiss chard, chopped
1 large tomato or 1 cup canned tomatoes, chopped
1 clove garlic, minced
1 1/2 teaspoons rosemary
1 1/2 teaspoons chopped parsley
1/2 teaspoon thyme leaves
Salt
Freshly ground pepper
6 thick slices Italian or French bread, toasted
1/2 cup freshly grated Parmesan cheese

• Place beans in large saucepan and add enough cold water to cover. Let stand at room temperature overnight. Drain beans well and return to saucepan.

• Add ham hock and enough water to cover generously. Bring to boil over high heat. Reduce heat and simmer until beans are tender, about 1 1/2 hours. Drain, reserving liquid and ham hock.

• Transfer half of beans to food processor or blender and puree (or put through strainer). Reserve whole beans. Remove and discard bone from ham hock. Cut meat into small pieces and reserve.

• Heat 1/4 cup olive oil in Dutch oven or large saucepan over medium-high heat. Add chopped onion, carrot and celery and saute about 5 minutes. Stir in kale, potato, pureed beans and about 6 cups reserved bean cooking liquid, adding water if necessary to make 6 cups. Bring to simmer over medium heat until all vegetables are tender, about 30 minutes.

CONTINUED☛

• Add Swiss chard, tomato, garlic, rosemary, parsley, thyme and reserved ham. Season to taste with salt and pepper. Simmer until chard is tender and flavors are well blended, at least 1 hour, adding more bean cooking liquid or water if soup is too thick.

• Stir in reserved whole beans and reserved ham hock. Simmer until heated through, 5 to 10 minutes. Cool. Cover and refrigerate overnight. Arrange toast in bottom of large oven-proof soup tureen. Sprinkle with Parmesan cheese. Bring soup to boil. Ladle soup over toast. Top with remaining 1/2 cup olive oil. Bake at 375 degrees until bubbling, about 25 to 30 minutes. Serve in individual terra cotta bowls.

6 to 8 servings. Each of 8 servings: 448 calories; 488 mg sodium; 9 mg cholesterol; 24 gram fat; 45 grams carbohydrates; 15 grams protein; 3.14 gram fiber.

Note: Ribollita means reboiled, so make large amount and simply reheat, or reboil when needed.

KAMABOKO UDON SOUP

THIS IS A WONDERFUL QUICK TWIST on the popular Japanese soup. It was developed by Times Test Kitchen intern Jet Tila and can be prepared in 20 minutes. You can find dashi and kamaboko at Japanese markets, most Asian markets and some supermarkets with well-stocked Asian aisles.

4 cups water
1 tablespoon dashi (instant soup base)
1 tablespoon soy sauce
1/2 cup spinach leaves, stemmed
1 (7-ounce) package udon noodles
3-4 (1/8-inch-thick) slices kamaboko (fish cake)
3 (2 x 1-inch) pieces firm tofu
1 green onion, chopped

• Bring water to boil in large saucepan, then add dashi and soy sauce. Add spinach and allow to wilt about 2 minutes. Add noodles and cook until soft, 1 to 2 minutes. Add kamaboko slices; blanch 1 minute. Divide soup between 2 bowls and top with green onion.

2 servings. Each serving: 176 calories; 790 mg sodium; 4 mg cholesterol; 1 gram fat; 31 grams carbohydrates; 9 grams protein; 0.65 gram fiber.

RUSSIAN CABBAGE SOUP

1989

THIS RECIPE CAME FROM food section reader Marian Bonner. "In an effort to duplicate a fabulous Russian cabbage soup I had when living in Moscow in 1936, I located a book of Russian recipes put out by the Russian War Relief in 1942. Never-fail, here it is," she wrote. If desired, the beef may be removed and served separately as boiled beef.

1 (28-ounce) can tomatoes
6 cups water
3 pounds beef brisket
2 soup bones
1 (6-ounce) can tomato paste
2 pounds cabbage, coarsely shredded
2 tablespoons coarse salt
3/4 cup sugar
Juice of 1 lemon, or to taste
Cayenne pepper
Paprika

• Combine tomatoes and water in large stockpot and bring to boil. Remove all but thin layer of fat from beef and cut into large chunks.

• Add beef, bones, tomato paste, cabbage, salt, sugar, lemon juice, dash cayenne and dash paprika to stockpot, stirring to blend. Simmer, with lid ajar, 2 to 2 1/2 hours or until meat is tender.

• Remove bones before serving.

6 to 8 servings. Each of 8 servings: 345 calories; 2,227 mg sodium; 82 mg cholesterol; 11 grams fat; 33 grams carbohydrates; 29 grams protein; 1.58 grams fiber.

SHIITAKE MUSHROOM *and* BARLEY SOUP

THIS RECIPE COMES FROM longtime food section contributor Judy Zeidler, a well-known local cooking teacher and author. She says it is especially good to break the fast on Yom Kippur.

2 tablespoons olive oil
1 onion, diced
2 stalks celery, diced
2 carrots, diced
3/4 pound fresh shiitake mushrooms, thinly sliced
2 cloves garlic, minced
6 cups vegetable stock
2 tablespoons soy sauce
3 tablespoons pearl barley
2 tablespoons minced fresh thyme
1 tablespoon dry Sherry
Salt
Freshly ground pepper

• In large heavy pot, heat olive oil over medium-high heat. Add onion, celery and carrots, stirring occasionally, until tender, about 10 minutes. Add mushrooms and garlic. Cook, uncovered, stirring occasionally, until lightly browned, about 5 minutes.

• Add vegetable stock, soy sauce, barley, thyme and Sherry. Reduce heat to low, cover partially, and simmer 45 minutes. Season to taste with salt and pepper. Ladle into heated soup bowl.

4 to 6 servings. Each of 6 servings: 328 calories; 459 mg sodium; 0 cholesterol; 6 grams fat; 67 grams carbohydrates; 9 grams protein; 2.5 grams fiber.

SPRING CHOWDER

———

THIS IS ONE OF THOSE SOUPS inspired by whatever happened to be at the farmers market on one particular day. It is by Times Food Editor Russ Parsons.

———

2 tablespoons butter
4 slices bacon, chopped
4 stalks green garlic, chopped
1 pound skinless salmon, raw or cooked
4 cups fish broth, or 2 cups chicken broth diluted with 2 cups water
1/2 pound small boiling potatoes, cut in 1-inch chunks
2 cups half-and-half
1 teaspoon salt
Freshly ground pepper

• Melt butter over medium heat in bottom of large soup pot. Add bacon and cook until soft. Add chopped garlic and continue cooking until garlic is soft, about 5 minutes.

• If using raw salmon, cut in chunks and add with broth and potatoes. Bring to boil over medium-high heat and immediately reduce heat to simmer. Cook until potatoes are tender, 15 to 20 minutes. Salmon should be moist but flaking. If using cooked salmon, add after potatoes are tender.

• Add half-and-half and salt and increase heat to high. Bring to simmer, then reduce heat immediately and cook until soup thickens slightly, about 5 minutes. (Soup will never become as thick as flour-thickened chowder.)

• Grind pepper generously over top and serve.

———

6 to 8 servings. Each of 8 servings: 367 calories; 878 mg sodium; 75 mg cholesterol; 27 grams fat; 11 grams carbohydrates; 20 grams protein; 0.19 gram fiber.

BLACK BEAN SOUP

THIS IS ONE OF THE MOST POPULAR DISHES at Mr. Stox restaurant in Anaheim.

1 pound dry black beans
Water
1 pound bacon, cut crosswise into thin strips
1 onion, diced
1 red bell pepper, diced
1 carrot, diced
1 stalk celery, diced
1 teaspoon chopped cilantro
1 large head garlic, minced
16 cups chicken stock
Chili powder
Salt
Freshly ground pepper
Salsa, optional
Mexican crema or sour cream, optional

• Soak beans in water to cover in refrigerator overnight. Drain and rinse in colander. Set aside.

• Cook bacon in large pot until almost browned. Add onion, bell pepper, carrot, celery, cilantro and garlic and saute over medium-high heat until vegetables are tender, 10 to 12 minutes.

• Add beans and chicken stock and bring to boil over medium-high heat.

• Reduce heat and simmer until beans are soft, about 1 hour.

• Puree soup in batches in blender. Strain back into pot. Season to taste with chili powder, salt and pepper. Serve in wide-rimmed soup bowls and garnish with salsa and crema if desired.

8 servings. Each serving, without salsa and crema: 528 calories; 1,912 mg sodium; 30 mg cholesterol; 28 grams fat; 42 grams carbohydrates; 26 grams protein; 3.36 grams fiber.

TOM YUM SOUP

1999

♥

IN THE THAI LANGUAGE "yum" refers to a special flavor that combines sour, salty and spicy. It makes an especially wonderful contribution to soups, such as this one from Times Test Kitchen intern Jet Tila. Look for straw mushrooms, Thai chiles and Kaffir leaves at Asian markets. This Thai chicken broth is the base for many delicious soups.

■ THAI CHICKEN BROTH

1 chicken carcass
8-10 cups water
3/4-1 cup thinly sliced galangal
6 stalks lemon grass, lower thick portion only, pounded
10 kaffir (Thai) lime leaves

• Place chicken carcass in stockpot. Add water, galangal and lemon grass. Roll lime leaves and crush lightly with hand, then add to pan.

• Bring to boil, then reduce heat and simmer 45 minutes to 1 hour. Strain.

■ ASSEMBLY

1/2 cup peeled shrimp
1 (15-ounce) can straw mushrooms, drained and rinsed
6-8 roasted dried Thai chiles
3 tablespoons fish sauce
3 tablespoons lime juice
1 1/2 tablespoons chile paste in soybean oil
2-4 kaffir (Thai) lime leaves
Cilantro sprigs

• Bring Thai Chicken Broth to simmer over medium-high heat in large pot. Add shrimp, mushrooms and chiles and cook until shrimp turn pink, about 1 minute. Stir in fish sauce, lime juice and chile paste. Garnish with lime leaves and cilantro.

4 to 6 servings. Each of 6 servings: 76 calories; 1,089 mg sodium; 22 mg cholesterol; 1 gram fat; 7 grams carbohydrates; 9 grams protein; 0.59 gram fiber.

TORTILLA SOUP

THERE ARE MANY DIFFERENT KINDS of tortilla soups. What makes Mayi Brady's special is the smokiness from the chipotle chiles. That and the fact that it can be prepared in less than half an hour.

1999

1 tablespoon oil
2 onions, sliced
6 cloves garlic, chopped
1 ear corn, husk and silk removed
1 (6-ounce) can tomato paste
1 chipotle chile packed in adobo sauce, or more to taste
4 (14 1/2-ounce) cans vegetable broth
1 avocado
1/4 pound Jack cheese, grated
1/2 cup chopped cilantro
1 cup tortilla strips

• Heat oil over medium-high heat, add onions and cook, stirring, 2 minutes. Add garlic, reduce heat to medium-low and continue cooking, covered, 10 minutes.

• While onions and garlic cook, roast corn in dry skillet over high heat until slightly charred, turning so it does not burn, about 5 minutes. Cut kernels from cob and set aside.

• Add tomato paste and chipotle to onions and cook over medium-high heat, stirring, 3 to 4 minutes. Add vegetable broth and bring to boil. Simmer 5 minutes. While soup simmers, chop avocado.

• Puree soup in blender. Divide cheese, avocado, cilantro, corn and tortilla strips among four bowls and ladle soup over top.

4 to 6 servings. Each of 6 servings: 300 calories; 1,713 mg sodium; 16 mg cholesterol; 18 grams fat; 29 grams carbohydrates; 9 grams protein; 2.36 grams fiber.

BAKED ONION SOUP

1987

THIS RECIPE COMES FROM former Times Food Editor Betsy Balsley.

4 cups sliced onions
3 cloves garlic, minced
1/4 cup (1/2 stick) butter or margarine
2 (14 1/2-ounce) cans beef broth
1 (14 1/2-ounce) can chicken broth
1/4 cup dry Sherry
Salt, pepper
12 small slices French bread
Grated Parmesan cheese
1/2 pound Jack cheese, shredded

• Saute onions and garlic in butter in large Dutch oven over low heat until browned and tender. Stir occasionally to prevent scorching. Add beef and chicken broths. Heat to boiling, reduce heat and simmer about 5 minutes to blend flavors. Add Sherry and season to taste with salt and pepper.

• Toast bread slices and sprinkle with Parmesan cheese. Ladle hot soup into 4 individual ovenproof casseroles. Place 3 slices toasted bread on top of soup in each. Sprinkle with Jack cheese. Bake at 375 degrees until soup is bubbly and cheese is browned, about 30 minutes.

4 servings. Each serving: 403 calories; 1804 mg sodium; 41 mg cholesterol; 18 grams fat; 45 grams carbohydrates; 16 grams protein; 1.10 grams fiber.

RICE *with* CHICKEN BROTH
(*Arroz con Caldo de Pollo*)

THIS IS FORMER TIMES TEST KITCHEN DIRECTOR Minnie Bernardino's version of a soup served often in the Philippines. The key to its success is simmering the chicken to make the broth. Garlic and ginger root provide flavor accents; rice turns this into a substantial, yet light soup. A squeeze of lemon and a sprinkling of chopped green onions add the finishing touch.

1989

1 (3-pound) whole chicken
Water
Celery leaves
6 black peppercorns
2 teaspoons minced garlic
2 tablespoons oil
1 tablespoon minced ginger root
1 onion, chopped
1 cup rice
Salt
White pepper
Lemon wedges
Chopped green onions

• Place chicken in large stock pot and cover with 3 quarts water. Add few celery leaves and peppercorns. Bring to boil, reduce heat and simmer until tender, about 1 hour.

• Remove chicken, strain and reserve broth. Cool chicken enough to handle, then bone and skin. Chop or shred meat and set aside.

• Saute garlic in oil in large stock pot until light golden. Remove 1 teaspoon and reserve for garnish. Add ginger to remaining garlic in pan and saute about 1 minute. Add onion and saute until tender.

• Add rice, stirring to coat with oil. Add reserved broth. Season to taste with salt and white pepper. Bring to boil, cover, reduce heat and simmer until rice is tender, 10 to 15 minutes. Add chicken and heat through.

• Serve with lemon wedges to squeeze into soup as desired. Garnish with reserved garlic and green onions.

10 to 12 servings. Each of 12 servings: 196 calories; 65 mg sodium; 43 mg cholesterol; 11 grams fat; 12 grams carbohydrates; 12 grams protein; 0.07 gram fiber.

CREAM *of* CAULIFLOWER SOUP

A RICH, CREAMY WINTER SOUP with only 185 calories and 8 grams of fat? It's not magic, it's the thickening power of the potato, which also lends a subtle earthy flavor to this soup from Times Food Editor Russ Parsons. Be generous with salt; because of the amount of starch from the potato, it takes more than you might think.

1 large leek
1/4 cup (1/2 stick) butter
1 shallot, minced
2 cups dry white wine
1 (1 1/2-pound) head cauliflower, trimmed to small florets
1 (3/4-pound) baking potato, peeled and cut in small dice
2 cups chicken stock
4 cups water
1 1/2 tablespoons Dijon mustard, plus more to taste
1/4 cup sour cream
2 teaspoons salt, plus more to taste
Grated nutmeg

• Trim root end and tough green leaves from leek. Quarter lengthwise, leaving attached at root end. Wash well under running water, pulling leaves apart to remove all grime. Slice thin.

• Combine leek and butter in 4- to 6-quart soup pot, cover and heat slowly over medium heat. Stir occasionally to keep from sticking. Cook 10 minutes and add shallot. Continue cooking, covered, stirring occasionally, until leeks are very soft, about 10 more minutes.

• Increase heat to medium-high and add wine. Cook, stirring, until wine has reduced by about half. Add cauliflower and potato and mix well until coated with leek-wine mixture. Add chicken stock and water, cover and bring to boil, about 5 minutes. Remove lid and reduce heat to simmer.

• Cook gently until potatoes and cauliflower are very tender, about 30 minutes. Cauliflower should smash with spoon.

• Remove half of soup to blender. Add half of mustard, sour cream and salt. Pulse to grind, then increase to puree. Remove to clean 3-quart saucepan and repeat with remaining cauliflower mixture and mustard, sour cream and salt.

• Bring back just to simmer (don't boil or sour cream will curdle) and season to taste with additional salt and mustard. Ladle into bowls and grate fresh nutmeg over top.

8 servings. Each serving: 185 calories; 935 mg sodium; 19 mg cholesterol; 8 grams fat; 16 grams carbohydrates; 4 grams protein; 1.08 grams fiber.

GARLIC SOUP
(*Nam Tom Gratiem*)

TIMOTHY EVANS, OWNER OF *Clos du Lac* winery, is a great lover of Thai food. In fact, when he makes his wine, he has spicy Thai food in mind. He makes the soup with fish wontons, sliced fried fish cake and fish balls that he orders from a Thai restaurant. In The Times Test Kitchen, we substituted frozen dumplings from a Chinese market. Notice that cilantro stems are used to make an herb paste; in Thailand cilantro roots would be used, but Thais in this country have adapted the technique to what's available in supermarkets.

2 heads garlic
10 cups water
11 large fresh sage leaves
9 sprigs flat-leaf parsley
7 sprigs thyme
1 1/2 bay leaves
2 whole cloves
1/4 cup cilantro stems
1 1/2 teaspoons white peppercorns
1/4 cup fish sauce, plus more if needed
1/4 cup cilantro leaves
Sliced deep-fried Thai fish cake, fish balls, frozen won tons, dumplings or seafood ravioli

• Break apart garlic heads. Lightly smash cloves with knife blade and peel.

• Bring water, garlic, sage, parsley, thyme, bay leaves and cloves to rapid boil in large pot. Reduce heat and simmer slowly 45 minutes.

• While broth boils, smash cilantro stems and peppercorns to paste in mortar with pestle.

• Strain broth after 45 minutes and return to pot. Add cilantro paste and fish sauce and bring to boil. Taste and add more fish sauce if needed.

• Add sliced deep-fried Thai fish cake, fish balls, frozen won tons, dumplings or seafood ravioli to taste. Boil 1 to 3 minutes until heated through. Garnish with cilantro leaves.

4 servings. Each serving without fish cake, fish balls, won tons or ravioli: 44 calories; 695 mg sodium; 0 cholesterol; 0 fat; 9 grams carbohydrates; 3 grams protein; 0.61 gram fiber.

POTATO, LEEK *and* FENNEL SOUP

1988

THIS RECIPE COMES FROM CHRISTOPHER BLOBLAUM, the former chef at Colette restaurant in the Beverly Pavilion Hotel.

1 1/2 cups coarsely chopped onion
4 cups sliced leek, white part only
2 baking potatoes, peeled and diced
1/2 pound fennel, fronds removed and reserved, bulb sliced
3 tablespoons butter or oil
4 cups chicken stock
Salt
Freshly ground white pepper
1 cup half-and-half

• Saute onion, leek, potatoes and fennel bulb slices in butter over medium heat 8 to 10 minutes. Add stock and bring to boil. Simmer 20 minutes.

• Puree potato-leek mixture in blender, or pass through food mill until smooth. Adjust seasoning with salt and pepper. Add half-and-half. Return to heat and heat through. Serve in heated soup plates, garnished with reserved fennel fronds, if desired, or serve chilled.

6 servings. Each serving: 233 calories; 699 mg sodium; 31 mg cholesterol; 12 grams fat; 26 grams carbohydrates; 8 grams protein; 1.41 grams fiber.

TWO

Salads

CHICKEN CURRY SALAD

1989

IN THE 1980S, BUTTERFIELD'S restaurant in Hollywood was a great favorite of many readers.

8 cups water
1/4 cup Sherry wine vinegar
6 chicken breasts, skin removed
1 large green bell pepper, diced
1 large Pippin apple, diced
3 large stalks celery, diced
5 green onions, green parts only, sliced
1 cup mango chutney
1 cup plain yogurt
6 tablespoons mayonnaise, preferably homemade
1 tablespoon curry powder, preferably Madras, or to taste
1/4 cup raisins
1/2 cup sliced almonds
1 1/2 teaspoons freshly ground pepper, or to taste
Mixed baby lettuces

• Combine water and vinegar in large saucepan. Add chicken, bring to boil, then simmer over medium heat 10 minutes or until chicken is tender.

• Remove chicken from water and cool, then cut into cubes or pieces.

• Combine green pepper, apple, celery, green onions and all but 2 tablespoons chutney in large bowl. Add chicken, yogurt, mayonnaise, curry powder, raisins and almonds. Mix to coat chicken well. Add pepper. Chill 1 hour.

• Serve over mixed baby lettuces and garnish each serving with 1 teaspoon of remaining chutney.

6 servings. Each serving: 576 calories; 836 mg sodium; 110 mg cholesterol; 22 grams fat; 53 grams carbohydrates; 46 grams protein; 1 gram fiber.

AUTUMN CRISP SALAD
with PERSIMMON DRESSING

THIS DISTINCTLY CALIFORNIAN SALAD was developed by Times Test Kitchen Director Donna Deane for a Thanksgiving story.

1998

■ PERSIMMON DRESSING

1 very ripe persimmon, peeled
1/4 cup oil
1 to 2 tablespoons rice vinegar (depending on tartness of persimmon)
1/2 teaspoon sugar
2 teaspoons minced fresh sage
1 clove garlic, minced
1/4 cup mayonnaise
2 to 4 tablespoons orange juice
Salt, pepper

• Process persimmon pulp in blender until smooth. Remove from blender and place in small bowl. Mix in oil, rice vinegar, sugar, sage, garlic and mayonnaise.

• Add orange juice to desired consistency. Season to taste with salt and pepper. Makes about 1 cup.

■ AUTUMN SALAD

1 chayote, peeled, pitted and thinly sliced
1 bunch spinach, stemmed, washed and dried
1 small red onion, thinly sliced
2 oranges, peeled and sliced
Salt, pepper
1/2 cup toasted chopped Brazil nuts
4 ounces ricotta, formed into balls

• Combine chayote, spinach, red onion and orange slices in salad bowl. Season to taste with salt and pepper.

• Just before serving, top with toasted nuts and ricotta balls. (Or compose salad on large platter.) Serve with Persimmon Dressing.

6 servings. Each serving: 288 calories; 246 mg sodium; 12 mg cholesterol; 23 grams fat; 18 grams carbohydrates; 7 grams protein; 1.54 grams fiber.

CAESAR SALAD

THERE ARE THOUSANDS OF Caesar salad recipes, but this one from famed cookbook author and longtime Times columnist Marion Cunningham has an impeccable pedigree. It is based on Julia Child's recollection of the salad she was served when she visited the original Caesar's restaurant in Tijuana with her parents in 1925. One-half cup vegetable oil may be mixed with 1/2 cup of olive oil instead of using all olive oil. Use a 2-cup jar with lid to mix and store the dressing. If dressing will not be used immediately, the egg should either be omitted entirely or added just before dressing the greens. To coddle the egg, if using, gently drop it into a pan of boiling water and immediately remove pan from heat to coddle. Cover and let stand 5 minutes. Remove from water and gently remove yolk from shell and white. It's easier than it sounds.

3 heads romaine lettuce
2 slices white bread
3 cloves garlic, finely chopped or pressed
1 teaspoon salt
1 cup olive oil
1 or 2 anchovy filets, optional
1 teaspoon Worcestershire sauce
1/4 teaspoon hot pepper sauce
4 teaspoons lemon juice
1 1/2 tablespoons red wine vinegar
1 teaspoon coarsely ground pepper
3 tablespoons whipping cream
1 coddled egg yolk, optional
1/3 cup grated Parmesan cheese

• Remove tough, discolored outer leaves from romaine. Rinse and thoroughly dry tender, more delicate leaves. Loosely wrap in towel and refrigerate.

• Remove crusts from bread and cut into 3/4-inch squares. Place on baking sheet and bake at 350 degrees, tossing every 5 minutes, until golden, 15 to 20 minutes.

• Put garlic, salt and olive oil in 2-cup jar with lid. Screw on lid and shake well.

• Put anchovies and 2 tablespoons garlic oil in small bowl and mash with fork or spoon to mix well. Add to jar. Add Worcestershire, hot pepper sauce, lemon juice, vinegar, pepper, cream and yolk. Screw on lid and shake thoroughly until dressing is completely blended. Makes 1 cup dressing.

• Remove lettuce from refrigerator and tear or cut into bite-size pieces and put in large salad bowl. Drizzle 1/3 cup dressing over salad and toss gently to coat all leaves. Add more dressing if needed. Sprinkle with cheese, add croutons and toss again. Taste and add more salt if needed. Serve at once.

4 servings. Each serving: 614 calories; 834 mg sodium; 90 mg cholesterol; 62 grams fat; 10 grams carbohydrates; 6 grams protein; 0.36 gram fiber.

BROCCOLI SALAD

THIS RECIPE CAME FROM TIMES FOOD SECTION reader Lisa O'Kane of Toluca Lake in response to a plea for potluck recipes for holiday entertaining. You can use regular or golden raisins.

■ DRESSING

1 cup mayonnaise
1 teaspoon white wine vinegar
1/4 cup sugar

• Mix together mayonnaise, vinegar and sugar. Cover and refrigerate 2 hours for flavors to meld.

■ ASSEMBLY

1 1/2 to 2 pounds broccoli florets
1 cup golden raisins
1 cup salted sunflower seeds
1 small red onion, chopped
8 slices bacon, cooked and crumbled

• In large serving bowl, combine broccoli, raisins, sunflower seeds, onion and bacon.
• Just before serving, add Dressing to broccoli mixture and stir well.

10 to 12 servings. Each of 12 servings: 230 calories; 296 mg sodium; 8 mg cholesterol; 14 grams fat; 25 grams carbohydrates; 6 grams protein; 1.03 grams fiber.

CELERY SALAD *with* WALNUTS *and* BLUE CHEESE

CELERY MAY BE REGARDED by many as the spinster aunt of the vegetable world, but Times Food Editor Russ Parsons paired its crunch and slightly astringent flavor with rich blue cheese and walnuts for this winter salad that is almost compulsively edible.

3/4 teaspoon minced shallots
1 tablespoon Sherry vinegar
3/4 cup walnuts
1 bunch celery, bottoms and leafy tops trimmed
1/4 cup olive oil
1 cup crumbled blue cheese
Salt
Freshly ground pepper

• Combine shallots and vinegar in small bowl and set aside.

• Toast walnuts on baking sheet in 350-degree oven or over medium heat in small skillet. When walnuts become fragrant, remove from heat. Do not scorch walnuts. Set aside.

• Slice celery on bias, making exaggerated V-shaped pieces. Place in large serving bowl.

• Whisk together shallots, vinegar and oil in small bowl. (Do not add salt and pepper at this time; many blue cheeses are very salty.)

• Coarsely chop walnuts and add to celery. Pour over 1/2 to 2/3 of dressing and toss to coat well. Add more dressing as needed; salad should be moistened, but there shouldn't be leftover dressing in bottom of bowl.

• Add blue cheese and toss lightly to combine. Taste and add salt, if needed, and pepper to taste.

6 servings. Each serving: 269 calories; 434 mg sodium; 17 mg cholesterol; 25 grams fat; 6 grams carbohydrates; 8 grams protein; 1.33 grams fiber.

CUCUMBER SALAD

1999

THIS SALAD WAS DEVELOPED by Times Food Editor Russ Parsons to be served alongside the Oven-Steamed Salmon (page 139), but it is quite good on its own.

5 cucumbers
Salt
2 tablespoons snipped chives
1 teaspoon toasted sesame seeds
1 tablespoon rice vinegar
1/2 teaspoon sesame oil
2 tablespoons chopped cilantro

• Peel cucumbers, cut in half lengthwise and scoop out seedy center with spoon. Cut each half in three lengthwise strips, then in 2-inch sections. Salt, and place in colander to drain 20 minutes.

• When cucumbers have drained, rinse under cold running water and drain again. Transfer to work bowl, add chives, sesame seeds, rice vinegar and sesame oil and mix well. Taste and adjust seasoning—sesame oil should be almost undetectable, cucumbers should be slightly tart from vinegar, and herbs should be in balance. Just before serving, add cilantro and mix well.

6 servings. Each serving: 39 calories; 54 mg sodium; 0 cholesterol; 1 gram fat; 7 grams carbohydrates; 3 grams protein; 1.58 grams fiber.

CRISP SALMON SALAD

SALMON IS PLENTIFUL IN CALIFORNIA, particularly during the spring. Not many people know that one of the best parts of the salmon, the fatty belly flap, is frequently discarded. In this recipe by Times Food Editor Russ Parsons, those delicious, moist strips are broiled crisp and then tossed with a tart mustardy dressing.

1 pound salmon filets, preferably belly cut
Salt, pepper
2 tablespoons Dijon mustard
1 tablespoon red wine vinegar
1/4 cup olive oil
1/2 pound mixed salad greens

• Cut salmon in lengthwise strips about 1/2 inch wide. Salt and pepper generously on both sides. Broil, skin side up, until skin is crisp and dark brown, 7 to 10 minutes, depending on thickness of meat.

• While salmon is broiling, beat together mustard and vinegar in small bowl. Gradually add oil, beating steadily until dressing forms smooth emulsion.

• Add half of dressing to salad greens and toss well to mix. Add enough extra dressing that greens are lightly but thoroughly coated.

• Divide greens among 4 plates and arrange salmon strips on top. Serve immediately with extra dressing to pass.

4 servings. Each serving: 268 calories; 299 mg sodium; 50 mg cholesterol; 19 grams fat; 2 grams carbohydrates; 19 grams protein; 0.60 gram fiber.

EXQUISITE SALAD

THIS RECIPE IS FROM the late cookbook author Bert Greene.

---

1 cup white and brown rice mix
1/4 cup white wine vinegar
3/4 cup olive oil
1 teaspoon sugar
1 clove garlic, minced
1 cup cilantro leaves
Salt
White pepper
2 cups shredded cooked chicken, chilled
1/2 cup sliced green onions
1 cup diced tomato
2 cups chopped escarole
1 1/2 cups chopped cooked asparagus, chilled
1 avocado, peeled and chopped

• Prepare rice according to package directions. Chill. Place vinegar, oil, sugar, garlic and cilantro in blender container. Blend until smooth.

• Season to taste with salt and white pepper.

• Combine rice, chicken, green onions, tomato, escarole, asparagus and avocado. Toss with dressing. Serve immediately or chill to blend flavors.

---

6 servings. Each serving: 390 calories; 77 mg sodium; 31 mg cholesterol; 27 grams fat; 24 grams carbohydrates; 14 grams protein; 1.26 grams fiber.

CHINESE DUCK SALAD

PICK UP A BARBECUED DUCK in Chinatown, take it home, cut it into pieces and you've got a great dinner, quack as a wink. This recipe was developed by Times Test Kitchen Director Donna Deane.

1 whole Chinese duck
1/2 head iceberg lettuce, shredded
4 green onions, sliced
1/2 cup whole toasted almonds
1/2 cup cilantro leaves
1/2 cup oil
1/4 cup vinegar
2 tablespoons hoisin sauce
1 1/2 teaspoons sugar
1 tablespoon minced ginger root
1 clove garlic, crushed
1/2 teaspoon sesame oil
Salt, pepper

- Remove meat from duck. Cut in bite-size pieces and toss together with lettuce, green onions, almonds and cilantro.
- Combine oil, vinegar and hoisin sauce in bowl. Whisk until blended.
- Stir in sugar, ginger, garlic and sesame oil. Season to taste with salt and pepper.
- Add amount of dressing desired to salad and toss. Serve any additional dressing with salad.

6 servings. Each serving: 743 calories; 651 mg sodium; 13 mg cholesterol; 66 grams fat; 7 grams carbohydrates; 31 grams protein; 0.89 gram fiber.

ISAAN-STYLE GRILLED BEEF SALAD

ISSAN FOOD, FROM THE NORTHEASTERN CORNER of Thailand, is wildly flavored, with lots of spice, garlic and fish sauce. This salad from cookbook author Nancy McDermott is typical of the region's delicious cooking. To make roasted rice powder, place 1/2 cup raw glutinous rice or other rice in a small skillet over high heat and dry-fry until the grains are wheaty golden brown. Shake the pan back and forth frequently to turn the grains so they brown evenly, 3 to 5 minutes. Remove from heat and set aside. When the rice is cool, transfer to a jar, seal tightly and keep at room temperature until needed. To use in recipes, grind roasted rice in heavy mortar and pestle or a coffee or spice grinder. The ideal texture is midway between sand and powder, with a discernible crunch.

1993

1 (1 pound) rib-eye or flank steak, grilled rare
1/3 cup chicken stock
Several lettuce leaves
2 small cucumbers, peeled and sliced crosswise into ovals
5 cherry tomatoes, halved
1 bunch fresh mint
3 green onions, thinly sliced crosswise
1/4 cup finely chopped shallots
1 bunch cilantro, coarsely chopped
2 tablespoons roasted rice powder
1 teaspoon coarsely ground dried red chile
1 teaspoon sugar
1/4 cup fish sauce
1/4 cup freshly squeezed lime juice

• Thinly slice beef crosswise into 2-inch-long strips and set aside.

• Bring chicken stock to gentle boil in small saucepan over medium heat. Add sliced beef and turn occasionally, moistening and warming steak in stock, 1 to 2 minutes. Set aside.

• Prepare small serving platter with lettuce, cucumber, tomatoes and few sprigs mint, then set aside.

• Add green onions, shallots, cilantro, roasted rice powder, chile, sugar, fish sauce and lime juice to saucepan. Toss well. Taste dressing, and adjust to taste with additional fish sauce, lime juice, sugar or chiles.

• Transfer beef to serving platter using slotted spoon. Mount on lettuce leaves. Drizzle with additional dressing. Garnish with cucumber, tomatoes and mint. Serve at once, warm or at room temperature.

4 to 6 servings. Each of 6 servings: 123 calories; 532 mg sodium; 28 mg cholesterol; 4 grams fat; 8 grams carbohydrates; 13 grams protein; 0.44 gram fiber.

SHREDDED CUCUMBER *and* GARLIC *in* SOUR CREAM

THIS IS A FAVORITE FAMILY RECIPE of Times food section reader Ildiko Kalu of Agoura Hills. The cucumbers, along with the sour cream, mellow out the huge amount of garlic, but it's still a great accompaniment for barbecued meats. The secret of the recipe is to pour off half the cucumber juice so the sour cream sauce is not too thin yet there is enough juice left to flavor the sauce

2 pounds (about 3 large) cucumbers, peeled
3 tablespoons sliced garlic cloves
2 teaspoons salt
1 (16-ounce) carton sour cream
Hungarian sweet paprika

• Shred cucumbers on medium shredder into glass bowl. Stir in garlic and salt. Cover and refrigerate 1 hour.

• Pour off 1/2 juice from cucumbers. (Do not squeeze cucumbers.) Stir in sour cream. Taste and add additional salt, if necessary.

• Serve in bowls and sprinkle with paprika.

8 servings. Each serving: 141 calories; 623 mg sodium; 25 mg cholesterol; 12 grams fat; 7 grams carbohydrates; 3 grams protein; 0.74 gram fiber.

LIMA BEAN *and* BACON SALAD

THIS RECIPE IS ONE of Test Kitchen Director Donna Deane's family favorites. Her mother would almost always make this salad for barbecues and family gatherings. As is common in the Midwest, she would toss the salad with Miracle Whip salad dressing, not mayonnaise. If you prefer mayonnaise, add more pickle or a dash of vinegar for flavor.

1 (1-pound) package frozen lima beans
1/2 cup water
2 tablespoons minced onion
3 hard-boiled eggs, diced
1 cup diced celery
1/4 cup diced dill pickle
6 strips bacon, cooked crisp, crumbled
1/2 cup salad dressing or mayonnaise
1/2 teaspoon salt
1 head iceberg lettuce, cut up

• Microwave beans with water in covered casserole 12 to 15 minutes, stirring twice during cooking. Drain and rinse under cold water.

• Toss together beans, onion, 2 diced eggs, celery, dill pickle and 4 slices crumbled bacon. Stir in salad dressing or mayonnaise and salt.

• Just before serving, add lettuce and toss. Spoon into serving bowl and sprinkle with remaining hard-cooked egg and 2 slices crumbled bacon.

6 servings. Each serving: 306 calories; 597 mg sodium; 121 mg cholesterol; 21 grams fat; 18 grams carbohydrates; 11 grams protein; 2.19 grams fiber.

CHINESE CHICKEN SALAD

CHINESE CHICKEN SALAD has to be one of the most popular dishes in Southern California restaurants. At one time, it seemed like almost every place in town had one on the menu. This one from Obachine is typical.

■ DRESSING

1/3 cup soy sauce
1/2 cup rice vinegar
1/3 cup Chinese hot mustard
1 egg yolk
2 tablespoons honey
1 tablespoon sesame paste
2 tablespoons chopped pickled ginger
1 tablespoon chile oil
Salt
Freshly ground pepper
3/4 cup peanut oil

• Combine soy sauce, vinegar, mustard, egg yolk, honey, sesame paste, ginger and chile oil in blender. Season with salt and pepper. Blend thoroughly. Slowly blend in peanut oil. Taste and adjust seasonings. Set aside. Makes about 2 cups.

■ SALAD

1 mango, peeled and cut into thin strips
5 cups nappa cabbage, cut into thin strips
2 carrots, peeled and cut into thin strips
1 head radicchio, cut into thin strips
4 cups mixed greens or watercress
3 pounds boneless skinless chicken breasts, cooked, cooled and diced
Oil
1 (12-ounce) package square won ton wrappers
2 tablespoons toasted sesame seeds

• In large salad bowl, mix mango, cabbage, carrots, radicchio, greens and chicken.
• Heat 1/2 inch oil in small skillet over medium-high heat. Cut wonton wrappers into 1/2-inch wide strips. Fry strips until golden brown, about 30 seconds each side. Drain on paper towels and let cool. (You need about 2 cups won ton strips.) Toss with salad.
• Toss Salad with 1 cup Dressing. Add more Dressing, if needed, a little at a time, so that salad is not overly sauced. Sprinkle with sesame seeds.

8 servings. Each serving: 741 calories; 522 mg sodium; 92 mg cholesterol; 56 grams fat; 26 grams carbohydrates; 42 grams protein; 3.75 grams fiber.

TOFU SALAD

MISHIMA HAS LONG BEEN one of the more popular Japanese restaurants in Los Angeles. It is justly famous for this salad. You can buy the sesame seed paste, sesame seasoning mix, dried bonito flakes and seaweed at Japanese markets, as well as already fried won ton skins.

Oil
2 cups rice noodles or thinly sliced fresh won ton skins
2 tablespoons sesame seed paste or creamy peanut butter
2/3 cup mayonnaise
1/4 cup rice vinegar
1/4 cup sugar
2 tablespoons sesame seasoning mix, optional
1 1/2 teaspoons grated ginger root
1 tablespoon soy sauce
1 1/2 teaspoons mirin (sweet rice wine)
1 tablespoon water
1 (14-ounce) package tofu
2 Japanese cucumbers, sliced thin
2 tomatoes, sliced thin
Radish sprouts, optional
Dried bonito flakes, optional
Dried seaweed (nori), minced, optional

• Heat enough oil for deep frying in skillet. Add rice noodles and fry until puffed, about 10 seconds. Remove immediately from oil with slotted spoon and drain on paper towels. Set aside.

• Combine sesame seed paste, mayonnaise, vinegar, sugar, seasoning mix, ginger, soy sauce, mirin and water and mix well. Cover and refrigerate until ready to use.

• Drain excess water from tofu and cut into 3/4-inch cubes. Divide tofu, cucumber and tomato slices among 6 to 8 plates. Garnish with sprouts, fried noodles and bonito flakes. Chill 20 minutes.

• Just before serving, pour dressing over salad and sprinkle with dried nori.

6 to 8 servings. Each of 8 servings: 356 calories; 294 mg sodium; 5 mg cholesterol; 16 grams fat; 46 grams carbohydrates; 9 grams protein; 0.58 gram fiber.

ORZO VEGETABLE SALAD

1998

TIMES FOOD SECTION READER Lucille Martin created this salad based on something she saw in a magazine at the beauty shop.

4 quarts water
3 beef bouillon cubes
2 cups orzo
3 green onions, sliced
1 cup sliced pitted black olives
1 cup thinly sliced celery
1/2 cup thinly sliced green bell pepper
2 large tomatoes, peeled and cubed
1 (6-ounce) jar marinated artichokes, drained and sliced
1 cup mayonnaise (or enough to coat orzo)
Salt
White pepper

• Bring water and bouillon cubes to boil. Add orzo. Reduce heat, cover and simmer 10 to 12 minutes, stirring several times. Drain and cool. Combine orzo, green onions, olives, celery, green bell pepper, tomato and artichokes. Stir in mayonnaise. Season to taste with salt and white pepper. Chill at least 2 hours. Makes about 10 cups.

8 to 10 servings. Each of 10 servings: 269 calories; 1,289 mg sodium; 6 mg cholesterol; 18 grams fat; 26 grams carbohydrates; 5 grams protein; 0.65 gram fiber.

COLESLAW

THE PANTRY IS DEFINITELY a downtown institution. And it was well before owner Richard Riordan was elected mayor. This is that venerable landmark's version of the classic diner specialty.

3/4 cup mayonnaise
3 tablespoons sugar
1 1/2 tablespoons white wine vinegar
1/3 cup oil
1/8 teaspoon garlic powder
1/8 teaspoon onion powder
1/8 teaspoon dry mustard
1/8 teaspoon celery salt
Dash black pepper
1 tablespoon lemon juice
1/2 cup half-and-half
1/4 teaspoon salt
1 large head cabbage, very finely shredded

• Blend together mayonnaise, sugar, vinegar and oil. Add garlic and onion powders, mustard, celery salt, pepper, lemon juice, half-and-half and salt. Stir until smooth. Pour over cabbage in large bowl. Toss until cabbage is well coated.

8 to 10 servings. Each of 10 servings: 185 calories; 223 mg sodium; 9 mg cholesterol; 15 grams fat; 14 grams carbohydrates; 2 grams protein; 0.73 gram fiber.

RARE NICOISE SALAD

In Nice, you will never find a Nicoise salad made with anything but canned tuna. But this is Southern California, and we do things a little differently. This recipe is from frequent contributor Diane Morgan.

4 small red boiling potatoes (about 3/4 pound)
Salt
3/4 pound green beans
6 leaves romaine lettuce
3 tomatoes, cut into 8 wedges
2 (6-ounce) cooked pepper-crusted tuna steaks, cut into 1/4-inch slices
2 hard-boiled eggs, each cut into 8 slices or wedges
8 cured black olives, pitted and halved
1/2 cup minced parsley
1/2 cup olive oil
3 tablespoons lemon juice
1 teaspoon anchovy paste
2 teaspoons Dijon mustard
1/2 teaspoon salt
Freshly ground pepper

• Boil potatoes in lightly salted water until tender when pierced with a knife, about 20 minutes. Drain, let cool, slip off skins and cut each into 8 wedges.

• Cook beans in plenty of boiling, lightly salted water until just tender, about 5 minutes. Drain, place in ice water to chill about 1 minute, drain again and blot dry on paper towels.

• Arrange salad on large serving plate by first covering plate with romaine leaves. Arrange potatoes in row, with row of green beans next to potatoes. Follow with row of tomatoes, then tuna, then eggs. Scatter olives and parsley over top.

• Whisk together olive oil, lemon juice, anchovy paste, mustard, salt and pepper to taste. Pour over composed salad and serve immediately.

4 servings. Each serving: 554 calories; 613 mg sodium; 149 mg cholesterol; 36 grams fat; 25 grams carbohydrates; 33 grams protein; 1.74 gram fiber.

SEAFOOD RICE SALAD

THE SECRET TO THIS tasty salad from Food Editor Russ Parsons is dressing the rice while it is still warm so the flavors have a chance to penetrate.

2 cups long- or medium-grain rice
2 lemons, plus more to taste
1 1/2 teaspoons salt
1 teaspoon dried red pepper flakes
1/2 cup olive oil
1 pound mixture of raw peeled small shrimp and cleaned calamari
1 pound mussels or clams
1/4 cup dry white wine
1/4 pound sliced soppressata or other spicy salami, cut in thin strips
1 red onion, diced small
Minced fresh herbs, such as basil, mint and parsley, optional

• Cook rice as you would pasta, adding it to plenty of rapidly boiling, lightly salted water and cooking until tender, about 13 minutes. Do not overcook rice, but do not undercook either. Rice should be soft completely through, but should not begin to "explode" at ends. Drain immediately and place in large mixing bowl, cover with towel and set aside 5 minutes.

• To rice, add juice of 1 lemon, salt, red pepper flakes and olive oil and stir gently to mix well. Do not stir too rapidly or rice can be crushed, becoming sticky. Chill 1 to 2 hours.

• Cook shrimp or calamari in rapidly boiling water just until firm: 1 to 2 minutes for small shrimp, 30 to 45 seconds for calamari. Drain, and if calamari are not cut in small pieces, do so. Place in small bowl with juice of 1/2 lemon and chill 30 minutes.

• When almost ready to serve, bring mussels or clams, white wine and juice of remaining 1/2 lemon to boil over high heat. Cover tightly and cook just until clams or mussels open, about 5 minutes.

• Remove rice from refrigerator and strain mussel cooking juice over top. Add cooked shrimp and calamari, salami and onion and toss well to mix.

• Adjust seasonings to taste. Salad should be pleasantly tart with just a hint of olive oil flavor. If desired, you can add some minced herbs, but this is a seafood salad, so be gentle. Just before serving, place mussels or clams in their shells in rice.

8 to 10 servings. Each of 10 servings: 333 calories; 750 mg sodium; 89 mg cholesterol; 16 grams fat; 29 grams carbohydrates; 15 grams protein; 0.09 gram fiber.

WARM ROSEMARY CHICKEN SALAD

ANDREW MURRAY VINEYARDS is one of the best of the Rhone-style producers on the Central Coast. Owner James Murray is also quite a cook. For this salad, he smokes the chicken for 20 minutes the day before he makes this dish. If you don't have a home smoker, simply roast the chicken as directed. Murray says the lemony flavors go well with Viognier or Roussanne, and the herbs and chicken match well with Esperance (Murray's Rhône blend).

■ ROSEMARY CHICKEN

2 lemons
9 sprigs rosemary
1 (4- to 5-pound) chicken
Salt
Freshly ground pepper

• Cut lemons crosswise into 1/4-inch-thick slices. Place lemon slices and 4 rosemary sprigs in chicken cavity. Insert additional 4 rosemary sprigs under skin of breast. Rub entire bird with salt, pepper and remaining rosemary. Roast chicken at 350 degrees until golden brown, about 1 hour, basting several times with pan juices.

• Remove chicken from oven, reserving pan juices. Keep chicken warm.

■ SALAD

1/2 cup plus 2 tablespoons Viognier or other white Rhône wine
1 clove garlic, crushed
1 tablespoon extra-virgin olive oil
Juice of 1 lemon
16 Kalamata olives
Salt
Freshly ground pepper
6 cups mixed salad greens

• Skim fat from roasting juices, then pour juices into skillet. Deglaze roasting pan with 2 tablespoons wine, scraping up brown bits, then add bits and sauce to skillet with juices. Reduce mixture over medium heat about 5 minutes.

• In separate pan, saute garlic in olive oil. Add to juices in skillet along with 1/2 cup wine, lemon juice, olives and salt and pepper to taste. Boil over high heat until reduced by half, about 10 minutes.

• Arrange greens on 4 serving plates. Slice Rosemary Chicken. Divide chicken, lemon slices from chicken cavity and olives from dressing among plates and arrange on greens. Pour warm dressing over salads and serve at once.

4 servings. Each serving: 665 calories; 1,234 mg sodium; 195 mg cholesterol; 47 grams fat; 6 grams carbohydrates; 50 grams protein; 1.04 grams fiber.

CHICKEN-CELERIAC-POTATO SALAD

THIS UNUSUAL COMBINATION was developed by former Times Test Kitchen Director Minnie Bernardino.

1998

1 pound yellow or red boiling potatoes, cooked, peeled and diced
2 cups finely diced peeled celeriac, parboiled until tender-crisp
4 cups cubed cooked chicken
1/2 cup chopped sweet pickles
1/4 cup sweet pickle juice
1 cup mayonnaise
1 cup thinly sliced snow peas
1/2 cup chopped green onions
Salt, pepper
Bibb lettuce
Red radishes

• Cool potatoes, celeriac and chicken. Combine in bowl with pickles, pickle juice, mayonnaise, Chinese peas and green onions. Season to taste with salt and pepper. Cover and let stand in refrigerator overnight. Mound on Bibb lettuce and garnish with red radishes.

8 to 10 servings. Each of 10 servings: 266 calories; 340 mg sodium; 56 mg cholesterol; 12 grams fat; 21 grams carbohydrates; 18 grams protein; 1.03 grams fiber.

THAI WATERFALL SALAD

IN THAI, THIS RECIPE is called Nam Thok, but Test Kitchen intern May Parich liked the more poetic translation. The salad is dressed while the meat is still warm and the mingled juices are what make it so special.

3/4 pound beef skirt steak
Salt
Freshly ground pepper
2 tablespoons jasmine rice
1 cup Thai basil leaves, torn into pieces
1/4 cup mint leaves, torn into pieces
1 red onion, thinly sliced
1 cucumber, peeled, seeded and thinly sliced
1/2 cup cilantro leaves, coarsely chopped
1/2 cup lime juice
1/4 cup fish sauce, or to taste
1 tablespoon dried red pepper flakes
Sugar

• Season steak with salt and pepper and grill over medium-high heat until browned, 30 seconds each side. Let rest 5 minutes before slicing against the grain into 1/4 inch slices.

• While meat rests, toast rice in dry skillet over medium-low heat until lightly colored, about 5 minutes. Grind into powder using spice grinder or food processor.

• Combine steak, rice powder, basil, mint, onion, cucumber, cilantro, lime juice, fish sauce, red pepper flakes and dash sugar. Taste for seasoning.

• Serve with cooked rice.

4 servings. Each serving: 171 calories; 814 mg sodium; 32 mg cholesterol; 5 grams fat; 16 grams carbohydrates; 17 grams protein; 0.93 gram fiber.

THREE

Appetizers

BAKED CRISP ROSEMARY CHIPS

THIS RECIPE COMES FROM cookbook author and longtime Food section columnist Abby Mandel. If you don't have two ovens, it's best to bake the chips in sequence.

24 wonton wrappers
Olive oil cooking spray
1 egg white
1 teaspoon dried rosemary
Generous 1/4 teaspoon coarse salt

• Lay 12 wonton wrappers in single layer on baking sheet sprayed with cooking spray. If there is any flour left on them, lightly brush off.

• Put egg white in small bowl; froth with fork or small whisk. Break up rosemary in mortar with pestle or on wax paper with rolling pin.

• Lightly brush each wrapper with egg white. Sprinkle 1/2 rosemary evenly over wrappers, then 1/2 salt.

• Bake at 400 degrees until medium brown, 6 to 7 minutes. Transfer to rack to cool. Repeat with remaining ingredients. (Can be made a week ahead, kept at room temperature in an airtight container.)

8 servings. Each serving: 55 calories; 137 mg sodium; 2 mg cholesterol; 0 grams fat; 12 grams carbohydrates; 2 grams protein; 0.03 gram fiber.

BRUSCHETTA *with* FRESH SHELL BEAN PUREE *and* MIXED MUSTARD GREENS
(*Bruschetta 'n Capriata*)

EVAN KLEIMAN, CHEF AND OWNER of Los Angeles' landmark Angeli Caffe on Melrose Avenue, developed this easy appetizer for a story on cooking from the garden.

1997

1 cup dried flageolet, Great Northern or cannellini beans
1/2 onion
Water
Salt
Extra-virgin olive oil
5 cloves garlic, plus 1 to 2 optional cloves garlic
2 large bunches or 4 small bunches greens (such as spinach, mustard greens, chard, tat soi)
2 anchovy filets
Salt
12 slices bread

• Soak beans overnight in water. Drain. Place beans and onion in small saucepan. Add water to cover by 2 inches, bring to rolling boil and boil 5 minutes, then reduce heat and simmer until beans are very tender, about 40 minutes, adding just enough water if necessary to keep beans covered.

• Add salt to taste during last few minutes of cooking.

• When beans are very tender, remove onion and drain off nearly all water, leaving just enough for mashing beans into fluffy puree. Mash beans with potato masher, adding olive oil to taste. Press 1 to 2 cloves optional garlic and mix into beans.

• Wash and dry greens and remove fibrous stems or ribs. Stack leaves, roll up and slice across to make thin strips. Mince 2 cloves garlic. Heat 2 tablespoons oil in skillet over medium heat. Add minced garlic, anchovies, greens and salt to taste. Cover pan and cook until greens wilt and are tender. Remove pan from heat. Drain off excess liquid.

• Grill or lightly toast bread. Rub each slice with remaining garlic cloves and drizzle with olive oil.

• To serve, put toast, greens and bean puree on serving platter. Let each guest spoon beans onto toast and top with bit of greens.

6 servings. Each serving: 363 calories; 588 mg sodium; 3 mg cholesterol; 7 grams fat; 60 grams carbohydrates; 15 grams protein; 2.60 grams fiber.

EGGPLANT INVOLTINI

TIMES TEST KITCHEN ASSISTANT MAYI BRADY developed these wonderful little bits of finger food for a story on elegant New Year's entertaining.

2 large eggplants
Salt
1/2 cup olive oil
Salt
Freshly ground pepper
1/2 pound herbed goat cheese
1/2 cup whipping cream
1 clove garlic, minced
30 small basil leaves

• Cut eggplants crosswise into very thin slices. Put slices in large bowl and sprinkle with salt. Let stand 30 minutes. Drain off excess liquid and dry eggplant slices with paper towels. Brush eggplant slices with olive oil and season lightly to taste with salt and pepper. Grill eggplant slices on both sides until lightly browned. Remove to paper towels to drain.

• Beat goat cheese in mixing bowl until fluffy. Beat in cream until light and fluffy. Stir in garlic. Season to taste with salt and pepper. (Cheese mixture can be made 1 day in advance.)

• Using pastry bag, pipe about 1 tablespoon cheese mixture onto each slice of grilled eggplant. Top each with basil leaf and fold over 2 sides to form horn or bugle shape. Serve at room temperature.

24 servings. Each serving: 85 calories; 62 mg sodium; 7 mg cholesterol; 8 grams fat; 1 gram carbohydrates; 2 grams protein; 0.09 grams fiber.

FONDUTA *with* TRUFFLE BUTTER

EVERYTHING OLD IS NEW AGAIN. Fondue, that hallmark of 1960s entertaining, is popular once more. This recipe comes from Campanile chef Nancy Silverton. The egg yolks in this fondue will cause it to curdle if kept at too high a heat. Truffle butter is available at specialty stores, but 3/4 cup butter and 1/2 pound chopped sauteed mushrooms can be substituted.

18 ounces Fontina d'Aosta cheese, cut into 1/4-inch dice
1 1/2 cups milk
8 egg yolks, beaten
3/4 cup truffle butter, room temperature
3/4 pound aged Provolone, grated
2 teaspoons lemon juice

• Place Fontina in heat-proof mixing bowl and cover with milk. Set aside at room temperature to soften at least 4 hours or overnight.

• Place cheese and milk mixture over pot of barely simmering water and stir constantly until cheese is melted. Mixture will separate with melted cheese on bottom and milk on top. Remove bowl from water and cool about 15 minutes, stirring occasionally to release heat.

• Combine egg yolks and truffle butter. Whisk egg yolks and truffle butter into cheese and milk mixture very quickly. Place over pot of simmering water and stir until warm and combined, about 5 minutes.

• Gradually add Provolone by the handful, stirring constantly, until each addition is melted. Add lemon juice and cook 2 to 3 minutes. Taste and adjust seasoning as needed.

• Pour into warmed fondue pot and set over warmer. Serve with grilled ciabattini or other bread rubbed with garlic and grilled potatoes.

6 servings. Each serving without bread or potatoes: 511 calories; 961 mg sodium; 301 mg cholesterol; 44 grams fat; 2 grams carbohydrates; 28 grams protein; 0 fiber.

CRACKERJACK SHRIMP

1998

KOSHER CHINESE FOOD? Why not? This is L.A., after all. Genghis Cohen was a kosher Chinese restaurant in the heavily Jewish Fairfax District.

■ GINGER SAUCE

1 tablespoon ketchup
1 tablespoon chicken broth
2 tablespoons sugar
1/2 teaspoon chili sauce
3 cloves garlic, thinly sliced
1/2 teaspoon chopped ginger root

• Combine ketchup, chicken broth, sugar, chili sauce, garlic and ginger.

■ MARINADE

1 pound shrimp (41 to 50)
1 tablespoon Shaoxhing wine or Sherry
1/2 teaspoon salt
1 small egg white, beaten
1 tablespoon cornstarch
1/2 tablespoon oil
1 cup cornstarch
2 cups cottonseed or peanut oil
2 cups shredded lettuce

• Shell and devein shrimp. Rinse in cold water and pat dry. Combine wine, salt, beaten egg white, cornstarch and oil. Marinate shrimp in egg white mixture 30 minutes.

• Place cornstarch in bowl. Coat shrimp well with cornstarch, using colander to remove excess cornstarch from shrimp.

• Heat wok until very hot, then add 2 cups oil. Heat to 375 degrees.

• Drop half of shrimp into hot oil and cook 2 minutes. Remove with strainer and add remaining shrimp. Cook until golden. Drain.

• Drain oil from wok (reserving for future use). Place Ginger Sauce in hot wok. Bring to boil. Add shrimp and toss to coat evenly with sauce.

• Pour shrimp mixture over lettuce.

6 servings. Each serving: 191 calories; 224 mg sodium; 74 mg cholesterol; 11 grams fat; 12 grams carbohydrates; 11 grams protein; 0.27 gram fiber.

GREEN OLIVE CAKE

THIS APPETIZER FROM ALAIN GIRAUD, executive chef at Citrus and then Lavande, should be sliced and served with green olives and a pastis liqueur. The Green Olive Cake can be baked a few days in advance. If firmly wrapped, it will keep very well in the refrigerator.

9 ounces cooked ham
7 ounces Swiss cheese
1/2 cup green olives, pitted
1 (1/4-ounce) package dry yeast
1/4 cup lukewarm milk
1 cup plus 3 tablespoons flour
4 eggs, lightly beaten
1/4 cup olive oil
Pepper

• Cut ham and Swiss cheese into 1/4-inch cubes. Slice olives in half. Set aside.

• Dissolve yeast in lukewarm milk in small bowl.

• Mix flour, dissolved yeast, eggs and oil on low speed with paddle attachment. Stir in ham, cheese, olives and pepper to taste.

• Line 11x5x3-inch mold with parchment paper and lightly grease. Pour in batter and bake at 325 degrees until pale golden brown, about 1 hour.

• Unmold on wire rack. Let cool, then refrigerate at least 4 hours.

8 servings. Each serving: 313 calories; 531 mg sodium; 146 mg cholesterol; 19 grams fat; 16 grams carbohydrates; 19 grams protein; 0.13 gram fiber.

LOBSTER CUSTARD *with* CAVIAR

1998

REMEMBER "IRON CHEF?" The Japanese cooking series debuted on Los Angeles' international television station before moving over to the Food Network. This recipe comes from Ron Siegel, an American who won the Iron Chef title.

■ LOBSTER STOCK

Shells from 2 lobsters
5 black peppercorns
1 bay leaf
1 sprig parsley
1 clove garlic
1/2 onion
5 cups water

• Put lobster shells, peppercorns, bay leaf, parsley, garlic, onion and water in saucepan and bring to boil. Lower heat to simmer and cook until liquid is reduced to 2 cups, about 2 hours.

• Strain liquid into clean pot and simmer until reduced to 1 cup, about 1 hour.

■ LOBSTER CUSTARD

1 cup milk
1 cup whipping cream
1/2 cup Lobster Stock
Salt, pepper
1 dozen eggs
2 pounds rock salt, optional
1 pound mixed spices (fresh bay leaves and peppercorns), optional
1 ounce Beluga or other caviar

• Bring milk and cream to boil with Lobster Stock. Season with salt and pepper to taste.

• Take 3 eggs and cut off tops of small ends with kitchen shears or sharp knock of large knife. Put yolks and whites in bowl. Set empty shell cups aside.

• Stir small amount of hot cream mixture into eggs in bowl to temper them. Then stir eggs into remaining cream mixture. Strain through fine mesh strainer or cheesecloth.

• Cut tops off remaining 9 eggs as above. Reserve shell cups; yolks and whites may be reserved for another use. Clean egg shells and carefully remove interior membrane with your finger. Once membrane is removed, shells will be very brittle.

• Rinse shells in warm water. Place shells back in egg carton, then place carton in large baking pan. Fill pan with water just until level reaches 1/4 way up side of eggs. Fill shells with custard. Cover and bake at 275 degrees until custard sets but is still soft, 40 minutes.

CONTINUED ☞

• Remove from oven and place custard-filled eggs on bed of rock salt decorated with spices. Top with caviar and serve.

---

12 servings. Each serving: 161 calories; 173 mg sodium; 255 mg cholesterol; 13 grams fat; 2 grams carbohydrates; 8 grams protein; 0 fiber.

HELEN'S CHILES RELLENOS

THIS RECIPE, PROBABLY PART of thousands of cooks' standard party repertoire, came to us from Sheilah Palacios of San Gabriel, in response to a story on favorite pot-luck dishes.

1/2 cup (1 stick) butter
1 (7-ounce) can diced green chiles, drained
1/2 pound Cheddar cheese, shredded
1/2 pound Jack cheese, shredded
3 eggs
2 cups milk
3/4 teaspoon salt
1 cup biscuit mix

• Melt butter in 13x9-inch baking dish. Arrange chiles in layer in bottom of pan. Cover with Cheddar and Jack cheeses.

• Blend eggs, milk, salt and biscuit mix in mixing bowl. Pour over cheese in baking dish.

• Bake at 350 degrees until golden, 35 to 40 minutes. Let cool slightly and cut into squares. Serve warm.

---

12 servings. Each serving: 291 calories; 598 mg sodium; 113 mg cholesterol; 22 grams fat; 10 grams carbohydrates; 13 grams protein; 0 fiber.

SQUASH *and* BEAN SPROUTS FRITTERS *with* SHRIMP
(*Ukoy*)

1999

TIMES TEST KITCHEN INTERN Rommel delos Santos grew up in the Philippines, where the midday snacks called meryendas are traditional. This is one of his mother's meryenda recipes. Dried shrimp are available at Asian markets.

■ SAUCE

1/4 cup light soy sauce
1/2 cup vinegar
1 small onion, diced
2 cloves garlic, minced
1/2 teaspoon pepper

• Combine soy sauce, vinegar, onion, garlic and pepper and mix well.

■ SQUASH

1 1/2 pounds kabocha squash, unpeeled
3 carrots
1/2 cup baby dried shrimp
1/2 pound large shrimp, peeled and deveined
1/2 pound bean sprouts
1/2 bunch green onions, chopped
1 1/2 teaspoons salt
1 1/2 teaspoons pepper

• Wash and quarter squash and remove seeds. Coarsely grate squash and carrots in food processor or with hand grater. Transfer to large bowl and add baby dried shrimp, shrimp, bean sprouts, green onions, salt and pepper.

■ BATTER

2 cups flour
1 tablespoon salt
2 eggs
1/2 teaspoon cayenne pepper
2 1/2 cups water
Oil for frying

• Combine flour, salt, eggs, cayenne and water and mix thoroughly.

CONTINUED☞

- Add batter to Squash and mix well. Form into palm-size 2-inch-thick fritters.
- Heat 1/4 inch oil in skillet over medium heat. Fry fritters until golden brown, about 2 minutes per side. Drain on paper towels.
- Spoon Sauce over fritters.

15 palm-size fritters. Each fritter: 143 calories; 1,031 mg sodium; 63 mg cholesterol; 6 grams fat; 16 grams carbohydrates; 7 grams protein; 0.44 gram fiber.

BRIE *with* SUN-DRIED TOMATO TOPPING

SANTA BARBARA CATERER Stephen Singleton created this recipe for an event featuring the photographs of Julia Child's husband Paul.

1989

2 pounds Brie
5 tablespoons minced parsley leaves
5 tablespoons freshly grated Parmesan cheese
10 sun-dried tomatoes, packed in oil, minced
2 1/2 tablespoons oil from sun-dried tomatoes
12 cloves garlic, mashed
2 tablespoons minced fresh basil
3 tablespoons toasted pine nuts, coarsely chopped

- Chill Brie well before handling. Remove rind from top and place cheese on serving platter. Combine parsley, Parmesan, tomatoes, oil, garlic, basil and pine nuts. Spread on top of Brie.
- Serve at once or refrigerate for later use. For optimum flavor, allow Brie to stand 30 to 60 minutes when removed from refrigerator.

16 servings. Each serving: 235 calories; 429 mg sodium; 58 mg cholesterol; 19 grams fat; 3 grams carbohydrates; 14 grams protein; 0.17 gram fiber.

PRAWN ROLLS
(*Prataad Lom*)

1987

THESE INCREDIBLE APPETIZERS came from a cooking class Barbara Hansen took in Bangkok at the Oriental Hotel from famed teacher Chalie Amyatakul. She took the class in order to learn more about Thai cuisine, which was just becoming popular in Southern California at that time. Sriracha, which is Thai hot sauce, bean curd sheets, and dried preserved plums are available in Asian markets.

■ PLUM SAUCE

1 cup water
1 cup sugar
1 1/2 tablespoons rice vinegar
1/4 teaspoon salt
6 Chinese dried preserved plums

• Combine water, sugar, rice vinegar, salt and whole plums in small saucepan. Bring to boil and boil until liquid is reduced to 3/4 cup. Remove plums and cool sauce to room temperature.

■ PRAWN ROLLS

Dried bean curd sheets
1 pound shrimp with heads
1 teaspoon coriander root
1 teaspoon minced garlic
1 teaspoon white pepper
1 tablespoon fish sauce or soy sauce
2 egg yolks, beaten
Oil for deep frying

• Sprinkle or brush bean curd sheets with water and allow to soften.
• Shell and clean shrimp, retaining tails. Make slits in inner curve so shrimp will lie flat. Combine coriander root, garlic and pepper in mortar and pound to make paste. Stir in fish sauce. Combine mixture with shrimp and marinate 5 minutes.
• Cut bean curd sheet into 3-inch squares. Place 1 shrimp on each square near top, allowing tail to extend over edge. Fold top of square over shrimp. Roll up tightly. Brush lower edge of bean curd sheet with egg yolk to seal. Place rolls on rack until ready to fry. Fry in deep hot oil until golden brown. Drain on paper towels. Serve at once with bowls of Plum Sauce or Sriracha sauce for dipping.

2 dozen rolls. Each roll: 66 calories; 91 mg sodium; 41 mg cholesterol; 2 grams fat; 9 grams carbohydrates; 3 grams protein; 0 fiber

SPICY MIXED NUTS

THIS IS THE KIND OF THING that should be on the table at every cocktail party. Cookbook author and longtime columnist Abby Mandel notes you can vary the heat on these according to your taste.

1 tablespoon sugar
1 1/2 teaspoons ground cumin
1 1/2 teaspoons cayenne pepper
1 1/4 teaspoons salt
1/2 pound walnut halves
1/2 pound pecan halves
1/2 pound unsalted cashews
1/4 cup oil

• Combine sugar, cumin, cayenne and salt. Set aside.

• Spread walnuts, pecans and cashews in single layer in jellyroll pan. Roast at 375 degrees until fragrant, about 7 minutes; shake pan several times during roasting to prevent sticking and browning. Transfer hot nuts to large bowl.

• Toss with oil (use 2 large spoons) until nuts are well coated.

• Immediately add spices, tossing again until well mixed. Serve warm or cool completely for storage. (Can be made up to a week ahead and kept in an airtight container at room temperature. Can be frozen up to 1 month, wrapped airtight. Before serving, let come to room temperature by spreading on baking sheet, then bake at 350 degrees 5 minutes.)

24 to 30 servings. Each of 30 servings: 157 calories; 100 mg sodium; 0 cholesterol; 15 grams fat; 6 grams carbohydrates; 4 grams protein; 0.70 gram fiber.

STUFFED SHRIMP *in a* SILK WRAPPER

1998

THIS IS ANOTHER RECIPE that came from Times Test Kitchen intern May Parich's talented mother, Surapee, a fabulous Thai cook. Thin soy sauce is sold at Asian markets.

■ DIPPING SAUCE

3 tablespoons Thai chili paste
1/3 cup vinegar
3/4 cup water
1 1/2 cups sugar
1 tablespoon plus 3/4 teaspoon salt

• Combine chili paste, vinegar, water, sugar and salt in medium saucepan. Boil until slightly thick, about 10 minutes. Let cool and set aside. Makes about 1 1/2 cups.

■ STUFFED SHRIMP

1/2 pound ground pork
1 (4 1/2-ounce) can lump crab meat
2 tablespoons thin soy sauce
1/4 teaspoon freshly ground pepper
1 teaspoon garlic powder
1/3 cup chopped cilantro
1/2 cup chopped water chestnuts
1 tablespoon sesame oil
2 tablespoons water
1 cucumber, peeled
48 large shrimp
24 spring roll wrappers
1 egg, lightly beaten
Oil for deep frying

• Combine pork, crab meat, soy sauce, pepper, garlic powder, cilantro, water chestnuts, sesame oil and water. Slice cucumber into 1/4-inch-thick rounds.

• Peel shrimp to tail. Butterfly along back, removing vein. Stuff cut portion of each shrimp with 1 teaspoon filling, mounding filling over shrimp.

• Cut wrappers diagonally to make triangles. Cover with damp towel to prevent drying.

• Place 1 shrimp on 1 wrapper triangle about 1/4 of way from corner with tail hanging over longest edge. Carefully wrap corner over shrimp and roll shrimp in wrapper about 3 times. Fold top corner over shrimp and continue rolling and tucking to achieve snug fit around shrimp with shrimp tail hanging out. Brush beaten egg where edges come together to seal wrapper.

CONTINUED ☛

- Fill medium-sized, heavy saucepan halfway with oil and heat on medium-high until 400 degrees. Fry shrimp until golden brown, about 3 minutes. Drain on paper towels.
- Serve with Dipping Sauce and cucumber slices.

48 shrimp rolls. Each shrimp roll with 1 teaspoon sauce: 79 calories; 229 mg sodium; 18 mg cholesterol; 2 grams fat; 12 grams carbohydrates; 4 grams protein; 0.05 gram fiber.

STUFFED CHERRY TOMATOES

MARION CUNNINGHAM SAYS SHE hates hors d'oeuvres. You couldn't tell it by these delicious little bites. Use the smallest cherry tomatoes you can find for this recipe.

1 pound cherry tomatoes, stems removed
1/2 cup mayonnaise
4 strips cooked bacon, crumbled

- Wash and dry tomatoes. Cut thin slice from top stem end of each tomato. Using small spoon, scoop out juice and seeds from inside each tomato and discard.
- Stir together mayonnaise and bacon in small bowl. Fill each tomato cavity with mayonnaise mixture.

16 to 20 tomatoes. Each tomato: 58 calories; 86 mg sodium; 5 mg cholesterol; 5 grams fat; 3 grams carbohydrates; 1 gram protein; 0.18 gram fiber.

TORTA RUSTICA

1987

AT ONE TIME, IT SEEMED almost impossible to go to a dinner party where you didn't find one of these, kind of a cross between a sandwich and a tart.

■ OMELET LAYER

1 tablespoon butter
3 eggs, beaten
1 clove garlic, minced
1/4 teaspoon dried tarragon leaves
Salt, pepper

• Melt butter in 10-inch nonstick skillet. Combine eggs, garlic and tarragon. Season to taste with salt and pepper. Pour egg mixture into skillet and cook over medium heat, lifting edges to allow uncooked portion of egg to flow underneath to cook. Cook until set. Slide onto plate and cool. Makes 1 (10-inch) omelet.

■ ASSEMBLY

2 loaves frozen bread dough, thawed
20 slices provolone
8 (7-inch diameter) slices mortadella with pistachios
1 (1-pound) jar roasted sweet red peppers, drained, seeded and halved lengthwise
25 slices mozzarella
10 slices cappicola
6 (4-inch diameter) slices mortadella
1 (1-pound) jar Macedonian golden peppers, drained, seeded and halved lengthwise
1 (10-ounce) package frozen collard greens, thawed and well drained
1/4 pound thinly sliced prosciutto
1 (6-inch long) link Italian dry sausage, cut in thin diagonal slices
13 slices spicy, hard salami
1 egg white
Water

• Roll 1 loaf thawed bread into circle large enough to fit in bottom and up sides of 10-inch springform pan. (If dough is too elastic to retain shape when rolled, let rest a few minutes, then try again.)
• Press rolled dough onto bottom and up sides of oiled pan.
• Arrange 7 slices provolone over dough in bottom of pan, overlapping slightly. Top provolone with 4 slices 7-inch mortadella with pistachios.

CONTINUED☞

• Flatten sweet red peppers on paper towels to remove any additional moisture and arrange half of peppers over mortadella. Add layer of 7 slices mozzarella, all cappicola and all slices 4-inch mortadella. Press layers down firmly each time new one is added.

• Slide Omelet Layer over mortadella. Flatten golden peppers on paper towels and arrange over Omelet Layer. Add 6 slices mozzarella. Spread drained collard greens over mozzarella. Press each layer down firmly while continuing to add layers of 6 slices provolone, prosciutto, 6 slices mozzarella, dry sausage slices, remaining half of sweet red peppers, remaining 7 slices provolone, all spicy hard salami, remaining 4 slices 7-inch mortadella and remaining 6 slices mozzarella.

• Roll remaining loaf of dough into large enough circle to fit top of torta. Pinch edges of dough together at sides, sealing well. Brush with egg white mixed with water. Bake at 350 degrees 1 hour or until bread case is golden brown and pulls away from sides of pan slightly.

• Completely cool in pan on rack. Refrigerate and serve cold. Cut in wedges to serve.

---

16 to 20 servings. Each of 20 servings: 365 calories; 1,086 mg sodium; 76 mg cholesterol; 41 grams fat; 30 grams carbohydrates; 18 grams protein; 0.27 gram fiber.

TUNA TARTARE
on MARINATED CUCUMBERS

THIS RECIPE FROM A STORY on noted cooking teacher Jacques Pepin is delicious and attractive, simple but sophisticated. The tuna should be chopped by hand rather than in a food processor. When mixed with vinegar, the chopped tuna will "whiten" somewhat, becoming opaque. This is because the acetic acid in the vinegar coagulates, thus "cooking" the protein in the tuna.

■ TUNA TARTARE

1 pound tuna
Salt
1 large shallot, finely chopped (2 tablespoons)
2 cloves garlic, crushed and finely chopped (1 teaspoon)
1/2 teaspoon pepper
2 tablespoons olive oil
1 1/2 teaspoons white vinegar
1/4 teaspoon hot pepper sauce

• Reserve 4 small slices (1 ounce each) tuna, and chop remainder by hand into 1/4-inch dice. Place 1 reserved tuna slice between 2 sheets of plastic wrap, and pound into thin round about 4 inches in diameter.

• Repeat with remaining slices.

• Remove top sheet of plastic wrap from slices and season lightly with salt to taste. Set aside.

• Mix chopped tuna with shallot, garlic, 1 teaspoon salt, pepper, oil, vinegar and hot pepper sauce.

■ CUCUMBER GARNISH

1 cucumber (about 3/4 pound)
1 teaspoon vinegar
1 teaspoon peanut oil
1/4 teaspoon salt
3 tablespoons minced chives
1 1/2 teaspoons drained capers

• Peel cucumber, and cut into long thin strips with vegetable peeler on all sides until you come to seeds. Discard seeds and mix strips with vinegar, oil and salt.

• To serve, divide garnish among 4 plates. Form chopped tuna mixture into 4 balls, and place 1 ball on top of cucumber on each plate. Wrap slice of tuna around each tuna ball, sprinkle with chives and capers, then serve.

4 servings. Each serving: 247 calories; 292 mg sodium; 43 mg cholesterol; 14 grams fat; 3 grams carbohydrates; 30 grams protein; 0.60 gram fiber.

PERFECT POTATO LATKES

NOBODY KNOWS MORE ABOUT latkes than Judy Zeidler, who has made quite a reputation for her classes and cookbooks on Jewish cooking. These are incredibly good. How good? They are so good we published them two years in a row.

1997

4 baking potatoes, peeled
1 large onion, grated
1 tablespoon lemon juice
4 eggs
3 tablespoons flour
Baking soda
1 teaspoon salt
Freshly ground pepper
Oil
Sour cream, optional

• Grate potatoes using food processor or fine shredder. Immediately transfer to large bowl and add onion, lemon juice, eggs, flour, dash baking soda, salt and pepper to taste. Mix well.

• Heat 1/8 inch oil in 4-inch nonstick skillet over medium heat. Ladle batter into hot oil with large spoon, and flatten latkes with back of spoon. Cook on 1 side just until golden brown, 3 to 5 minutes, then turn and cook other side. Turn once only. Drain well on paper towel and serve immediately, plain or with sour cream.

1 dozen latkes. Each latke: 75 calories; 220 mg sodium; 71 mg cholesterol; 3 grams fat; 9 grams carbohydrates; 3 grams protein; 0.23 gram fiber.

SAVORY MINCED PORK
on PINEAPPLE (*Mah Haw*)

★

1993

♥

THIS RECIPE FROM COOKBOOK AUTHOR Nancy McDermott is an example of Central Thai court cuisine. The spark is a cilantro "pesto," hot with black pepper rather than chiles. Look for Thai chiles at Asian markets.

■ CILANTRO PESTO

1 teaspoon white or black peppercorns
2 tablespoons coarsely chopped fresh cilantro roots or leaves and stems
2 tablespoons coarsely chopped garlic

• In mortar, small blender or food processor, combine pepper, cilantro roots and garlic and work into fairly smooth paste. If using blender or food processor, adding some oil or water may ease grinding. Makes 1/4 cup.

■ MINCED PORK

1 teaspoon oil
3 tablespoons Cilantro Pesto
1/2 pound coarsely ground pork
2 tablespoons fish sauce
2 tablespoons palm sugar or brown sugar, packed
3 tablespoons finely chopped dry roasted peanuts
1 small to medium pineapple
2 fresh red Thai chiles, cut into long, thin strips, or 6 long, thin sweet red pepper strips 1 bunch small cilantro leaves

• Heat wok or medium skillet over medium heat. Add oil and swirl to coat surface. When oil is hot, add Cilantro Pesto. Stir-fry paste until quite fragrant, about 2 minutes. Increase heat to medium-high and crumble in ground pork. Stir-fry pork until it breaks into small lumps, renders some fat and is no longer pink, about 2 minutes.

• Add fish sauce and palm sugar and continue cooking, stirring and scraping often to brown and coat meat evenly. After about 4 minutes, when meat is browned, remove pan from heat and taste sauce for salty-sweet balance. Add more fish sauce and palm sugar if needed and return to heat to reduce. Remove from heat, transfer to medium bowl and let cool to room temperature.

• Peel pineapple and cut crosswise into 1/4-inch-thick slices. Remove hard core from center of each slice and cut slices into 1-inch squares. There should be about 2 cups of squares.

• To serve, mound spoonful of savory pork onto each pineapple square.

• Garnish each mound with chile strips and cilantro leaves. Transfer to platter and serve at room temperature as finger food.

10 to 12 servings. Each of 12 servings: 88 calories; 125 mg sodium; 10 mg cholesterol; 3 grams fat; 12 grams carbohydrates; 4 grams protein; 0.68 gram fiber.

FOUR

Meat

BEEF TATAKI

1986

ROY YAMAGUCHI, NOW FAMED AS one of the pioneers in Hawaiian cuisine, got his start in Los Angeles. He worked at L'Ermitage for Jean Bertranou, one of the founding fathers of modern Southern California cooking. Yamaguchi's first restaurant on his own was 385 North on La Cienega Boulevard. Shiso leaf is available in Asian markets.

1 1/2 teaspoons grated ginger root
3/4 teaspoon grated garlic
1/2 cup dark soy sauce
1 bunch shiso leaf, cut in thin strips
1/4 cup lime juice
14 ounces culotte or New York steak
Pepper
2 tablespoons peanut oil
Green onions, thinly sliced diagonally

• Combine ginger, garlic, soy sauce, shiso and lime juice in flat glass dish just large enough to hold steak. Set aside.

• Trim steak to remove excess fat and season to taste with pepper on top and bottom. Sear beef quickly in hot peanut oil on all sides over high heat. Cook to rare stage only.

• Place in dish with marinade and turn to coat well. Refrigerate, turning occasionally, at least 1 hour. Steak should be very cold and firm before slicing. To serve, thinly slice diagonally. Sprinkle steak slices with green onions and spoon small amount of marinade over, or serve on bed of carrots, Chinese pea pods or other thinly sliced vegetable, if desired.

4 servings. Each serving: 181 calories; 2,051 mg sodium; 42 mg cholesterol; 10 grams fat; 4 grams carbohydrates; 18 grams protein; 0.02 gram fiber.

BARBECUE RIBS, MISSOURI-STYLE

We called this recipe the ultimate home-made rib. Because the ribs start off with a rub and a slow bake, the meat does not shrink from the bone. What you get are crisp, chewy and satisfyingly spicy ribs. If you like a saucier rib, you can simply brush the ribs with your favorite barbecue sauce just before you serve them. From Chris Schlesinger and John Willoughby.

1993

Salt
Sugar
2 tablespoons ground cumin
Freshly ground pepper
2 tablespoons chili powder
4 tablespoons paprika
2 (3 pounds each) full racks pork spareribs
1 3/4 cups white vinegar
2 tablespoons hot pepper sauce

• Combine 2 tablespoons salt, 4 tablespoons sugar, cumin, 2 tablespoons pepper, chili powder and paprika in bowl and stir well. Rub dry rub mixture over ribs.

• Place ribs on baking sheets and bake at 180 degrees 3 hours.

• Remove ribs from oven. (Ribs can be done up to 2 days ahead to this point and then refrigerated.)

• Over very low charcoal fire, with rack set as high as possible, grill ribs until light crust forms on outside, up to 30 minutes per side. Turn ribs over and repeat.

• Combine vinegar, hot pepper sauce, 2 tablespoons sugar, 1 tablespoon salt and 1 tablespoon pepper and baste ribs with mixture just before removing from grill. (If "dry" ribs are desired, sauce can be served on side.)

6 servings. Each serving: 769 calories; 3,787 mg sodium; 186 mg cholesterol; 58 grams fat; 21 grams carbohydrates; 42 grams protein; 1.65 grams fiber.

BOUDIN BLANC *aux* HERBES

THE OLD LE ST. GERMAINE RESTAURANT was one of the landmarks of Hollywood dining. This recipe is from Eric Gerber, chef-charcutier at Le St. Germain To Go. Casings are available from some butcher shops. Sheep casings will be finer and more tender than pork casings.

1 1/2 cups milk
1/4 cup whipping cream
1/2 bunch tarragon
1/2 bunch basil
1/2 bunch parsley
2 green onions, chopped
2 shallots
14 ounces lean veal, trimmed
14 ounces lean chicken meat, trimmed
14 ounces pork fatback or veal fat
1 pound ice cubes with a little cold water
1 1/4 tablespoons salt
3/4 teaspoon ground white pepper
1/8 teaspoon ground allspice
1/8 teaspoon ground mace or nutmeg
Pork or sheep casings
Butter

• Bring milk and cream to boil. Add tarragon, basil, parsley, green onions and shallots. Let boil 1 minute. Drain. Chill herbs and cream mixture separately until cold, 30 minutes to 1 hour.

• Grind veal, chicken meat and fat separately through fine grinding plate. Repeat to grind even more finely.

• Place herbs in food processor or sausage chopper and finely grind. Add veal, chicken and 1/3 of ice and water mixture. Grind until water is absorbed. Add salt, white pepper, allspice and mace. Add another 1/3 of ice and water and process until almost smooth. Add milk mixture and remaining ice and water. Process until emulsion is smooth, fine and creamy. Remove mixture and keep cold.

• Place ground fat in processor and process until smooth and creamy.

• Slowly add meat mixture, processing until smooth and creamy (temperature should not exceed 55 degrees).

• Slide wet casings onto stuffing horn or funnel tube. Tie knot in end.

• Feed in sausage meat, filling casing loosely. Pinch sausage at 5- to 6-inch lengths, then twist or twirl twice to make links.

CONTINUED ☞

• Poach sausages in large kettle, covered with cheesecloth, 20 minutes for larger pork casings and 7 to 10 minutes for smaller sheep casings. Water temperature should be about 180 degrees. Transfer sausages from poaching water to ice cold water to cool quickly 5 to 12 minutes. (If not grilling immediately, store, covered, in refrigerator 4 to 5 days.)

• Saute in small amount of butter until lightly golden. If desired, add small amount of wine to remaining drippings and pour over sausages upon serving. Serve with butter-sauteed onions and cooked potatoes, if desired.

20 pork-casing sausages or 40 sheep-casing sausages. Each of 20 sausages: 164 calories; 477 mg sodium; 34 mg cholesterol; 14 grams fat; 2 grams carbohydrates; 7 grams protein; 0.07 gram fiber.

CHORIZOS ENTOMATADOS

ANA OVIEDO, A TIMES TEST KITCHEN WORKER, contributed this wonderful El Salvadoran sausage dish. Salvadoran chorizos are available at Latino markets.

1993

18 (2-inch) Salvadoran chorizos
1/2 cup water
1 onion, thinly sliced
4 serrano chiles, quartered lengthwise, seeded
2 large tomatoes
2 teaspoons oregano
1 teaspoon salt
Salvadoran-Style Frijoles, optional (See Page XX)

• Place chorizos in single layer in skillet. Add water. Boil, uncovered, until water cooks away. Cook chorizos in drippings remaining in skillet until browned on each side. Add onion and chiles.

• Break apart tomatoes with fingers and add to skillet. Crumble oregano into pan. Add salt and stir. Cover and simmer 10 minutes, or until onion is tender and tomatoes have cooked down to sauce. Serve with Salvadoran-Style Frijoles.

4 to 6 servings. Each of 6 servings, without Frijoles: 500 calories; 1,849 mg sodium; 89 mg cholesterol; 39 grams fat; 11 grams carbohydrates; 26 grams protein; 1.33 grams fiber.

BEEF POT PIES

THIS RECIPE IS FROM Times Test Kitchen Director Donna Deane.

■ BEEF FILLING

2 tablespoons oil
1/2 cup chopped onion
1 clove garlic, minced
1/2 cup chopped celery
1/2 cup chopped peeled carrot
1 (14 1/2-ounce) can beef broth
1 (14 1/2-ounce) can chicken broth
Water
1/2 cup flour
4 cups diced cooked beef, drippings reserved
2 tablespoons prepared horseradish
1 cup frozen peas, thawed and drained
1 cup frozen corn, thawed and drained
Salt, pepper
1/2 cup shredded Swiss cheese

• Heat oil in skillet. Saute onion, garlic, celery and carrot in oil until tender. Combine beef and chicken broths. Add water to measure 4 cups. Add to vegetables. Cover and simmer until vegetables are tender, about 10 minutes.

• Combine flour and 2/3 cup water, stirring until smooth. Stir into simmering broth. Heat and stir until boiling and thickened. Stir in meat, horseradish, peas and corn. Add any beef drippings left from roasting meat to broth. Simmer about 5 minutes, stirring occasionally, to blend flavors. Season to taste with salt and pepper. Spoon mixture into 2 1/2-quart oven-proof casserole or individual 4- to 5-inch oven-proof casseroles. Set aside while making Pastry.

■ PASTRY

1 1/2 cups flour
3/4 teaspoon salt
10 tablespoons shortening
1/2 cup shredded Swiss cheese
4 to 5 tablespoons ice water

• Combine flour and salt. Cut in shortening until size of peas. Stir in cheese.

• Add enough water so dough clings together. Gather into ball. Roll Pastry to 1/4-inch thickness. Cut round or rounds of dough 1/2 inch larger than tops of casserole. Press Pastry against edges of each casserole to seal. Cut vent holes on top. Sprinkle cheese over Pastry.

CONTINUED ☞

• Place casserole on baking sheet. Bake at 400 degrees about 30 minutes or until pastry is golden.

---

6 to 8 servings. Each of 8 servings: 473 calories; 559 mg sodium; 50 mg cholesterol; 28 grams fat; 33 grams carbohydrates; 23 grams protein; 0.97 gram fiber.

BEEF PAPRIKASH *for* TWO

3/4 pound beef sirloin
2 tablespoons oil
1/2 cup chopped onion
1 clove garlic, minced
1 1/2 teaspoons butter or margarine
2 cups beef stock
2 tablespoons sweet Hungarian paprika
1/2 cup sliced mushrooms
Salt, pepper
1 tablespoon flour
1/2 cup sour cream
1 1/2 teaspoons lemon juice
Cooked noodles for two

1986

• Chill beef until very firm but not frozen. Slice in thin strips about 3 inches long. Brown in 1 tablespoon oil in heavy skillet. Remove beef from skillet and set aside.

• Pour off excess fat. Saute onion and garlic in same skillet in remaining 1 tablespoon oil and butter until tender, but not browned.

• Return beef to pan and add beef stock, paprika and mushrooms. Season to taste with salt and pepper. Bring mixture to boil, reduce heat, cover and simmer until meat is tender, 45 minutes to 1 hour.

• When beef is tender, stir flour into sour cream and add to beef mixture. Bring to boil and cook, stirring, until thickened. Stir in lemon juice. Serve at once over hot noodles.

---

2 servings. Each serving: 520 calories; 1,069 mg sodium; 109 mg cholesterol; 37 grams fat; 14 grams carbohydrates; 34 grams protein; 1.73 grams fiber.

GRILLED PORK CHOPS
with POBLANO CREAM SAUCE

1999

This dish from Test Kitchen Director Donna Deane is perfect dinner-party fare.

■ POBLANO CREAM SAUCE

4 poblano chiles
1 tablespoon butter
1 clove garlic, minced
1/3 cup chopped onion
1/2 cup chicken broth
1 cup whipping cream
Salt
Freshly ground pepper

• Roast poblano chiles on rack over gas burner or on pan beneath broiler until charred on all sides. Put roasted peppers in paper bag and fold end over to seal. Let stand to allow peppers to sweat, about 15 minutes. Peel peppers, then cut each in half and remove ribs and seeds.

• Cut 2 pepper halves lengthwise into strips and set aside for garnish.

• Chop remaining peppers coarsely and set aside.

• Melt butter in skillet over medium heat. Add garlic and onion and saute until onion just begins to brown, 4 to 5 minutes. Stir in broth and whipping cream. Bring to boil, reduce heat and simmer until sauce begins to thicken slightly, about 5 minutes.

• Stir in chopped chiles and simmer 1 minute. Pour into blender and puree. Return Sauce to skillet, add salt and pepper to taste and keep warm.

■ PORK CHOPS

4 loin pork chops, about 3/4-inch-thick
1/2 teaspoon crumbled Mexican oregano
Salt
1/3 cup garlic oil
2 cloves garlic, sliced
Chopped cilantro, for garnish

• Season pork chops with oregano and with salt to taste. Arrange chops in glass baking dish in single layer, pour garlic oil over and add sliced garlic. Cover and marinate several hours or overnight.

• Grill chops on hot outdoor grill or heavy cast-iron grill pan set on stove until brown on outside yet light pink in center, 3 to 4 minutes per side. Serve with warm Poblano Cream Sauce and garnish with cilantro and reserved pepper strips (from Cream Sauce).

4 servings. Each serving: 640 calories; 307 mg sodium; 172 mg cholesterol; 58 grams fat; 5 grams carbohydrates; 27 grams protein; 0.32 gram fiber.

ELOY MENDEZ'S ALBONDIGAS

ELOY MENDEZ WORKED AT CAMPANILE restaurant, where this recipe quickly became a favorite at staff meals. It's a bit thicker than the typical albondigas soup, more of a stew. If you want all-beef meatballs, use 2 pounds beef.

1 1/2 onions
4 cumin seeds
1 pound ground beef
1 pound ground pork
6 whole peppercorns, freshly ground
6 whole cloves, freshly ground
5 mint leaves, chopped
2 to 3 hard-boiled eggs, coarsely chopped
2 pounds tomatillos
4 cups boiling water
5 cloves garlic
1/4 pound long green chiles, roasted and peeled
1 1/2 cups cilantro sprigs
Salt, pepper
1/4 cup oil

• Chop 1 onion. Grind 2 cumin seeds to make about 1/8 teaspoon. Combine beef, pork, ground cumin, ground peppercorns and cloves, chopped onion and mint in bowl. Mix thoroughly with hands. Form into 1-inch meatballs, putting pieces of hard-cooked egg inside each meatball. Set aside.

• Place tomatillos in boiling water with garlic, remaining 1/2 onion and 2 cumin seeds. Cook until tomatillos are tender. Place in blender with green chiles and 1 cup cilantro. Season to taste with salt and pepper.

• Puree mixture.

• Heat oil in 5-quart Dutch oven. Add pureed chile sauce and meatballs.

• Season to taste with salt and pepper. Simmer about 20 minutes. Stir in remaining cilantro.

6 servings. Each serving: 530 calories; 384 mg sodium; 169 mg cholesterol; 39 grams fat; 14 grams carbohydrates; 32 grams protein; 1.33 gram fiber.

BAKED HONEY HAM

HAMS GLAZED WITH HONEY and brown sugar are always popular at the holidays. But buying commercial ones can be expensive. This homemade version comes from reader Mrs. Jerry Fleming of Canoga Park.

---

2 cups honey
2 cups brown sugar, packed
1/3 cup cider vinegar
2 teaspoons ground nutmeg
2 teaspoons ground cinnamon
2 teaspoons ground cloves
1 (5- to 6-pound) cooked ham, bone in, or 3- to 4- pound boneless ham

• Combine honey, brown sugar, vinegar, nutmeg, cinnamon and cloves. Bake bone-in ham at 350 degrees 1 hour to heat thoroughly, basting with honey sauce occasionally. Place in broiler to glaze top.

• To cook boneless ham, slice halfway through at 1/4-inch intervals, then tie with string. Place in roasting pan. Heat honey sauce and pour over ham to marinate 24 hours before baking. Then bake at 350 degrees 1 hour or until heated through. Glaze top under broiler, if desired.

---

8 to 10 servings. Each of 10 servings: 554 calories; 2,907 mg sodium; 120 mg cholesterol; 19 grams fat; 55 grams carbohydrates; 42 grams protein; 0.02 grams fiber.

HOBO STEAK

THIS WAS ONE OF THE STANDARD entrees at Chasen's, one of the glory spots of Beverly Hills dining in the middle of the century.

1 (3-inch-thick) New York steak
Freshly ground pepper
1 (1/4-inch-thick) strip beef fat, as wide as steak is thick or several smaller pieces of fat
1 cup salt
2 tablespoons water
Sourdough French bread, cut into 3x1 1/2x1/4-inch slices, toasted
1/2 cup unsalted butter

• Season steak to taste with pepper. Wrap fat around steak to cover sides completely but not top or bottom of steak. Tie around sides with 1 string near top or bottom or steak. Tie another string over steak to hold fat securely. Combine salt and water to make mush. Mound mush over top of steak, covering meat completely.

• Place steak under broiler and broil 8 to 10 minutes, depending on size. Remove salt crust, keeping crust in 1 piece. Turn steak over and place salt on other side. Broil another 8 to 10 minutes.

• Remove steak from oven and discard salt and fat. Slice meat, cutting slightly on diagonal. Heat butter in chafing dish or large skillet until foaming and lightly browned. Place meat, few slices at time, in foaming butter. Cook to desired degree of doneness. Allow about 1 minute on each side for rare. Place each slice of meat on 1 slice of toast and spoon some of hot butter over.

2 servings. Each serving: 415 calories; 863 mg sodium; 111 mg cholesterol; 23 grams fat; 19 grams carbohydrates; 30 grams protein; 0.07 gram fiber.

LAMB SHANK KORMA

LUCKNOW, A CITY RENOWNED among India's Muslims for its elegant way of life, is where this refined, highly aromatic dish comes from. The recipe calls for kewra essence, an exotic flavoring reminiscent of roses, jasmine and sandalwood that is made from one of the many varieties of pandanus leaves. It can be overwhelming, so be careful not to add too much. Buy it at Indian grocers and import shops or use rose water instead. And be sure to use yogurt without thickeners like gelatin or tapioca, which could change the texture of the dish. Serve this dish over rice.

■ GARAM MASALA

1/4 teaspoon ground cinnamon
1/4 teaspoon ground cloves
1/4 teaspoon pepper
1/8 teaspoon ground cardamom or 1 green cardamom pod

• Mix cinnamon, cloves, pepper and cardamom. If using green cardamom pod, remove seeds from husk and pound to powder before adding.

■ LAMB SHANKS

Saffron
2 to 3 teaspoons kewra essence or rose water
2 onions
1/2 cup oil
1 1/2 ounces (1/3 cup) raw cashews
4 serrano chiles, chopped
2 bay leaves
1 tablespoon minced ginger root
1 tablespoon minced garlic
2 to 3 lamb shanks, about 2 to 2 1/2 pounds total
2 teaspoons ground coriander
1 1/2 teaspoons salt
2 teaspoons cayenne
3 tablespoons plain yogurt
3/4 teaspoon ground mace
1/2 teaspoon ground cardamom or 3 green cardamom pods, husked and crushed
4 cups water
Juice of 1 lime

• Lightly crush several threads of saffron and soak in kewra essence at least 15 minutes. Set aside.

CONTINUED ☞

- Slice onions thin and heat 1/4 cup oil in skillet. Add onions and fry until medium brown, 8 to 10 minutes. Add cashews and fry until onions are quite brown, 5 minutes longer. Tip skillet up and use spatula to press oil out of onion mixture. Discard oil and transfer onion mixture to bowl.

- When cool, puree in food processor.

- Heat remaining 1/4 cup oil in skillet and add chiles, bay leaves, ginger, garlic, lamb shanks, coriander, 1/2 Garam Masala and salt. Saute over medium heat 10 minutes, stirring continuously.

- Reduce heat to low. Add cayenne and yogurt, stir continuously 3 minutes and simmer until yogurt is absorbed, 3 to 5 minutes. Add remaining 1/2 Garam Masala, mace and cardamom and saute 2 to 3 minutes.

- Add water, bring to boil, reduce heat to medium-low, cover and cook until lamb shanks are tender, 2 hours.

- When lamb is done, remove to warm oven; debone if wished. Stir reserved onion mixture into sauce and reduce over medium-high heat, stirring constantly, until silky brown gravy forms, about 10 minutes. Add lime juice and saffron-kewra mixture. Stir meat in sauce to coat.

4 servings. Each serving: 330 calories; 921 mg sodium; 32 mg cholesterol; 27 grams fat; 15 grams carbohydrates; 11 grams protein; 1.22 grams fiber.

LAMB BASTIDS

Melissa Manchester is famous for her singing. Her mom, Ruth, is famous for her cooking. This is an example (you have to say the recipe title with a New York accent to understand it).

1992

Juice of 3 lemons (about 1/2 cup)
2 (14-ounce) bottles Chris & Pitts barbecue sauce
2 (5-ounce) bottles red horseradish
1 (18-ounce) jar apricot-pineapple jam
60 lamb riblets (about 7 pounds)

- Combine lemon juice, barbecue sauce, horseradish and jam in large bowl. Add riblets, cover and marinate in refrigerator overnight.

- Line large pan with foil. Place riblets in pan and bake at 350 degrees 1 hour until glazed. Turn riblets, brush with sauce and bake 30 minutes to 1 hour more or until dark brown.

8 servings. Each serving: 583 calories; 723 mg sodium; 148 mg cholesterol; 20 grams fat; 60 grams carbohydrates; 44 grams protein; 1.69 grams fiber.

CHILORIO

1995

WHEN KATHIE JENKINS STARTED exploring cooking under pressure for a story on the return of the pressure cookers in 1995, one of the real winners was this Mexican-flavored stew. After an hour, the meat becomes flavorful and so tender that it literally falls apart.

1 (3- to 4-pound) pork shoulder or loin roast
Salt
Black pepper
1 onion, sliced
3 cups boiling water
3 medium jalapenos, seeded and sliced
2 cloves garlic
1/4 teaspoon cumin seeds
1 teaspoon fresh oregano
1/4 cup lemon juice
Cayenne pepper
2 tablespoons chopped cilantro
2 dozen corn or flour tortillas
Chopped lettuce, optional
Chopped tomatoes, optional

• Place cooking rack in 6-quart pressure cooker. Trim as much surface fat from meat as possible. Sprinkle entire roast with salt and black pepper to taste. Place meat and sliced onion on rack. Add boiling water. Lock lid in place, bring up to full pressure and cook 60 minutes. Allow pressure to come down naturally. Remove meat and rack.

• Boil juices rapidly to reduce to about 1 1/2 cups. Add jalapenos, garlic, cumin, oregano and 1/2 teaspoon black pepper. Lock lid in place, bring to full pressure and cook 2 minutes. Reduce pressure quickly.

• Puree liquid with hand blender or in standard blender or food processor. Add lemon juice and 1/2 teaspoon salt.

• Remove meat from bones, discarding bones and fat. Coarsely chop meat with knife and then place meat in bowl. Add half of sauce to meat, mixing well. Add dash cayenne and cilantro to remaining sauce.

• To make tacos, heat tortillas over griddle or low flame. Place about 2 tablespoons meat mixture in each tortilla. Top with remaining sauce, lettuce and tomatoes.

24 tacos. Each taco: 132 calories; 101 mg sodium; 28 mg cholesterol; 4 grams fat; 14 grams carbohydrates; 11 grams protein; 1.14 grams fiber.

FAJITAS

1985

LA PARILLA, ON FIRST STREET in East Los Angeles, is one of that neighborhood's land-mark restaurants. This recipe for their fajitas comes from 1985, when that dish was just beginning to become popular.

1 to 1 1/4 pounds skirt steak or rib-eye steak
1 (8-ounce) bottle Italian dressing
4 slices bacon, cut into 1-inch squares
Oil
2 teaspoons Worcestershire sauce
1/2 teaspoon garlic salt
2 poblano chiles, cut into strips
1 onion, cut into 1/4-inch slices
5 plum tomatoes, quartered
4 yellow chiles
4 green onions
1/2 small lemon
Tortillas
Salsa

• Marinate steak overnight in dressing. When ready to cook, drain meat and cut into strips. Cook meat with bacon on large griddle or in heavy skillet 4 minutes, sprinkling with small amount oil. Season with Worcestershire and some of garlic salt while cooking.

• Cook poblano chiles and onion alongside meat on griddle or in separate skillet for same amount of time, sprinkling with oil and remaining garlic salt. Add tomatoes to vegetables and cook about 2 minutes.

• Place yellow chiles on griddle or in skillet and cook until brown in spots. Dip green onions in oil, place on griddle or in skillet and char lightly.

• Combine meat and vegetables except green onions on sizzling hot griddle or on heat-ed platter. Arrange green onions over top. Squeeze lemon juice over before serving. Accompany with tortillas and salsa.

4 servings. Each serving: 349 calories; 468 mg sodium; 54 mg cholesterol; 27 grams fat; 8 grams carbohydrates; 20 grams protein; 0.61 gram fiber.

ARISTA

1985

EVAN KLEIMAN, WHOSE ANGELI CAFFE was one of the first places in Los Angeles to serve real Italian cooking, contributed this dish in 1985—a year after the restaurant opened.

6 cloves garlic, minced
1 to 2 tablespoons fennel seeds
1 teaspoon coarse salt
Freshly ground pepper
1 (7-pound) boneless pork rib roast
Fruity olive oil

• Make paste of minced garlic, fennel seeds, salt and pepper to taste with mortar and pestle or mash with side of chef's knife. Unroll roast, if tied. Spread most of paste over meat, reserving 1 tablespoon or more.

• Roll and tie roast so that white tenderloin is in center and dark meat is outside. Make a few incisions with sharp knife about 1/2 inch deep in roast and stuff some paste into incisions. Rub olive oil over meat and place in roasting pan.

• Roast, uncovered, at 350 degrees, 2 1/2 to 3 hours or until thermometer inserted in center registers 170 degrees. Baste roast 2 or 3 times with pan juices. Remove roast from oven and cool slightly. Slice into 1/2-inch slices and drizzle olive oil over meat, if desired.

10 to 12 servings. Each of 12 servings: 629 calories; 271 mg sodium; 129 mg cholesterol; 53 grams fat; 1 grams carbohydrates; 35 grams protein; 0.10 gram fiber.

LAURA VERA'S TINGA

READER LAURA VERA CONTRIBUTED this recipe for a story on "dad food." She says her father cooked to celebrate the birth of each of his children..

1 pound flank steak
1 onion
Salt
2 ounces guajillo chiles
1 large tomato, peeled
1 clove garlic
1 pound onions, sliced
2 tablespoons oil
1 to 2 canned chipotle chiles
Dried oregano
8 tostada shells
1/2 pound queso fresco, crumbled
Sour cream

• Place flank steak, whole onion and salt to taste in large saucepan.

• Add water to cover. Bring to boil, reduce heat and simmer 30 to 45 minutes or until tender. Remove meat, cool slightly, then shred and set aside.

• Place guajillo chiles in small saucepan. Add water to cover and bring to boil. Reduce heat and simmer until tender. Drain chiles, discard seeds and place in blender container. Add tomato and garlic. Puree.

• Saute sliced onions in oil. Add chipotle chiles and 2 teaspoons salt. Simmer 10 minutes. Add reserved meat, dash oregano and guajillo chile mixture. Cook 10 to 15 minutes. Spoon meat mixture on tostada shells and garnish with queso fresco and sour cream.

8 servings. Each serving: 268 calories; 502 mg sodium; 49 mg cholesterol; 16 grams fat; 17 grams carbohydrates; 15 grams protein; 0.63 gram fiber.

LEG *of* LAMB *a la* TAMAS

1995

BUDAPEST-BORN TAMAS VETRO gave the Times Test Kitchen this recipe in which 2-inch deep cuts are made all over the surface of the lamb then filled with slivers of garlic that have been rolled in small pieces of bacon. With the bacon, there is no need to season with salt or to baste with oil. All you need to do is brush the lamb occasionally so that the melting bacon fat spreads over the whole surface. If the garlic and bacon start to pop out of the slits, just push them back in.

1 (6- to 7-pound) leg of lamb
Garlic cloves, cut into slivers
1/4 pound bacon, cut crosswise into 2-inch pieces
Dijon mustard, optional

• Make deep 2-inch cuts at regular intervals over entire surface of lamb. Roll 1 sliver garlic in 1 (2-inch) piece bacon and insert completely into lamb slit. Repeat until all bacon is used.

• Place lamb on spit over hot charcoals or in electric rotisserie. Cook until lamb reaches desired doneness, about 3 hours for medium-rare to medium. Brush surface of lamb during cooking as bacon juices begin to come out. If bacon starts to pop out of slits, push back in. Serve with mustard.

12 servings. Each serving: 228 calories; 141 mg sodium; 90 mg cholesterol; 12 grams fat; 1 gram carbohydrates; 28 grams protein; 0.05 gram fiber.

MICHAEL ROBERTS' BIRRIA

1998

MICHAEL ROBERTS WAS ONE of the founding chefs in Los Angeles' new wave. His Trumps restaurant in West Hollywood was one of the first places to serve what became known as "California Cuisine." This is a recipe he developed while working as a consultant at Cabo San Lucas' stylish Twin Dolphins resort. Look for goat leg at Latino markets.

1 (24-ounce) can enchilada sauce
2 cups red wine
1 teaspoon ground cumin
1/2 teaspoon cinnamon
1/4 teaspoon ground cloves
1 (7-pound) goat leg, cut into 8 large pieces with bone
2 tablespoons lard
2 onions, chopped
4 dried ancho chiles, stemmed and seeded
4 branches epazote
Water
8 cloves garlic
3 tablespoons prepared adobo sauce
4 to 5 whole canned chipotle chiles in adobo sauce
2 teaspoons salt
3 jalapenos, seeded and finely chopped
1/4 cup finely chopped cilantro leaves

• Combine enchilada sauce, wine, cumin, cinnamon and cloves. Pour over goat, cover and marinate in refrigerator 8 hours or overnight.

• Place lard, 1 onion, ancho chiles and epazote in heavy cast-iron pot or Dutch oven and place on coals of barbecue or bake at 375 degrees until onion is soft but not brown, 10 to 15 minutes. Add meat and marinade and enough water to barely cover meat. Add garlic, adobo, chipotle chiles and salt. Cook on just enough coals to maintain slow simmer or bake at 300 degrees, stirring occasionally, until meat is tender and falling off bones, 6 to 7 hours. Add water to pot as necessary to keep meat barely covered.

• Combine jalapenos, remaining chopped onion and cilantro in small bowl and serve as accompaniment to goat.

10 to 12 servings. Each of 12 servings: 237 calories; 727 mg sodium; 87 mg cholesterol; 6 grams fat; 5 grams carbohydrates; 31 grams protein; 0.13 gram fiber.

MIENG KWAYTEOW

1993

BANGKOK-BORN PIPATPONG ISRASENA learned to cook this dish from his father. To make this recipe, cut a sheet of fresh rice noodles into strips and pile them on a plate. Another plate holds thinly sliced pork tenderloin, and small bowls contain roasted peanuts, dried shrimp and a bold sauce that is sweet, hot and loaded with garlic. A little bit of each of these ingredients goes into the center of a large leaf of super-fresh lettuce along with a little mint, red-stemmed basil and bean sprouts. Bite into the bundle and you'll experience a wonderful accumulation of flavors. Look for palm sugar, Thai chiles, fresh rice noodles and dried shrimp at Thai markets.

1 (2- to 3-pound) pork tenderloin
2 tablespoons palm sugar
1 tablespoon granulated sugar
2 tablespoons fish sauce
2 tablespoons lime juice
4 to 5 cloves garlic, finely chopped
5 tiny Thai chiles, chopped
1 (16-ounce) package uncut fresh rice noodles
Lettuce leaves, such as romaine or other leafy lettuce
Bean sprouts
Red-stemmed basil sprigs
Mint sprigs
1/2 cup roasted peanuts
1/2 cup dried shrimp

• Place pork in large saucepan or Dutch oven. Cover with water. Simmer until fully cooked, about 30 minutes. Cool and refrigerate.

• Combine sugars, fish sauce and lime juice in small saucepan. Boil until sugars are dissolved. Cool. Add garlic and chiles. Turn into sauce dish.

• Cut rice noodles into 3x1 1/2-inch rectangles and place on serving plate. Arrange lettuce, bean sprouts, basil and mint on large platter.

• Place peanuts and shrimp in separate bowls.

• To eat, tear large lettuce leaf into smaller pieces. Top with 1 noodle rectangle, opened flat. Place few peanuts, couple shrimp and slice pork on top of noodle. Add spoonful sauce. Top with bean sprouts and herbs.

• Fold lettuce into bundle and eat.

8 servings. Each serving: 384 calories; 218 mg sodium; 55 mg cholesterol; 7 grams fat; 57 grams carbohydrates; 24 grams protein; 0.73 gram fiber.

OXTAILS *with* ORANGE

THIS RECIPE FROM NOVELIST Michelle Huneven, a frequent contributor to the Times Food section, is notable for the way the orange juice and zest add a subtle citrus under-taste that balances the fatty richness of the oxtails.

1994

2 cups fresh orange juice
20 whole cloves
5 whole allspice
2 teaspoons peppercorns
2 teaspoons coarse salt
2 tablespoons olive oil
4 pounds oxtails
4 medium-large onions, chopped
2 carrots, peeled, chopped
2 tablespoons orange zest
1 cup beef stock

- Reduce orange juice to 1 cup in skillet over medium heat, stirring often. Set aside.

- Grind cloves, allspice, peppercorns and salt. Rub oxtails with ground spices, using only as much as needed.

- Heat olive oil in heavy Dutch oven or enameled cast-iron pan with lid. Brown oxtails thoroughly on all sides over medium-high heat, about 20 minutes. Set aside. Unless oil is scorched, use same oil, adding more if necessary, to fry onions, carrots and orange zest quickly until just brown at edges.

- Add enough stock to fill pan scant 1/2 inch, about 1 cup. Loosen particles sticking to pan and bring to boil. Set oxtails on top of vegetables and simmering stock. Drizzle reduced orange juice over each oxtail. Cover and bake 2 1/2 to 3 hours at 300 degrees, until meat on bones is tender and caramelized.

- Remove oxtails to platter or individual plates. Skim fat off pan drippings. Serve oxtails with pan drippings spooned over them.

6 servings. Each serving: 230 calories; 960 mg sodium; 35 mg cholesterol; 8 grams fat; 17 grams carbohydrates; 22 grams protein; 0.66 gram fiber.

PORK *and* TOMATILLO CHILI

1992

THIS IS ONE OF FORMER FOOD EDITOR Ruth Reichl's standard party dishes. She wrote "This is one of those dishes that people just can't stop eating; friends have been known to have thirds and then smile with slight embarrassment and serve themselves some more." To make the lime sour cream, combine 1/2 cup sour cream and the grated zest and juice of 1 lime.

1 cup orange juice
1 (12-ounce) bottle dark beer
1 pound tomatillos, papery husks removed, quartered
1/4 cup peanut oil
1 head garlic, peeled
2 pounds boneless pork, cut into 1/2-inch cubes
Salt, pepper
2 large onions, thinly sliced
2 pounds Roma tomatoes, chopped
3 jalapenos, diced
1 teaspoon hot red pepper flakes, or more to taste
1 bunch cilantro, leaves chopped
1 (16-ounce) can black beans with liquid or 1 1/2 cups homemade cooked black beans with liquid
Cooked rice
1/2 avocado, peeled and sliced
Cilantro sprigs
Lime Sour Cream

• Combine orange juice, beer and tomatillos in large saucepan. Cook over medium heat about 20 minutes. Set aside.

• Heat peanut oil in large skillet. Add garlic cloves and cook 2 minutes. Stir in 1/4 of cubed pork and season to taste with salt and pepper. Brown pork on all sides, remove pork with slotted spoon and add to tomatillos. Cook remaining pork in skillet. Remove pork and garlic and add to tomatillos.

• Add onions and lightly brown. Add to tomatillo and pork mixture. Mix in tomatoes, jalapeno chiles, crushed red pepper and cilantro. Cover and cook over low heat 2 hours. (Chili can also be cooked in 350-degree oven 2 hours.) Add beans. Cook, uncovered, 1/2 hour more. Adjust seasonings to taste.

• Serve over rice, garnished with sliced avocado, sprigs of cilantro and lime sour cream.

6 servings. Each serving, without rice: 547 calories; 171 mg sodium; 86 mg cholesterol; 25 grams fat; 47 grams carbohydrates; 34 grams protein; 3.74 grams fiber.

ROAST PORK *with* MEXICAN OREGANO PASTE
(*Puerco con Pasta de Oregano*)

New York chef and cookbook author Zarela Martinez contributed this recipe based on a dish she remembers from growing up on a Chihuahua cattle ranch.

1994

■ PORK WITH OREGANO PASTE

8 cloves garlic, minced
1 tablespoon Mexican oregano, crushed between palms
2 teaspoons salt, preferably kosher
1 tablespoon freshly ground black pepper
1 (4 1/2-pound) pork butt

• Put garlic, oregano, salt and pepper in mortar, blender or food processor. Process into paste.

• Using small, sharp knife, make gashes 1 inch deep all over roast and rub Oregano Paste into gashes. Place meat in shallow roasting pan and roast at 475 degrees 20 minutes. Lower heat to 350 degrees and continue to roast until tender and thoroughly cooked, about 2 hours 15 minutes.

■ CHIPOTLE SALSA

2 tablespoons lard or vegetable oil
2 large cloves garlic, minced
1 onion, chopped
Pan drippings from roast pork, optional
5 to 6 large tomatoes, or 1 (28-ounce) can plain-style tomatoes
without puree
1 1/2 teaspoons Mexican oregano
Sugar
1/2 teaspoon salt, or to taste
2 to 3 canned chipotles en adobo, with sauce to taste

• Heat lard in medium saucepan until almost smoking. Add onion and garlic. Saute over medium-high heat, stirring often, until onion is translucent, about 2 to 3 minutes. Add pan drippings, tomatoes, oregano, sugar, salt and chipotles. Stir thoroughly and simmer uncovered over low heat 10 to 15 minutes, stirring often. Puree sauce in blender. With wooden spoon, force through sieve. May be frozen or stored, tightly covered, up to 3 days in refrigerator. Makes 3 to 4 cups.

• Remove roast from oven. Let stand 20 minutes. Carve into thin slices. Serve with Chipotle Salsa.

12 to 14 servings. Each of 14 servings: 334 calories; 501 mg sodium; 81 mg cholesterol; 27 grams fat; 5 grams carbohydrates; 19 grams protein; 0.55 gram fiber.

PROVENCAL ROAST LEG OF LAMB
(*Gigot d'Agneau Roti a la Provencale*)

1992

READER CLAUDIE CES makes this lamb the old-fashioned way, roasting it until the herb coating is crusty on the outside, while the meat remains tender and juicy. A local Provencal rose would accompany the lamb in Aix-en-Provence, where Ces' relatives live. If you can't find a Provencal rose, Ces suggests Beaujolais as an alternative. Serve this with ratatouille.

■ PROVENCAL LAMB

1 (5-pound) leg of lamb
3 cloves garlic, cut into slivers
1 tablespoon olive oil
2 teaspoons herbes de Provence, or combination of 1/2 teaspoon thyme,
1/2 teaspoon basil, 1/2 teaspoon marjoram, 1/2 teaspoon rosemary
1 teaspoon salt
1/2 teaspoon pepper

• Remove fat from leg of lamb. Make several slits in meat and insert sliver of garlic in each. Make paste with olive oil, herbs, salt and pepper. Rub all over leg of lamb. Bake at 350 degrees, allowing 20 minutes per pound, about 1 hour 40 minutes.

■ SAUCE PERNOD

2 tablespoons olive oil
3 tablespoons minced shallots
3 large tomatoes, peeled, seeded and finely chopped
1/3 cup fresh basil leaves, torn into small pieces
1 tablespoon herbes de Provence or combination of 3/4 teaspoon thyme,
3/4 teaspoon basil, 3/4 teaspoon marjoram, 3/4 teaspoon rosemary
1 teaspoon fennel seeds, crushed
Salt, pepper
3 tablespoons Pernod

• Heat olive oil in heavy skillet or saucepan. Add shallots and brown.
• Add tomatoes, basil, herbs and fennel seeds and season to taste with salt and pepper. Cook 15 minutes. Add Pernod and cook 15 minutes longer.
• Incorporate cooking juices reserved from lamb. Serve over sliced lamb. Makes about 2 1/2 cups.

6 servings. Each serving: 583 calories; 684 mg sodium; 242 mg cholesterol; 24 grams fat; 5 grams carbohydrates; 79 grams protein; 0 fiber.

TYCOON'S GULYAS
(*Magnas Gulyas*)

1993

THIS RECIPE CAME FROM a story on Hungary's Gundel restaurant that was written for us by Colman Andrews, a long-time contributor who is also editor of Saveur magazine. It is an example of the changes brought to the century-old restaurant by its new owner, New York restaurant impresario George Lang.

1 3/4 cups minced onions
2 cloves garlic, minced
1/3 cup plus 3 tablespoons oil
1 tablespoon sweet Hungarian paprika
1/2 teaspoon caraway seeds
Salt
Freshly ground pepper
1 veal bone, cracked in half
3 cups water
3 small green pepppers, seeded and thinly sliced
3 tomatoes, peeled and sliced
Spicy Hungarian paprika to taste
2 pounds beef tenderloin, cut into cubes

• In medium saucepan, saute onion and garlic in 1/3 cup oil over medium heat until golden brown, about 10 to 15 minutes. Stir in sweet paprika, caraway seeds and salt and pepper to taste. Add veal bone and water and reduce heat to low. Simmer, uncovered, 1 to 1 1/2 hours.

• Remove and discard veal bone. Add green peppers, tomatoes and hot paprika to taste to saucepan. Stir and simmer 20 minutes. If sauce is too thin at this point (doesn't coat back of spoon lightly), raise heat to medium-high to reduce to proper consistency. Adjust seasonings to taste. (Sauce can be made ahead to this point and reheated gently just before serving.)

• Just before serving, heat 3 tablespoons oil over high heat in large heavy skillet. Add meat and cook quickly, stirring constantly until outside of meat is browned and inside is rare. (Can do in batches in order not to crowd pan.) Remove meat with slotted spoon onto serving dish and pour heated sauce over meat. Serve immediately.

8 servings. Each serving: 302 calories; 89 mg sodium; 53 mg cholesterol; 22 grams fat; 8 grams carbohydrates; 19 grams protein; 0.83 gram fiber.

COWBOY STEAK

SONORA CAFÉ IS A DRESS-UP West Hollywood restaurant run by Ron Salisbury, whose family owns the landmark El Cholo restaurant near Downtown.

■ COWBOY SAUCE

5 tomatoes
1 dried pasilla chile
1/4 cup (1/2 stick) butter
1/2 onion, finely chopped
1 large clove garlic, minced
1/2 yellow bell pepper, chopped
1/4 cup red wine vinegar
1/4 cup dry white wine
1 cup chicken stock
2 tablespoons chopped fresh oregano or 2 teaspoons dried
1 tablespoon chopped fresh thyme or 2 teaspoons dried

• Char tomatoes over flame of gas burner or under broiler until skin begins to blacken. Transfer to bowl and let cool. Coarsely chop. Do not peel.

• Heat small skillet over medium-high heat. Add chile and cook until skin darkens, about 1 minute per side. Transfer to plate and cool. Remove seeds and cut into small pieces.

• Melt 2 tablespoons butter in large saucepan over medium-high heat. Add onion and saute until brown, about 12 minutes. Add garlic and bell pepper and saute until soft, about 4 minutes.

• Add vinegar and wine and bring to boil, scraping up any brown bits. Boil until liquid is reduced by half, about 5 minutes. Add charred tomatoes, chile and stock. Simmer until sauce thickens and is reduced to 2/3 cup, about 15 minutes. Puree sauce in blender until almost smooth. Add oregano and thyme. Cover and refrigerate. (Sauce may be made 1 day ahead.)

■ PARSNIP MASHED POTATOES

4 baking potatoes, peeled and each cut into 8 pieces
5 parsnips, peeled and cut into 1-inch slices
1 cup half-and-half or heavy whipping cream
Salt, pepper

• Boil potatoes in water to cover until tender, about 20 minutes. Boil parsnips in separate saucepan in water to cover until tender, about 15 minutes.

• Puree parsnips in food processor until smooth. Beat potatoes with electric mixer until smooth. Add parsnips and cream and mix. Season with salt and pepper to taste. Keep warm.

CONTINUED ☞

■ PARSNIP CHIPS

2 parsnips, peeled
2 tablespoons butter, or more if needed

• Slice parsnips diagonally about 1/8 inch thick. Heat butter to coat large skillet. Add parsnip slices and fry over medium-low heat, turning until browned on both sides, about 5 minutes.

■ STEAKS AND ASSEMBLY

6 to 8 (8-ounce) filet mignon steaks, about 1 1/4 inches thick
Salt, pepper
Chopped fresh oregano

• Season steaks with salt and pepper to taste. Cook under broiler or grill over medium-high heat on barbecue until done as desired, about 5 minutes per side for rare. Transfer to platter.
• Bring Cowboy Sauce to simmer. Remove from heat and whisk in remaining 2 tablespoons butter.
• To serve, place large dollop of Parsnip Mashed Potatoes on each serving plate. Season steaks with salt and pepper to taste and place 1 steak on top of potatoes on each plate. Spoon Cowboy Sauce alongside.
• Garnish with Parsnip Chips and sprinkling of chopped oregano.

6 to 8 servings. Each of 8 servings: 433 calories; 393 mg sodium; 118 mg cholesterol; 22 grams fat; 28 grams carbohydrates; 32 grams protein; 2.07 grams fiber.

STEAMED CORNED BEEF *and* CABBAGE

TIMES TEST KITCHEN DIRECTOR Donna Deane developed this recipe, which has quickly become the standard for a number of our readers. Steaming the beef rather than boiling it yields a texture that is much firmer and less stringy.

1998

1 head cabbage
1 (3 1/2-pound) corned beef
1 bunch carrots, tops removed

• Remove outer leaves from cabbage and use to line steamer basket. Put corned beef on top of leaves in basket and steam 2 1/2 hours.
• Cut cabbage into 6 wedges. Put cabbage and carrots on top of corned beef in steamer basket, and steam until corned beef and cabbage are fork tender, about 30 minutes.

6 servings. Each serving: 409 calories; 263 mg sodium; 93 mg cholesterol; 26 grams fat; 16 grams carbohydrates; 28 grams protein; 1.96 grams fiber.

CHAP CHAE

THE WORDS CHAP CHAE MEAN thin-sliced, indicating the uniformly thin slicing of the ingredients. Sweet-potato starch noodles, which are essential to this dish, are readily available in Korean markets. This recipe is from Korean home cook Mary Min.

■ BULGOGI MARINADE

3/4 cup soy sauce
1/3 cup sugar
1/2 head garlic, finely chopped
4 or 5 green onions, finely chopped
1 tablespoon sesame oil
1 teaspoon minced ginger root
1 teaspoon toasted sesame seeds

• Combine soy sauce, sugar, garlic, green onions, sesame oil, ginger root and sesame seeds. Makes about 1 1/4 cups.

■ BARBECUED BEEF

1/2 pound ground beef or pork
1 onion
1/2 pound carrots
6 to 7 large dried shiitake mushrooms, soaked until softened, drained and sliced
1/2 pound small pickling cucumbers, seeded
4 green onions
2 eggs
Oil
8 ounces Korean sweet-potato starch noodles
4 teaspoons sesame oil
1 teaspoon sugar

• Marinate beef in Bulgogi Marinade 1 1/2 to 2 hours. Cut onion, carrots, mushrooms, cucumbers and green onions into thin julienne strips about 2 inches long.

• Beat eggs in bowl and pour into small, lightly oiled skillet or omelet pan. Cook gently until firm. Loosen edges from pan. Carefully turn over and finish cooking. Remove from pan and cool. Cut into same-size strips as vegetables.

• Heat 1 teaspoon vegetable oil in skillet. Add and saute beef with marinade until just done. Drain well, reserving liquid. Cook noodles in boiling water until al dente and translucent, about 12 minutes. Drain.

CONTINUED ☞

• Heat 1 tablespoon oil in large skillet or wok. Add and saute onion and carrots until onion is tender. Add mushrooms and meat. Add noodles and toss with sesame oil and sugar. Add reserved liquid from beef. Lastly, add egg strips and cucumber and toss to mix. Arrange on serving platter and garnish with green onion strips.

6 to 8 servings. Each of 8 servings: 373 calories; 1,550 mg sodium; 69 mg cholesterol; 18 grams fat; 46 grams carbohydrates; 10 grams protein; 1.58 gram fiber.

WALDORF DEVILED BEEF RIBS
with MUSTARD SAUCE

THIS IS A GREAT WAY TO USE the rib bones left after cooking a rib roast. It comes from chef John Doherty of New York's Waldorf-Astoria Hotel.

1987

8 pounds beef ribs (from standing rib roast of beef, about 2 racks)
Salt, pepper
About 1/4 cup extra-virgin olive oil
1 cup Dijon mustard
2 1/2 cups fine dry bread crumbs
10 ounces veal or beef stock
1/2 cup Madeira
1/2 teaspoon cornstarch
1/2 teaspoon water
2 tablespoons butter

• Lightly season ribs with salt and pepper. Place on baking tray and roast at 325 degrees 1 1/2 hours. Allow to cool until easy to handle, about 15 minutes.

• Combine 3 tablespoons olive oil and all but 3 tablespoons mustard, blending well. Separate beef into rib sections and lightly coat with mustard mixture. Dredge each piece in bread crumbs and place on baking tray. Sprinkle lightly with more olive oil. Bake at 375 degrees until golden brown.

• Combine stock and Madeira in skillet over medium heat. Cook until reduced by half. Combine cornstarch with water until smooth. Stir into sauce and cook until sauce coats back of spoon. Continue to simmer several minutes to blend flavors over low heat. Add butter and 3 tablespoons reserved mustard. Stir until smooth.

6 to 8 servings. Each of 8 servings: 364 calories; 460 mg sodium; 55 mg cholesterol; 23 grams fat; 19 grams carbohydrates; 18 grams protein; 0.07 gram fiber.

FIVE

Poultry

ROAST BRINED TURKEY

RARELY HAS SUCH A SIMPLE recipe won so many converts so quickly. Almost everyone who tries this recipe by Food Editor Russ Parsons quickly admits that it is one of the moistest, tastiest turkeys he or she has ever made.

2/3 cup salt
1 gallon water
1 (12- to 14-pound) turkey

- Combine salt and water and stir until salt dissolves. Pour brine over turkey in pot just large enough to hold both. If turkey is completely covered, don't worry about using all of brine. Cover with foil and refrigerate 6 hours or overnight, turning 2 or 3 times to make sure turkey is totally submerged.

- Remove turkey from brine and pat dry with paper towels. Refrigerate, unwrapped, 6 hours or overnight.

- Place turkey on its side on rack in shallow roasting pan. Roast at 450 degrees 15 minutes. Turn turkey to other side and roast another 15 minutes. Turn breast-side up and roast another 15 minutes.

- Reduce heat to 325 degrees and roast until meat thermometer inserted in center of thickest part of thigh registers 160 to 165 degrees, about 2 hours. Remove from oven and set aside 20 minutes before carving.

10 to 12 servings. Each of 12 servings: 394 calories; 792 mg sodium; 236 mg cholesterol; 12 grams fat; 1 gram carbohydrates; 65 grams protein; 0 fiber.

TURKEY ROLL

ADRIANA PACIFICI, A SOUTHERN CALIFORNIA caterer, specialized in Northern Italian Jewish cooking.

1990

1 whole breast turkey, boned
3 cloves garlic, cut in half
Salt, pepper
6 slices prosciutto or cooked ham
4 eggs
2 tablespoons chopped parsley
Butter
6 slices mortadella
Fresh sprigs rosemary or dried rosemary leaves
1/2 cup olive oil
1 onion, sliced
1 shallot, sliced
1/2 cup wine

• Have butcher remove all turkey bones. Butterfly meat to spread out into a flat sheet. With sharp knife make 6 random incisions in breast and place garlic half in each. Sprinkle with salt and pepper to taste. Rub in garlic. Cover with layer of prosciutto slices.

• Beat eggs with salt and pepper to taste. Stir in parsley. Heat 1 to 2 tablespoons butter in large non-stick skillet placed over medium heat.

• Pour in eggs and cook to a soft, whole, round omelet or frittata (do not overcook). Cool slightly. Place omelet over prosciutto .

• Top with mortadella slices. Roll breast as tightly as possible, jellyroll fashion, and tie with string all around. If using fresh rosemary, insert sprigs under strings; if using dried, rub turkey roll with dried herb. Season to taste with salt, pepper.

• Heat olive oil in large Dutch oven or roasting skillet placed over low heat. Add turkey roll, and cook to brown evenly, turning occasionally.

• Raise heat and sprinkle with wine. After about 5 minutes or after wine has evaporated, add 1/3 cup butter, onion and shallot. Reduce heat to low, and simmer 1 hour and 15 minutes, basting top occasionally. Let stand about 15 minutes before carving. Cut into thin slices, and arrange on serving platter. At time of serving, heat sauce and pour some over slices and serve remainder on the side.

20 to 24 servings. Each of 24 servings: 125 calories; 114 mg sodium; 67 mg cholesterol; 7 grams fat; 1 gram carbohydrates; 12 grams protein; 0.06 gram fiber.

CHICKEN RELLENO

1986

READER ALICE AQUINO'S version of this popular Filipino dish is one of the best we've tasted.

1 (3-pound) chicken
Salt, pepper
1 to 2 tablespoons soy sauce
2 tablespoons lemon juice
3/4 pound ground pork
1/4 pound lean bacon, chopped or coarsely ground
6 ounces Cheddar cheese, shredded
1/2 cup raisins
3 tablespoons sweet pickle relish
1 egg
1 carrot, cooked and sliced into thin strips, or 1/2 cup green peas, cooked
3 ounces cooked ham, sliced into thin strips
2 Spanish chorizo de Bilbao or pepperoni, about 5 ounces
2 hard-boiled eggs, cut in halves
1 to 2 tablespoons butter, melted

• Bone chicken for stuffing, leaving wing and drumstick bones intact. Season chicken to taste with salt and pepper and rub with soy sauce and lemon juice. Let stand at least 30 minutes. (Refrigerate if marinating longer than this time.)

• Combine ground pork, bacon, cheese, raisins, pickle relish and egg. Mix well. Place chicken on board, skin side down. Place half of stuffing in boned cavity of chicken. Arrange carrot and ham strips, sausage and egg halves in rows on top of pork mixture. Cover with remaining mixture, stuffing boned thighs.

• Bring 2 cut sides of chicken together. Fasten edges at 1-inch intervals with wood picks or skewers, then lace with string. Turn bird over and mold it back to resemble original shape. Tie legs with string and tuck wings akimbo. Place on rack in roasting pan and cover with foil.

• Bake at 350 degrees 30 minutes and remove foil. Continue baking until golden brown, 1 hour, basting with melted butter.

• Collect drippings, if desired, and make flour gravy.

• Remove skewers and string. Place on serving platter and garnish as desired with vegetables or fruit. Carve into 1/2-inch-thick diagonal or crosswise slices, starting from wing sides.

10 to 12 servings. Each of 12 servings: 357 calories; 567 mg sodium; 143 mg cholesterol; 25 grams fat; 8 grams carbohydrates; 25 grams protein; 0.18 gram fiber.

TURKEY SCHNITZEL

THIS IS A GREAT WAY TO USE those turkey cutlets that are now so common in supermarkets. Test Kitchen Director Donna Deane says to serve them with the traditional German accompaniments: spaetzle, tiny German dumplings or buttered noodles along with garlicky spinach or sauteed red cabbage.

2 (4-ounce) turkey breast cutlets
1/4 cup flour, seasoned with 1/2 teaspoon salt and 1/8 teaspoon pepper
1 cup fine fresh bread crumbs, left out to dry
1 egg, lightly beaten
Coarse salt
Freshly ground pepper
1 tablespoon olive oil
1 tablespoon butter
1 tablespoon minced parsley, for garnish
2 teaspoons drained capers, for garnish
2 lemon wedges, for garnish

• Tear 4 sheets of plastic wrap. Put each cutlet between 2 sheets. Gently pound cutlet from center to edges until uniformly 1/4-inch thick.

• Put seasoned flour on 1 sheet waxed paper, bread crumbs on another and egg in shallow pie dish. Dip each cutlet into flour, beaten egg and then bread crumbs, coating cutlet evenly. Arrange cutlets on wax paper-lined baking sheet and refrigerate 30 minutes for coating to adhere and dry out slightly. Before cooking, generously season both sides cutlets with salt and pepper.

• Heat oil and butter in 10-inch heavy skillet over medium-high heat.

• When hot, saute cutlets until well-browned, about 3 to 4 minutes. Turn and brown other side, about 2 to 3 minutes. Serve hot garnished with parsley, capers and lemon wedges.

2 servings. Each serving: 302 calories; 932 mg sodium; 175 mg cholesterol; 16 grams fat; 38 grams carbohydrates; 26 grams protein; 0.20 gram fiber.

CHINESE AMERICAN THANKSGIVING TURKEY
with RICE *and* SAUSAGE STUFFING

1997

KEN HOM IS ONE OF THE WORLD'S great experts on Chinese cooking, but he was raised in the United States. This unusual turkey recipe reflects that blending of traditions.

■ STUFFING

3 cups sweet rice (also known as glutinous rice)
1 cup dried black mushrooms
1 1/2 pounds ground pork
3 tablespoons light soy sauce
1/4 cup Shaoxing rice wine or dry Sherry
2 teaspoons toasted sesame oil
Salt
Freshly ground pepper
2 tablespoons peanut oil
1/2 cup finely chopped green onions
2 tablespoons finely chopped ginger root
Turkey giblets (heart and gizzard only), chopped
1 pound Chinese pork sausage, chopped
1/2 pound fresh water chestnuts, peeled and coarsely chopped, or canned
3 cups low-sodium chicken broth

• Cover rice with cold water and soak overnight. Drain thoroughly.

• Soak mushrooms in warm water 20 minutes. Drain and squeeze out excess liquid. Remove and discard stems. Coarsely chop caps.

• Combine ground pork with 1 tablespoon soy sauce, 1 tablespoon rice wine, sesame oil, 1 teaspoon salt and 1/2 teaspoon pepper. Set aside 20 minutes.

• Heat wok or large skillet over high heat until hot. Swirl in peanut oil. When oil is very hot and smoking slightly, add green onions and ginger and stir-fry 3 minutes. Add pork mixture and turkey giblets and stir-fry 3 minutes, breaking up pork. Add mushrooms, Chinese sausage, rice and water chestnuts and continue to stir-fry, about 3 minutes.

• Add chicken broth, remaining 2 tablespoons soy sauce and remaining 3 tablespoons rice wine and mix well. Season to taste with salt and pepper. Reduce heat to low, cover and cook 20 minutes, stirring occasionally. Remove from heat and cool thoroughly.

CONTINUED☛

■ TURKEY

1 (12- to 14-pound) turkey
2 tablespoons toasted sesame oil
3 tablespoons kosher salt
1 tablespoon freshly ground pepper

• Carefully separate skin of turkey breast from meat with hands. Rub skin with sesame oil. Mix salt and pepper and rub evenly over turkey. Set aside. (This may be done a day ahead. Cover turkey with plastic wrap and refrigerate.)

• Insert thin layer of stuffing between turkey breast and skin.

• Loosely fill turkey cavity with stuffing and close with skewer. (Spoon any remaining stuffing into baking dish and steam 40 minutes before serving).

• Place turkey on deep heat-proof platter on rack in large roasting pan or turkey roaster. Add enough hot water to pan or roaster to come to 1 1/2 inches beneath rack. Cover pan tightly with lid or foil. Bring water to simmer, reduce heat to low and gently steam until thigh juices run clear when pricked with fork or tip of knife, 2 to 2 1/2 hours.

• Replenish steaming water as needed. Remove turkey from platter, reserving any juices that may have collected. Discard steaming water.

• Place steamed turkey on rack in roasting pan and roast at 350 degrees 25 minutes. Increase temperature to 450 degrees and roast until turkey is golden brown and thermometer inserted in thickest part of thigh registers 165 degrees, about 15 minutes.

• Remove turkey from oven and let rest 20 minutes before carving.

• Serve carved turkey and stuffing with sauce.

■ SAUCE

3 cups low-sodium chicken broth
Salt
Freshly ground pepper

• While turkey is roasting, combine chicken stock and reserved turkey juices in saucepan. Bring mixture to boil and reduce by half. Season to taste with salt and pepper.

10 to 12 servings. Each of 12 servings: 848 calories; 1,056 mg sodium; 286 mg cholesterol; 33 grams fat; 47 grams carbohydrates; 83 grams protein; 0.39 gram fiber.

CHICKEN *with* GINGER CITRUS TERIYAKI GLAZE

TIMES TEST KITCHEN INTERN Jet Tila specializes in Thai cooking, but his talents do not stop there. This Japanese-influenced dish made lots of friends when he tried it out. Look for citrus-flavored soy sauce at Asian markets.

■ GLAZE

1/4 cup soy sauce
1 cup mirin (sweet rice wine)
1/4 cup citrus-flavored soy sauce
1/4 cup sugar
1/4 cup water
1 (2-inch) piece ginger root, minced (about 1/2 cup)

• Combine soy sauce, mirin, citrus soy sauce, sugar, water and ginger root in small saucepan and simmer over medium heat until slightly thickened, 10 to 15 minutes. (Makes about 1 1/2 cups.)

■ ASSEMBLY

1 1/2 pounds boneless, skinless chicken breasts
Salt, pepper
3 to 4 tablespoons oil
Steamed white rice
2 green onions, thinly sliced

• Season chicken breasts with salt and pepper to taste. Saute in oil in medium skillet over high heat or grill chicken breasts on high heat for 3 to 5 minutes on each side.
• Serve chicken over steamed rice. Top each serving with sliced green onions, then drizzle about half of sauce over chicken. (Refrigerate leftover sauce for another use.)

4 servings. Each serving: 310 calories; 1,343 mg sodium; 74 mg cholesterol; 9 grams fat; 22 grams carbohydrates; 32 grams protein; 0.09 gram fiber.

CHICKEN *with* RICE

THERE MUST BE A MILLION recipes in the world combining chicken and rice. This unusually delicious version came from one of St. Sophia Greek Orthodox Cathedral's annual festivals in Los Angeles. Greek seasoning is a basic mixture found in most spice aisles.

Water
1 tablespoon butter
Salt
1 cup rice
1/4 onion, finely chopped
1 chicken, cut into 8 pieces
1 (8-ounce) can tomato sauce
1 (10 3/4-ounce) can tomato soup
Cinnamon
1/2 teaspoon Greek seasoning
Sugar
1 slice American cheese

• Boil 2 cups water. Add 1 1/2 teaspoons butter, 1 teaspoon salt and rice. Cover, reduce heat to low and simmer 5 minutes. Remove from heat and let stand, covered, 10 minutes.

• Saute onion in remaining 1 1/2 teaspoons butter in large pot over medium heat until tender, 5 minutes, adding dash of water as onion cooks.

• Place chicken in pot, add 1/2 cup water and salt to taste. Stir chicken until opaque. Add tomato sauce, tomato soup and 1/2 soup can of water. Cover and simmer over medium-low heat 15 minutes.

• Season with dash of cinnamon, Greek seasoning and dash of sugar. Cover and cook until tender, 30 minutes. Remove chicken from pot. When cool enough to handle, skin and debone; set aside.

• Add rice to pot and simmer until rice is tender and liquid is absorbed, 15 minutes. Return chicken to pot, add cheese and cook until melted, 5 minutes.

4 servings. Each serving: 701 calories; 1,819 mg sodium; 159 mg cholesterol; 38 grams fat; 47 grams carbohydrates; 40 grams protein; 0.76 gram fiber.

STEWED RABBIT *and* DUMPLINGS

1985

THIS MIDWESTERN FRICASSEED RABBIT is an old family favorite of Times Test Kitchen Director Donna Deane.

1 rabbit, cut up
Salt, pepper
Flour
2 tablespoons butter or margarine
Oil
1 clove garlic, crushed
1 cup minced onions
1/2 cup minced celery
1/2 cup minced carrots
1 (14 1/2-ounce) can chicken broth
1/2 cup white wine
1 small bay leaf
1 1/2 teaspoons baking powder
2 eggs
1/2 cup milk
1 teaspoon fresh thyme
Chopped parsley

- Sprinkle rabbit pieces with salt and pepper to taste. Dredge in flour.

- Melt butter with 2 tablespoons oil in Dutch oven and saute rabbit until brown.

- Remove rabbit. Add garlic, onions, celery and carrots to pan and saute until tender.

- Stir in chicken broth and wine. Add rabbit and bay leaf. Bring to boil, then cover, reduce heat and simmer until rabbit is tender, about 30 minutes.

- Mix together 1 1/2 cups flour and baking powder. Combine eggs, milk, 1/4 cup oil and thyme. Stir into flour mixture to form sticky dough. Drop dough by tablespoons onto rabbit and boiling liquid.

- Cover and simmer 15 minutes (do not remove cover). Uncover and sprinkle parsley over dumplings.

4 servings. Each serving: 560 calories; 801 mg sodium; 197 mg cholesterol; 38 grams fat; 17 grams carbohydrates; 34 grams protein; 0.84 gram fiber.

Note: Dumplings will absorb liquid as they cook. If additional gravy is desired, remove dumplings to warm platter and keep warm. Combine 1 1/2 teaspoons flour with 1 cup water or chicken broth and add to Dutch oven. Bring mixture back to boil, reduce heat and cook about 5 minutes. Return dumplings to pan and heat briefly before serving.

LEMON CHICKEN

LEMON CHICKEN IS ONE OF THE FIRST Chinese dishes many Americans try. This version came from the Universal City restaurant Fung Lum.

1998

1 pound boneless chicken pieces, cut into strips
1 egg, lightly beaten
Sesame oil
2 tablespoons cornstarch
Salt, pepper
Peanut oil for deep-frying
1/2 cup plus 1 tablespoon water
2 tablespoons white wine vinegar
2 tablespoons lemon juice
1/3 cup sugar
2 drops lemon extract

• Combine chicken, egg, 2 drops sesame oil, 1 tablespoon cornstarch, 2 teaspoons salt and dash pepper until chicken pieces are coated and ingredients are blended. Deep-fry in peanut oil at 400 degrees until browned. Drain chicken on paper towels. Cut into smaller pieces. Keep warm while preparing lemon sauce.

• Blend 1/2 cup water, vinegar, lemon juice, sugar, lemon extract, 1 drop sesame oil and dash salt in wok or small saucepan. Heat to boiling.

• Blend remaining 1 tablespoon water and remaining 1 tablespoon cornstarch until smooth. Stir into lemon mixture. Heat and stir until smooth and clear. Pour sauce over chicken and serve.

2 to 4 servings. 528 calories; 262 mg sodium; 193 mg cholesterol; 25 grams fat; 50 grams carbohydrates; 25 grams protein; 0.02 gram fiber.

GRANDMA'S PICKLED CHICKEN

THIS RECIPE COMES FROM longtime Food section contributor Judy Zeidler's mother, a well-known cook in Boyle Heights, Los Angeles' first Jewish neighborhood. The recipe is a turn on the flavor combination from gefilte fish. A bouquet garni is a combination of herbs, usually wrapped in cheesecloth, or you can wrap the herbs in leek leaves; they add flavor besides providing a holder for the herbs.

2 outer green leaves from 1 large leek
1 celery top
2 sprigs parsley
2 bay leaves
2 cloves
1/4 teaspoon dried thyme
1/3 cup extra-virgin olive oil
1 (3- to 4-pound chicken), cut into 8 pieces
3/4 cup white wine
3/4 cup vinegar
3/4 cup hot water
1 onion, cut into 1/8-inch wedges
2 carrots, thinly sliced into rounds
1 small leek, including 2 inches of green part, thinly sliced
1 teaspoon salt
Lemon slices, for garnish

• To make bouquet garni, place 1 leek leaf on work surface and flatten by pressing with palm of your hand. Arrange celery top, parsley, bay leaves, cloves and thyme in center. Cover with remaining leaf and tie with string to make a tight bundle. Set aside.

• In large heavy pot, heat oil over medium-high heat and brown chicken, skin-side down, turning once, about 5 minutes.

• Add wine, vinegar, water, onion, carrots, leek, salt and bouquet garni and bring to boil over high heat. Reduce heat to low, cover and simmer until chicken is tender but not falling apart, about 25 minutes.

• Remove bouquet garni and arrange chicken pieces in deep baking dish, just large enough to hold them snugly in 1 layer. Pour cooking liquid with vegetables over chicken. Cool to room temperature, about 15 minutes.

• Cover with plastic wrap and refrigerate 2 to 3 hours or overnight.

• Garnish with lemons when serving.

4 servings. Each serving: 673 calories; 751 mg sodium; 148 mg cholesterol; 50 grams fat; 13 grams carbohydrates; 36 grams protein; 0.98 gram fiber.

GRILLED CHICKEN BREAST SANDWICH
with TARRAGON MAYONNAISE

DENNIS BARRY WAS THE EXECUTIVE CHEF at Culbertson Winery, one of the first operations in the Temecula Valley.

1986

1/2 cup red wine vinegar
2 tablespoons crushed dried tarragon
2 tablespoons butter
4 teaspoons minced shallots
2 cups mayonnaise
1/2 teaspoon white pepper
6 (8-ounce) whole boneless chicken breasts, skinned
Salt, pepper
6 sandwich buns
6 lettuce leaves
6 slices tomato, optional

• Combine vinegar and tarragon in small saucepan. Bring to boil and cook until reduced by one-half. Melt butter in small skillet and saute shallots until tender.

• Combine mayonnaise, tarragon reduction, sauteed shallots and white pepper, mixing well. Set aside.

• Pound chicken breasts slightly with fine side of meat tenderizing mallet. Cut in half down natural seam, eliminating any cartilage at center. Season chicken with salt and pepper to taste.

• Grill chicken over moderate heat to internal temperature of 165 degrees, turning once and basting with about 1 tablespoon reserved mayonnaise mixture per side. Slice and warm sandwich buns.

• Spread inside of buns generously with mayonnaise mixture. Place 2 pieces chicken on bottom of bun and top with lettuce, tomato and other half of bun.

6 servings. Each serving: 667 calories; 1,008 mg sodium; 129 mg cholesterol; 34 grams fat; 44 grams carbohydrates; 45 grams protein; 0.20 gram fiber.

LOCO POLLO

THOUGH THE FAMOUS FAST-FOOD CHAIN whose name this recipe resembles is notoriously close-mouthed with its recipes, we pieced together this version of its most popular dish in the Times Test Kitchen. Annatto powder, natural reddish-yellow coloring from a tropical tree, is available at most Latin grocery stores.

1/4 cup corn oil
1/4 cup (1/2 stick) melted butter
1/2 teaspoon onion powder
1/2 teaspoon garlic powder
1 teaspoon annatto powder or few drops yellow food color
1/4 teaspoon ground cumin
2 teaspoons lemon juice
1 (2 1/2- to 3-pound) chicken, halved

• Combine oil, butter, onion powder, garlic powder, annatto powder, cumin and lemon juice in large shallow pan. Add chicken halves, turning to coat well. Cover and marinate in refrigerator several hours or overnight.

• Remove chicken from marinade and grill over medium coals or under broiler, 4 inches from heat source, until browned on both sides and meat is done, turning and basting frequently, about 25 minutes.

• Cut chicken halves into pieces to serve with beans and rice, corn or flour tortillas and salsa, if desired.

4 servings. Each serving: 562 calories; 227 mg sodium; 149 mg cholesterol; 49 grams fat; 1 gram carbohydrates; 29 grams protein; 0.04 gram fiber.

SAKE DUCK

THE NEW OTANI HOTEL is the predominant hotel in Little Tokyo in downtown Los Angeles. This recipe is from executive chef Robert Seabolt.

■ SAKE SAUCE

1 cup mirin (sweet sake)
1/2 cup soy sauce
1/4 cup orange juice
1 teaspoon grated ginger root
1/4 cup brown sugar, packed
1 tablespoon arrowroot or cornstarch
1 leek, cut into thin strips

• Combine mirin, soy sauce, orange juice and ginger in small saucepan. Heat until hot but do not boil. Remove from heat and stir in brown sugar.

• Stir arrowroot or starch with some of hot liquid until smooth and return to pan. Cook and stir until sauce thickens slightly. Strain sauce through fine strainer into another pot or sauce boat. Add leek to sauce and mix gently. Let stand 10 minutes to blend flavors. Makes about 2 cups.

■ DUCK

1 (2- to 4-pound) duckling
Honey
1 orange or mandarin orange
1/2 bunch green onions or 1 leek, cut into thin strips

• Place duckling in baking pan. Bake at 300 degrees 2 hours, basting with honey every 15 minutes. Remove from oven and cool to room temperature. Remove bones from duck and slice meat into desired slices.

• Grate orange over duck and sprinkle with green onions. Pour Sake Sauce over duck.

2 to 4 servings. Each of 4 servings: 566 calories; 2311 mg sodium; 151 mg cholesterol; 19 grams fat; 49 grams carbohydrates; 45 grams protein; 0.44 gram fiber.

CHEESE-STUFFED CHICKEN BREASTS

1988

THIS RECIPE COMES FROM Production Caterers which specialized in serving film and television workers on location.

■ BUTTER TOPPING

1/2 cup (1 stick) butter, melted
1 teaspoon paprika
1/4 teaspoon garlic powder
1/4 teaspoon salt
1/4 teaspoon white pepper

• Combine butter, paprika, garlic powder, salt and white pepper. Makes 1/2 cup.

■ YOGURT SAUCE

6 tomatoes, chopped
1/4 cup plain yogurt
1/2 (1/2-ounce) package basil leaves, finely chopped
4 drops red wine vinegar
Salt
White pepper

• Combine tomatoes, yogurt and basil. Add vinegar, dash salt and pepper to taste. Makes 2 1/2 cups.

■ STUFFED CHICKEN BREASTS

1/2 cup frozen chopped spinach, loosely packed
1/2 cup ricotta cheese
1/4 cup grated Parmesan cheese
1/4 cup cottage cheese
3 eggs, beaten
4 whole chicken breasts, boned, but not skinned

• Thaw spinach and drain thoroughly. Combine spinach, ricotta, Parmesan and cottage cheeses and eggs. Gently stuff mixture under skin of each chicken breast. Brush generously with Butter Topping.

• Bake at 350 degrees 20 to 25 minutes. Let cool and cut in half. Chicken may also be served hot. Accompany with bowl of Yogurt Sauce.

8 servings. Each serving: 340 calories; 409 mg sodium; 177 mg cholesterol; 25 grams fat; 4 grams carbohydrates; 25 grams protein; 0.28 gram fiber.

STEAMED CHICKEN

It might sound simple, but there is nothing plain about this succulent steamed chicken by Test Kitchen Director Donna Deane.

■ CHICKEN

1 (3 1/2-pound) chicken
Salt
2 green onions
3 (1/4-inch-thick) slices ginger root
4 sprigs cilantro
1/2 bunch watercress

• Season inside cavity of chicken with salt to taste. Cut white bulb end of green onions into eighths and put inside chicken cavity with ginger.

• Tie legs of chicken together and tuck wings under chicken.

• Put chicken on platter and place cilantro sprigs on top of chicken.

• Put 1 inch water in bottom of steamer and put platter on rack in steamer. Bring to simmer. Cover and steam until juice runs clear when pricked with fork, about 1 hour. Check water level periodically during steaming and add more water if needed.

• Remove chicken from steamer. Remove cilantro, green onions and ginger from chicken. Remove skin from chicken, cut into pieces and bone. Slice meat and arrange on platter. Garnish with watercress.

■ SAUCE

2 tablespoons light soy sauce
2 tablespoons chicken broth
2 tablespoons minced green onion
1 tablespoon lemon juice
1 tablespoon chopped cilantro
1 teaspoon minced ginger root
1 clove garlic, minced
1 teaspoon sesame oil
1/2 teaspoon sugar

• Combine soy sauce, broth, green onion, lemon juice, cilantro, ginger, garlic, sesame oil and sugar. Serve with chicken.

4 servings. Each serving: 423 calories; 987 mg sodium; 139 mg cholesterol; 29 grams fat; 3 grams carbohydrates; 36 grams protein; 0.14 gram fiber.

TURKEY OSSO BUCO

—————

YOU WON'T BELIEVE THIS recipe from former Chianti Cucina chef Fabio Flagiello.

—————

■ TURKEY OSSO BUCO

4 turkey drumsticks (14 ounces each after trimming)
1/4 cup flour
Salt, pepper
1/4 cup (1/2 stick) butter, plus 1 tablespoon softened butter
2 tablespoons olive oil
2 tablespoons dry white wine
1 cup finely chopped carrots
1 cup minced onion
1 cup minced celery
2 cups tomato sauce
1 1/2 teaspoons chopped fresh rosemary
1 1/2 teaspoons chopped fresh sage
2 cups chicken stock

• Have butcher chop 1/2 inch off meaty end of turkey drumsticks, leaving skin intact. Bone end, leaving 4 to 5 inches of meaty part of turkey with bone in. Season flour to taste with salt and pepper and dredge turkey in flour.

• Place 2 tablespoons butter and 1 tablespoon olive oil in skillet over medium-high heat. Add turkey and cook until skin is golden-brown and crisp, about 3 to 4 minutes on each side. Remove from heat and remove turkey from pan. Sprinkle 1 tablespoon white wine over turkey.

• Place 2 tablespoons butter and 1 tablespoon olive oil in large saucepan over medium heat. Add carrots, onion and celery and cook 3 to 5 minutes until tender-crisp. Add remaining 1 tablespoon white wine, tomato sauce, rosemary and sage. Bring to boil, stirring.

• Add chicken stock and turkey. Cover, reduce heat to low and simmer 45 minutes, stirring occasionally, until meat separates from bone. Cooking time depends on size of drumstick. Season to taste with salt and pepper.

• Add softened butter to thicken gravy, if necessary.

CONTINUED☞

■ CREAMY POLENTA

4 cups water
Salt
1 tablespoon olive oil
1 cup cornmeal

• Combine water, salt and olive oil in 4-quart saucepan and bring to boil. Reduce heat and slowly stir in cornmeal. Simmer, stirring frequently with wooden spoon, about 40 to 50 minutes, or until polenta is thick and creamy and pulls away from sides of pan.

• To serve, circle each serving plate with polenta, place turkey drumstick in center and top with sauce.

4 servings. Each serving: 786 calories; 1,458 mg sodium; 191 mg cholesterol; 41 grams fat; 52 grams carbohydrates; 49 grams protein; 1.91 grams fiber.

TARRAGON ROASTED CHICKEN

THIS RECIPE FROM longtime Food section columnist Abby Mandel is based on one she enjoyed on the island of St. Barth's.

3 tablespoons olive oil
2 (3-pound) chickens, fat trimmed
2 tablespoons seasoned salt
1 tablespoon lemon pepper
4 large shallots, halved
1 large bunch tarragon

• Rub oil on chickens inside and out. Combine seasoning salt and lemon pepper in small bowl and use to season chickens inside and out. (Chickens may be prepared to this point several hours ahead or overnight and refrigerated. Let stand at room temperature 30 minutes before roasting.)

• Place chickens breast side down on rack in shallow roasting pan. Fill cavity of each chicken with half of shallots and half of tarragon. Tuck wings under and tie legs together.

• Roast chickens at 425 degrees until lightly browned, about 30 minutes.

• Insert large kitchen fork into each chicken cavity and turn breast side up. Return to oven and roast until darkly browned and meat thermometer inserted into innermost part of thigh registers 165 degrees, about 30 minutes. Transfer chickens to platter and let rest 10 minutes before slicing. Chickens may be served warm, room temperature or chilled.

6 to 8 servings. Each of 8 servings: 431 calories; 183 mg sodium; 130 mg cholesterol; 31 grams fat; 3 grams carbohydrates; 33 grams protein; 0.25 gram fiber.

GARLIC MARINATED CILANTRO CHICKEN

PATRICK HEALY IS ONE OF Los Angeles' best chefs. This recipe comes from when he was working at Xiomara Ardolino's restaurant in Pasadena, Xiomara.

■ CHICKEN

4 (1/2-pound) boneless chicken breast halves
8 cloves garlic, minced
1/2 cup extra-virgin olive oil
1 bunch cilantro
Salt, pepper

• Marinate chicken breasts with garlic and 1/4 cup olive oil overnight in refrigerator.

• Reserve a few cilantro leaves for garnish. Blanch remaining cilantro in boiling salted water 10 seconds and immediately cool off in ice bath.

• Drain, pat dry and place in blender with remaining 1/4 cup olive oil. Blend until leaves are pureed. Set aside 1 hour.

• Strain cilantro oil through fine strainer, season to taste with salt and pepper and refrigerate.

• Just before serving, season chicken breasts with salt and pepper and grill or broil skin-side down 8 minutes. Turn and finish cooking 4 minutes.

■ RANCHERO RISOTTO

2 tablespoons extra-virgin olive oil
1 onion, diced
2 jalapenos, seeded and sliced
1 clove garlic, chopped
1 cup Arborio rice
3 cups chicken stock
Salt
Freshly ground pepper
2 tablespoons grated Parmesan cheese
2 plum tomatoes, diced
Juice of 2 limes

• Heat oil in large saucepan or heat-proof casserole and add onion and jalapenos. Cook over low heat without browning 2 minutes. Add garlic, and rice. Stir and add chicken stock with salt and freshly ground pepper to taste. Cook over medium heat while stirring until most of moisture is absorbed and rice is cooked al dente. Add Parmesan cheese.

CONTINUED ☛

• Mound risotto in center of each plate. Toss diced tomatoes in lime juice, and season with salt and pepper. Sprinkle tomato mixture over risotto. Place chicken breast on top, skin-side up, and sprinkle generously with cilantro oil mixture. Garnish with reserved cilantro leaves around chicken.

4 servings. Each serving: 801 calories; 883 mg sodium; 90 mg cholesterol; 49 grams fat; 52 grams carbohydrates; 38 grams protein; 1.13 grams fiber.

ZAHLEH-STYLE GRILLED CHICKEN
(*Farrouj Mashwi*)

THIS RECIPE, WHICH HAS MADE THE riverside restaurants of the Lebanese city of Zahleh famous, is similar to the one used by the popular Los Angeles restaurant chain Zankou Chicken. Serve it with Aioli. The meat is slashed to facilitate marinating and grilling.

6 cloves garlic
1/2 teaspoon salt
1/2 cup olive oil
Juice of 1 lemon
1 (3 1/2- to 4-pound) broiling chicken

• Grind garlic to paste in mortar or small food processor. Work in salt, olive oil and lemon to create mayonnaise-like consistency.

• Cut chicken into 6 to 8 pieces, slashing each piece (except wings) to the bone 2 to 3 times against grain of meat. Rub pieces with sauce, cover and refrigerate 1 to 3 hours.

• Grill chicken pieces over medium heat until juices run clear, 10 to 12 minutes per side.

4 servings. Each serving: 695 calories; 442 mg sodium; 156 mg cholesterol; 58 grams fat; 2 grams carbohydrates; 39 grams protein; 0.07 gram fiber.

TURKEY TONNATO SANDWICH

1998

ANOTHER CASE OF TURKEY MASQUERADING for veal, this recipe by Food Editor Russ Parsons takes advantage of the peculiarly cooling flavors of the tuna-flavored mayonnaise traditionally used with vitello tonnato.

Salt, pepper
1 (2- to 2 1/2-pound) turkey breast half, boned, rolled and tied
Olive oil
1 (6-ounce) can tuna in olive oil, undrained
4 to 6 anchovy filets in olive oil, drained
Juice of 1 lemon
1 cup mayonnaise
1/4 cup capers, drained
1 large flat ciabatta loaf or other flat round bread
2 ounces arugula

• Salt and pepper turkey breast to taste and rub with enough olive oil to coat meat. Place on rack in roasting pan and roast at 300 degrees until instant-read thermometer inserted in breast reaches 160 degrees, about 1 hour 30 minutes. Let rest 10 minutes at room temperature.

• Remove breast from rack and immediately wrap tightly in foil. Chill several hours or overnight.

• Puree tuna and anchovies in blender. Add 1/3 cup olive oil in thin stream with motor running to make smooth emulsion, scraping down sides as necessary. Add lemon juice and pulse to combine. Taste: Mixture should be very tangy; if necessary, add more lemon juice. If anchovies aren't salty enough, add salt to taste.

• Place mayonnaise in mixing bowl and pour tuna mixture over top.

• Whisk to combine. Add capers and whisk briefly just to mix. Pour half of tonnato sauce onto large platter and spread evenly across bottom. Remove turkey from refrigerator, unwrap and cut strings. Cut into 1/8- to 1/4-inch-thick slices, placing each slice on platter, overlapping to make all fit. Spoon remaining sauce evenly over top. Cover tightly with plastic wrap and refrigerate at least 2 hours or overnight.

• To prepare sandwiches, cut ends from ciabatta loaf and slice in half horizontally, leaving halves attached along 1 long side. Arrange turkey slices on bread and spoon over just enough sauce from platter to moisten meat. Scatter arugula over top and close sandwich. Wrap tightly in plastic wrap and then in foil. Refrigerate until ready to serve.

• Slice before serving.

---

8 to 10 servings. Each of 10 servings: 402 calories; 694 mg sodium; 60 mg cholesterol; 16 grams fat; 80 grams carbohydrates; 27 grams protein; 0.11 gram fiber.

CHICKEN *in* GARLIC BREAD SAUCE

BREAD-THICKENED SAUCES USED TO BE quite common before they fell out of style in the 1970s. Taste this recipe from longtime food section columnist Marion Cunningham, and you'll wonder why we ever let them go.

1 bay leaf
2 large cloves garlic
1 small onion
1 cup whole milk
2 cups chicken broth
2 tablespoons red wine vinegar
2 tablespoons butter
1 teaspoon salt
1/2 teaspoon pepper
3 or 4 slices white bread
2 cups spinach, loosely packed
2 1/2 to 3 pounds chicken pieces, washed and patted dry

• Break bay leaf into pieces and set aside. Peel and finely chop garlic. Cut ends off onion, then peel and chop onion into small pieces.

• Place garlic, onion, milk, broth, vinegar, butter, bay leaf pieces, salt and pepper in medium saucepan. Set pan over medium-low heat and slowly bring to almost boiling, about 25 minutes; this allows flavors to develop.

• While sauce is heating, tear bread into small pieces and set aside.

• Prepare spinach by rinsing and patting dry with paper towels. Chop leaves into pieces.

• When sauce is about to boil, reduce heat to low and stir in bread pieces and chopped spinach. Add chicken pieces to sauce. Cover pan and simmer 20 minutes, making sure sauce never boils. Remove lid and turn chicken pieces over. Cover and cook 20 more minutes or until chicken is done. Immediately serve in deep dishes or bowls, using enough sauce to cover chicken pieces.

3 to 4 servings. Each of 4 servings: 544 calories; 1,306 mg sodium; 149 mg cholesterol; 34 grams fat; 19 grams carbohydrates; 39 grams protein; 0.56 gram fiber.

SIX

Fish

ALICE'S OYSTERS

RUTH REICHL, FORMER RESTAURANT CRITIC and food editor at the Los Angeles Times, who became restaurant critic at the New York Times and then editor of Gourmet magazine, says this is one of her favorite all-time recipes. It comes from her mother's housekeeper, Alice.

12 oysters
Salt
1/2 cup cracker crumbs (about 15 crackers)
1 egg
2 tablespoons oyster juice
Pepper
Oil or shortening
1 cup fresh bread crumbs
Lemons, cut in eighths

• Open oysters. Sprinkle with salt to taste and let stand in colander to dry out, 1 hour. Reserve 2 tablespoons of liquid from oysters.

• Coat thoroughly with cracker crumbs and let dry 10 minutes.

• Beat egg with oyster juice and pepper to taste. Set aside.

• Heat oil 3 inches deep in deep skillet to 365 degrees. Dip oysters in egg mixture, then in bread crumbs. Throw into hot fat, 2 at a time, and cook until brown, about 1 minute.

• Sprinkle with lemon juice and eat immediately.

12 oysters. Each oyster: 49 calories; 271 mg sodium; 26 mg cholesterol; 2 grams fat; 5 grams carbohydrates; 2 grams protein; 0.02 gram fiber.

FRIED CATFISH

MARINA DEL REY MAY SEEM AN ODD SPOT for a soul food café, but Aunt Kizzy's Back Porch is one of the best in Los Angeles. This is its version of traditional fried catfish. Old Bay brand seafood seasoning is preferred.

1/2 cup yellow or white cornmeal
1/2 cup flour
1 1/2 teaspoons seasoned salt
1 teaspoon black pepper
1 teaspoon garlic powder
1/2 teaspoon cayenne pepper
1/2 teaspoon seafood seasoning, optional
4 to 6 (4- to 8-ounce) catfish filets
Peanut oil for deep frying

- Thoroughly mix cornmeal, flour, salt, pepper, garlic powder, cayenne and seafood seasoning in bowl. Dredge filets in mixture to coat completely.

- Heat 2 to 3 inches peanut oil in large skillet to about 375 degrees.

- Drop 2 filets at a time in hot oil. Fry fish until golden brown, 4 to 7 minutes, depending on thickness, or until cooked as desired. Drain on paper towels.

Variation: For fish fingers, cut each filet into strips, then dredge in dry cornmeal mixture.

---

4 to 6 servings. Each of 6 servings: 282 calories; 409 mg sodium; 61 mg cholesterol; 14 grams fat; 17 grams carbohydrates; 21 grams protein; 0.16 gram fiber.

BAKED CHILEAN SEA BASS
with TOMATILLO SAUCE

THIS RECIPE FROM TEST KITCHEN DIRECTOR Donna Deane is astonishingly delicious, especially when you consider that a serving has less than 165 calories and 6 grams of fat.

1 pound tomatillos
2 cups water
Nonstick cooking spray
1 clove garlic, minced
1/4 onion, chopped
1 serrano chile, minced
2 teaspoons oil
1 teaspoon salt
2 teaspoons lime juice
4 (1/4-pound) Chilean sea bass filets, each about 1-inch thick
1/4 cup low-fat sour cream
Chopped cilantro, for garnish

• Remove husks from tomatillos, then wash under running water. Combine tomatillos and water in saucepan. Bring to boil and simmer until tomatillos are tender, about 10 minutes. Puree with liquid; set aside.

• Coat skillet with cooking spray. Saute garlic, onion and chile in oil until tender, 1 to 2 minutes. Stir in tomatillo puree. Bring to simmer and cook until puree thickens slightly, about 5 minutes. Season with salt and lime juice.

• Place filets into 4 individual baking dishes. Pour tomatillo sauce over fish. Bake at 375 degrees until fish flakes easily when tested with fork, about 30 minutes. Just before serving, spoon sour cream over fish and sprinkle with cilantro.

4 servings. Each serving: 162 calories; 666 mg sodium; 42 mg cholesterol; 6 grams fat; 9 grams carbohydrates; 19 grams protein; 0.17 gram fiber.

HEARTY CALAMARI STEW

GLADSTONE'S FOR FISH IN MALIBU IS FAMOUS for its location and lively crowd, not necessarily for the quality of its cuisine. But this recipe, from chef Saverio Posarelli, is something else. Furthermore, it's adaptable. It works well with chicken breast substituted for the squid, you can easily omit the chiles if you don't like spicy food, and if you don't feel like cooking polenta, the stew is every bit as good served over rice.

1991

1 pound calamari, thawed if frozen
1 tablespoon olive oil
1 onion, diced
1 clove garlic, pressed
1 pound tomatoes, coarsely chopped
1 tablespoon lemon juice
1/2 teaspoon sugar
1/4 teaspoon pepper
3 tablespoons soy sauce
1/4 cup chopped parsley
Hot cooked rice

• To clean calamari, remove head from body sac and discard viscera. Set aside heads and tentacles. Remove transparent quill from inside sac and wash insides. Pull off speckled outer skin covering sac. Cut tentacles from head and discard hard beak.

• Slice calamari sacs crosswise into 1/2-inch rings. Set aside.

• Heat oil in large skillet over high heat. Add onion and garlic and saute 1 minute. Stir in tomatoes, lemon juice, sugar, pepper and 1/2 cup water. Cook, stirring constantly, until mixture boils. Reduce heat and simmer, covered, until onion and tomatoes are tender, 12 minutes.

• Stir in soy sauce and calamari rings and tentacles. Cook, uncovered, over medium heat until calamari is opaque, 5 minutes. Stir in parsley. To serve, ladle stew over rice in large soup bowls.

4 servings. Each serving: 158 calories; 803 mg sodium; 190 mg cholesterol; 5 grams fat; 13 grams carbohydrates; 16 grams protein; 1.03 gram fiber.

CRISP-SKINNED SALMON
on CREAMY LEEKS *and* CABBAGE

FOOD EDITOR RUSS PARSONS ADAPTED a technique from French chef Joel Robuchon and came up with this combination. The salmon skin cooks to an almost bacon-like crispness that contrasts perfectly with the moist flesh and creamy vegetables.

2 leeks
1 (3-pound) head cabbage
1 slice bacon
1/2 teaspoon cumin seeds
1/4 cup (1/2 stick) butter
3 to 3 1/2 pounds salmon filets, center-cut preferably, in 1 or 2 pieces
Salt, pepper
2 tablespoons oil
1/4 cup whipping cream

• Trim tough green tops from leeks, leaving only whites and pale green lower leaves. Leaving leeks attached at bottom, slice in quarters lengthwise. Rinse well under cold running water until all sand and mud are gone. Slice thinly crosswise.

• Quarter head of cabbage and remove tough white core. Slice thinly.

• Slice bacon in thin crosswise strips.

• Toast cumin seeds in dry pan over medium heat, shaking frequently until fragrant, about 5 minutes.

• Combine bacon and 2 tablespoons butter in bottom of large skillet and cook over medium-high heat until bacon is rendered and crisp, about 5 minutes.

• Reduce heat to medium, add toasted cumin and leek slices, then cook until leeks soften, about 5 minutes. Add half of cabbage and cook, stirring, until soft, about 10 minutes. Add half of remaining cabbage and cook until that is soft, 10 more minutes.

• While cabbage is cooking, score salmon on skin-side, cutting just deep enough to pierce skin. Cut salmon into 8 equal pieces. Salt and pepper to taste on both sides.

• Add remaining cabbage to first skillet along with cream. Cook, stirring occasionally, until cream is no longer visible when pan is tilted from side to side. Season to taste with salt. Just before serving, add remaining 2 tablespoons butter, and cook just until sauce thickens, less than a minute.

• Heat oil in wide nonstick skillet over high heat. Add salmon filets, skin side down, and cook until skin has crisped and flesh has lightened about one-third up side, 2 to 3 minutes. Turn filets over and remove skillet from stove to finish cooking off heat.

• Divide leek and cabbage mixture evenly among 8 plates or shallow bowls. Place salmon on top, skin side up. The skin should be very crisp.

• Serve immediately.

8 servings. Each serving: 358 calories; 201 mg sodium; 80 mg cholesterol; 21 grams fat; 11 grams carbohydrates; 32 grams protein; 1.45 grams fiber.

CILANTRO SHRIMP
with LEMON GRASS RICE *and* COCONUT

THIS RECIPE FROM TIMES TEST KITCHEN INTERN Danae Campbell tastes authentically Thai. It can be prepared in less than 30 minutes.

2 1/4 cups water
1 1/2 cups jasmine rice
1 stalk lemon grass, root end trimmed and cut into 2-inch pieces
1/4 cup sweetened flaked coconut
1 tablespoon peanut oil
1 1/2 tablespoons minced ginger root
1 1/2 tablespoons minced garlic
1 teaspoon Thai red curry paste
2 cups coconut milk
1 bunch cilantro, coarsely chopped
1 1/2 pounds shrimp, peeled
1/2 red bell pepper, chopped
1/2 teaspoon Thai fish sauce (nam pla)
2 teaspoons lime juice
Salt, pepper

• Combine water, rice and lemon grass in medium saucepan. Bring to boil, reduce to simmer and cook, covered, 15 minutes. Remove from heat and let stand, covered, 5 minutes. Remove lemon grass from rice and discard. Keep rice warm.

• Place coconut on baking sheet and toast at 375 degrees until golden brown, about 8 minutes, stirring once.

• Remove from oven and cool. In large skillet, heat oil over medium-high heat. Add ginger, garlic and curry paste and cook 1 minute, stirring constantly. Add coconut milk and simmer until thickened, about 3 minutes. Remove sauce from heat and place in blender with cilantro. Puree until smooth, 2 minutes. Return sauce to skillet, bring to simmer and add shrimp and red pepper. Simmer until shrimp are just pink, 4 to 6 minutes. Add fish sauce, lime juice and season with salt and pepper. Serve with rice. Top with toasted coconut.

4 servings. Each serving: 694 calories; 515 mg sodium; 332 mg cholesterol; 31 grams fat; 62 grams carbohydrates; 43 grams protein; 2.72 grams fiber.

CRAB CAKES FAIDLEY

HOW DO YOU MAKE THE PERFECT CRAB CAKE? Everyone's got a different take on it. This is longtime Food section columnist and cookbook author Marion Cunningham's favorite.

1 cup mayonnaise
1 tablespoon plus 1 teaspoon Dijon mustard
About 40 saltine crackers
2 cups cooked crab meat or any cooked fish with bones removed
2 tablespoons oil
2 lemons

• Place mayonnaise and mustard in mixing bowl and stir briskly with spoon until color is uniform pale yellow. Spread a piece of wax paper about 16 inches long on counter. Set crackers on top of it, and using a rolling pin or your hands, press crackers into coarse crumbs. You should have about 2 cups crumbs. Add 1 cup cracker crumbs to mayonnaise mixture and add crab meat. Mix gently so crumbs and crab are well distributed in mixture.

• Spread remaining cracker crumbs evenly across wax paper. Divide crab mixture into 8 equal portions and gently pat each into a ball. Lightly flatten each ball into 3-inch round cake. Lightly coat each cake in cracker crumbs that are on wax paper, top and bottom.

• Heat large skillet over medium heat. Add 1 tablespoon oil and tilt skillet so oil completely coats bottom. Place 4 cakes in skillet and pan-fry over medium heat until golden on each side, 2 to 3 minutes.

• Remove cakes, add 1 tablespoon oil and fry remaining cakes in the same manner.

• Cut each lemon in half lengthwise and each half in half. Remove seeds and serve lemon wedges with crab cakes.

8 (3-inch) crab cakes. Each crab cake: 258 calories; 555 mg sodium; 41 mg cholesterol; 16 grams fat; 20 grams carbohydrates; 9 grams protein; 0.07 gram fiber.

FRUTTI *di* MARE

GABRIELLE LONGHI, WHO WAS RAISED in a restaurant family in Hawaii but lives in Los Angeles, contributed this favorite recipe. She says that if you're in a real rush, you can poach the seafood in plain water rather than in the seasoned liquid called for in this recipe.

---

1 bay leaf
1 stalk celery, chopped
1 onion, chopped
Juice of 1 lemon plus 1/4 cup
1 1/2 teaspoons salt
5 black peppercorns
2 to 3 sprigs Italian parsley plus 1/4 cup chopped
1/2 pound squid, cleaned
1 pound scallops
1 pound shrimp, peeled and deveined
1/2 cup extra-virgin olive oil
1/2 teaspoon chopped garlic
1 teaspoon freshly ground pepper
1/4 cup Kalamata olives, pitted and sliced thin
1/2 cup roasted red peppers, peeled, seeded and sliced thin

• Fill 4-quart stockpot 3/4 full of water. Add bay leaf, celery, onion, juice of whole lemon, 1 teaspoon salt, peppercorns and 2 to 3 sprigs parsley. Cook over medium-low heat 20 minutes.

• Strain liquid and return to stockpot. Bring to slow simmer. Add squid and poach 2 to 3 minutes.

• While squid is poaching, fill large bowl with ice and add water just to cover. Remove squid from poaching liquid, plunge into ice bath and drain again. Cut into 1/4-inch rings, leaving tentacles whole.

• Poach scallops in poaching liquid 2 minutes, plunge into ice bath and drain.

• Poach shrimp 2 minutes, plunge into ice bath and drain.

• Combine 1/4 cup lemon juice, olive oil, garlic, 1/4 cup chopped parsley, pepper and remaining 1/2 teaspoon salt and mix well. Add olives and red peppers. Toss mixture with drained seafood until well coated. Chill at least 1 hour before serving.

---

4 servings. Each serving: 534 calories; 1,451 mg sodium; 294 mg cholesterol; 32 grams fat; 11 grams carbohydrates; 49 grams protein; 0.56 gram fiber.

GRILLED CALAMARI
with LEMON AIOLI SANDWICH

THE LEMONY AIOLI GIVES A TART counterpoint to the garlicky, smoky grilled calamari in this wonderful sandwich.

■ LEMON AIOLI

1/3 cup mayonnaise
1/2 teaspoon grated lemon zest
1 clove garlic, minced

• Mix mayonnaise, lemon zest and garlic.

■ GRILLED CALAMARI

1 tablespoon butter
1 tablespoon olive oil
1 to 2 cloves garlic, minced or pressed
4 calamari steaks
Salt, pepper
2 teaspoons lemon juice or to taste
4 large French rolls, split, buttered and grilled
Assorted greens

• Melt butter with olive oil in small skillet. Add garlic and saute until tender. Brush mixture over calamari steaks. Grill over hot coals until just done, about 2 to 3 minutes on each side, brushing with more garlic butter. Season to taste with salt and pepper. Sprinkle with lemon juice to taste.

• Spread Lemon Aioli over bread bottoms. Fill with greens, calamari and, if desired, sliced tomato, caviar or capers. Top with roll tops and serve.

4 servings. Each serving: 401 calories; 619 mg sodium; 229 mg cholesterol; 17 grams fat; 43 grams carbohydrates; 21 grams protein; 2.02 gram fiber.

MARINATED GRILLED BLACK COD

THE COMBINATION OF SAKE, MIRIN AND SUGAR gives an almost caramel flavor and lacquer to the oily fish. This version, from Asakuma restaurant in West Los Angeles, is one of the greatest hits of Southern Californian fusion cuisine.

1 cup sake
1 cup mirin (sweet rice wine)
1 cup soy sauce
3/4 cup sugar
Juice of 2 oranges
6 (1/2-pound) Alaskan black cod filets, skin on

• Cook sake and mirin in large saucepan over medium heat 15 to 20 minutes, being careful sake and mirin do not ignite. Add soy sauce and sugar. Cool slightly, then add orange juice. Pour into shallow pan. Place cod in sake mixture, turning to coat all sides. Marinate in refrigerator overnight.

• When ready to broil, place fish over grill or on broiler rack in oven.

• Cook under broiler or over coals until dark brown and well-glazed. Turn and grill on other side until dark brown. Fish is done if bone can be easily removed. (Do not heat in microwave.)

• Serve skin-side down.

6 servings. Each serving: 393 calories; 3,045 mg sodium; 63 mg cholesterol; 1 gram fat; 49 grams carbohydrates; 36 grams protein; 0.02 gram fiber.

LINGUINE *with* CLAMS

TIMES TEST KITCHEN ASSISTANT Mayi Brady learned to make this from Mario Martinoli of Mario's Cooking With Friends restaurant in Los Angeles.

3/4 pound linguine
3 tablespoons olive oil
2 tablespoons butter
2 cloves garlic, minced
1/4 teaspoon dried red pepper flakes
1 cup clam juice
1 1/2 pounds small clams, preferably Manila
1/4 cup white wine
1 (6 1/2-ounce) can chopped clams
2 tablespoons chopped Italian parsley

- Cook linguine in plenty of salted water until al dente, about 10 minutes.
- Heat oil and butter in large skillet over medium heat. Add garlic and red pepper flakes and cook until garlic is softened, about 3 to 4 minutes. Add clam juice and simmer 5 minutes.
- Add fresh clams, cover and cook until clams have opened, about 5 minutes. Be sure to discard any that didn't open completely. Remove clams and set aside.
- Add wine, canned clams and their juice and parsley. Simmer another 5 minutes.
- Toss cooked pasta with sauce and top with fresh clams.

---

4 servings. Each serving: 730 calories; 383 mg sodium; 131 mg cholesterol; 20 grams fat; 74 grams carbohydrates; 55 grams protein; 0.35 gram fiber.

MOROCCAN FISH

THE INTRICATE SPICING of North Africa makes this fish tajine special.

1/2 cup olive oil
8 to 10 cloves garlic, sliced
5 red bell peppers, sliced
4 medium tomatoes, diced
1 (12-ounce) can garbanzo beans
1 tablespoon turmeric
3 tablespoons paprika
1 teaspoon dried red pepper flakes
1/2 teaspoon pepper
1 tablespoon salt
1 cup chopped cilantro
1/4 cup lemon juice
2 cups water
8 (4-ounce) sea bass steaks

• Heat oil in large skillet over medium heat. When hot, add garlic and cook, stirring, until barely brown. Do not burn. Add bell peppers, tomatoes, garbanzo beans, turmeric, paprika, pepper flakes, pepper and salt. Cook mixture for 5 minutes. Add cilantro, lemon juice and water and cook until peppers are soft and fragrant, about 10 more minutes.

• Take 1/4 of sauce and spread on bottom of 13x9-inch baking pan. Place fish in pan over sauce, then pour remaining sauce over fish. Cover with foil and bake at 350 degrees until fish begins to flake, about 20 minutes.

8 servings. Each serving: 300 calories; 1,083 mg sodium; 37 mg cholesterol; 17 grams fat; 19 grams carbohydrates; 20 grams protein; 1.86 grams fiber.

OPEN-FACE LOBSTER SALAD SANDWICH

THIS RECIPE FROM LONGTIME FOOD SECTION COLUMNIST Abby Mandel may be the ultimate fish sandwich. Serve an extra piece of warm brioche toast on the side for those who may want to make a closed sandwich.

2/3 cup low-fat mayonnaise
2 tablespoons low-fat sour cream
2 tablespoons snipped chives or dill
1 tablespoon plus 1 teaspoon chili sauce
Few drops hot pepper sauce
Few drops lemon juice
4 cups large chunks cooked lobster
Salt
Freshly ground pepper
8 Boston lettuce leaves, ribs removed
8 (3/4-inch-thick) slices brioche bread, lightly toasted and buttered
12 thick slices large tomato
8 slices bacon, preferably applewood-smoked, cooked crisp

• Combine mayonnaise, sour cream, chives, chili sauce, hot pepper sauce and lemon juice in 2-quart bowl. Add lobster and toss gently until mixed.

• Season with salt and pepper to taste. (Recipe can be made to this point and refrigerated for a few hours before serving.)

• Arrange lettuce leaves on 4 pieces warm brioche toast. Put 3 slices tomato on each piece of lettuce. Spoon lobster salad on tomatoes, pressing down slightly. Top each with 2 bacon slices. Serve immediately.

4 servings. Each serving: 578 calories; 1,522 mg sodium; 117 mg cholesterol; 23 grams fat; 49 grams carbohydrates; 43 grams protein; 0.74 gram fiber.

PEPPERED TUNA *with* PONZU SAUCE *and* DEEP-FRIED WON TONS

THIS WAS ONE OF JOACHIM SPLICHAL'S early dishes at Patina restaurant on Melrose Avenue.

1 (1 1/2-pound) tuna loin
1/4 cup cracked black pepper
1/2 cup butter, clarified
12 whole green onions
6 heads baby bok choy
2 cups oil
15 won ton skins, sliced in thin strips
Ponzu Sauce

• Trim tuna and remove skin. Roll loin in black pepper. Sear sides of tuna in hot pan with clarified butter. Thinly slice tuna into about 16 slices.

• Cut green onions into 3-inch pieces and blanch with bok choy in boiling water. Refresh in ice water to keep bright green color. Cut each bok choy in half lengthwise.

• Heat oil in wok or deep-fryer. Deep fry won ton strips, few at time, until golden brown.

• Place seared tuna slices on tray and warm in 350-degree oven, 1 to 2 minutes, or longer to desired doneness.

■ PONZU SAUCE

8 cloves garlic, peeled
2 Roma tomatoes
2/3 cup chicken stock
2 tablespoons lemon juice
1/4 cup soy sauce
1/2 cup finely diced ginger root
1/4 cup thinly sliced green onions

• Blanch garlic cloves in boiling water 3 times, changing water each time. Drain and thinly slice garlic.

• Quickly blanch tomatoes in boiling water, then shock in ice water. Peel skin, seed and dice.

• Combine chicken stock, lemon juice and soy sauce in saucepan and bring to boil. Add garlic slices, ginger, green onions and tomatoes.

• Quickly reheat green onions and bok choy in boiling water and drain.

• Place bok choy at top of serving plate and top with green onions. Fan tuna slices attractively at bottom of plate, then cover with Ponzu Sauce. Place won ton strips in center of plate, piled high.

4 servings. Each serving: 495 calories; 1,618 mg sodium; 139 mg cholesterol; 25 grams fat; 21 grams carbohydrates; 46 grams protein; 0.93 gram fiber.

STEAMED ROCKFISH

THERE MAY BE NO GREATER EXAMPLE of the elegant simplicity of fine Chinese cooking than this dish. This version comes from cookbook author Bruce Cost.

1 (1 1/2-pound) whole rockfish, cleaned, with head left on
1 teaspoon salt
2 teaspoons soy sauce
1 tablespoon dry Sherry or Chinese rice wine
1 1/2 tablespoons peanut oil
Sugar
1 tablespoon finely shredded ginger root
2 green onions, sliced into 2-inch lengths
Cilantro sprigs

• Rinse fish and dry thoroughly. Score fish lightly at 1-inch intervals with sharp knife. Rub salt over entire fish. Combine soy sauce, wine, oil and dash sugar. Set aside.

• Pour enough water into steamer or wok to come within 1 inch of cooking rack. Cover and bring to boil. Place fish on heatproof platter. Pour sauce over fish. Decorate fish with ginger and green onion shreds. Steam 12 to 15 minutes or until fish is just firm to touch. Serve garnished with cilantro.

2 to 4 servings. Each of 4 servings: 185 calories; 861 mg sodium; 48 mg cholesterol; 7 grams fat; 2 grams carbohydrates; 26 grams protein; 0.04 gram fiber.

SICHUAN SHRIMP

CHINATOWN'S MON KEE WAS one of the first restaurants in Southern California to specialize in Cantonese seafood. This is their version of a now-standard dish.

♥

---

1 pound shrimp
1 teaspoon plus 1 tablespoon rice vinegar
1 tablespoon rice wine or Sherry
1/2 teaspoon salt
Pepper
Garlic powder
1/2 teaspoon sesame oil
1 teaspoon cornstarch
1/2 egg white
Vegetable oil
1 slice ginger root, minced
1 clove garlic, minced
2 green onions, finely chopped
1 small onion, finely chopped
1 green bell pepper, finely chopped
1/4 cup ketchup
1 tablespoon sugar
1 teaspoon soy sauce
1 teaspoon hot chili sauce

• Shell and devein shrimp. Place in pie plate, sprinkle with 1 teaspoon vinegar and toss to coat well. Rinse with cold water and drain several times. Pat dry with paper towels. Sprinkle rice wine over shrimp and toss lightly. Pat dry with paper towels. Combine shrimp, salt, dash pepper, dash garlic powder, sesame oil, cornstarch and egg white. Mix well and refrigerate at least 1 hour or overnight.

• Heat wok. Add small amount of oil and ginger, garlic and green onions. Add refrigerated shrimp mixture and stir-fry until pink.

• Remove shrimp. Add more oil. Stir-fry onion and bell pepper.

• Combine ketchup, sugar, soy sauce, 1 tablespoon vinegar and chili sauce. Add to wok and bring mixture to boil. Add shrimp, mixing thoroughly.

---

4 servings. Each serving: 153 calories; 531 mg sodium; 88 mg cholesterol; 7 grams fat; 9 grams carbohydrates; 13 grams protein; 0.25 gram fiber.

HOT SALMON PIE

THIS LOVELY RECIPE WAS DEVELOPED based on an idea by the famed 19th century French chef Antonin Careme. He said to serve it with a ragout of carp roe, crayfish tails, oysters, mushrooms, artichoke bottoms and truffles, which does seem like gilding the lily.

■ CRUST

1 1/2 cups flour, plus more for kneading
6 tablespoons butter
3 tablespoons shortening
4 to 5 tablespoons ice water

• Put flour in large mixing bowl. Cut butter and shortening into small pieces and add to flour. Work mixture with pastry cutter until it resembles coarse meal. Mix with hands or rubber spatula while adding ice water, 1 tablespoon at time, just until dough holds together. Turn dough out onto floured board and knead few times to combine ingredients thoroughly.

• Pinch off lemon-sized portion of dough, wrap in plastic wrap and set aside. Roll remaining dough out to fit 8-inch pie plate. Transfer dough to pie plate and crimp edges. Prick bottom of dough all over and bake at 375 degrees 10 minutes. Set crust aside to cool.

• Roll out reserved piece of dough and cut into decorative shapes such as fish or leaves to top pie filling. Keep decorative shapes covered in plastic wrap until use.

■ FILLING

2 pounds salmon filets
3 slices bacon, chopped
3 tablespoons butter
1/2 cup minced shallots
1 cup sliced fresh mushrooms
1/2 cup dried mushrooms, soaked in warm water
2 tablespoons minced parsley
Salt, pepper
1 egg, beaten with 1 teaspoon water

• Remove bones from salmon. Cut fish into 1-inch chunks and set aside.

• Saute bacon in butter until it starts to crisp. Add shallots and cook until shallots start to soften, about 5 minutes. Add fresh mushrooms and cook 5 minutes longer. Drain reconstituted mushrooms, chop and add to saute pan along with parsley and salt and pepper to taste. Cook until fresh mushrooms begin to brown and dried mushrooms soften, about 10 minutes.

CONTINUED ☞

• Remove from heat, add salmon pieces and stir gently. Transfer filling to prepared crust. Top filling with decorative crust shapes. Brush exposed crust and cutouts with egg wash. Bake at 375 degrees until crust is golden, about 15 to 20 minutes.

■ HOLLANDAISE

1/4 cup (1/2 stick) butter
3 egg yolks
2 tablespoons lemon juice
Cayenne pepper
Salt
White pepper

• Melt butter in small saucepan. Set aside.

• Put water in bottom of double boiler, bring to boil and lower heat to just below boiling. In top of double boiler, off heat, mix egg yolks and lemon juice, then set on bottom of double boiler and whisk eggs until smooth. Slowly whisk in melted butter until thick.

• Remove from heat and season to taste with cayenne, salt and white pepper. Serve wedges of pie while hot and pass hollandaise.

6 to 8 servings. Each of 8 servings: 493 calories; 328 mg sodium; 218 mg cholesterol; 35 grams fat; 20 grams carbohydrates; 23 grams protein; 0.43 gram fiber.

OVEN-STEAMED SALMON

THIS IS AN ADAPTATION OF A TECHNIQUE from Paula Wolfert. Food Editor Russ Parsons likes to serve the salmon whole; there's something about spooning it off the platter that emphasizes just how moist and rich it is. Feel free to experiment with accompaniments. He likes the cucumber salad (page 31) because of the way its cool green color and crisp texture complement the salmon.

1999

1 (3-pound) salmon filet
Salt, pepper

• Remove skin and pin bones from salmon filet. Trim sides to form roughly rectangular shape that is fairly consistent in thickness. Place salmon on baking sheet and salt and pepper liberally.

• Place roasting pan in bottom of 300-degree oven and fill with boiling water. Place baking sheet with salmon on middle rack of oven and cook until salmon flakes, about 20 minutes. Carefully slide onto serving platter, surround with Cucumber Salad and serve immediately.

6 to 8 servings. Each of 8 servings: 193 calories; 97 mg sodium; 75 mg cholesterol; 9 grams fat; 0 carbohydrates; 27 grams protein; 0 fiber.

SEAFOOD CASSEROLE
with MONGOLIAN SAUCE

JASMINE AND BASMATI ARE just a few of the specialty rices now available in Southern California markets. This recipe by cookbook author Nina Simonds uses a variety of seafood to make a sensational dish.

1/2 pound firm-fleshed fish filet, such as haddock, red snapper or lake trout
1/2 pound shelled shrimp
3 tablespoons rice wine or sake, plus 1/3 cup
1 1/2 tablespoons minced ginger root
1 teaspoon sesame oil
1 Chinese or nappa cabbage, about 1 1/2 pounds
1/2 pound fresh shiitake mushrooms
1 bunch (1/2 pound) enoki mushrooms
1 teaspoon canola or corn oil
4 cloves garlic, smashed lightly
4 cups Chinese chicken broth
1 teaspoon salt
2 1/4 cups jasmine or basmati rice
1/2 pound firm tofu, cut into 1/4-inch dice, optional
2 green onions, cut diagonally into 1/4-inch-thick slices

• Cut fish into 1-inch-square chunks and place in bowl. Cut shrimp along back to butterfly and add to bowl with fish. Whisk together 3 tablespoons rice wine, ginger and sesame oil, and add to seafood, stirring to coat. Marinate 20 minutes.

• Separate stem and leafy sections of cabbage, and cut into 2-inch squares. Remove stems from shiitake mushrooms and cut caps into thin slices. Trim stem ends from enoki mushrooms. Rinse lightly and drain.

• Heat Dutch oven or covered casserole over medium-high heat. Add oil and heat until hot, about 30 seconds. Add garlic and cabbage stems, and stir-fry over medium-high heat 1 minute. Add remaining 1/3 cup rice wine and lightly toss, cover and cook 1 1/2 minutes. Remove cover and add remaining cabbage, chicken broth and salt. Partially cover and bring to boil, then simmer 5 minutes.

• Rinse rice under cold, running water, using fingers as rake, until water runs clear. Drain rice in colander. Put rice in 4-quart casserole that can be used on stove top or in Dutch oven. Pour broth with cabbage into casserole, cover and cook on top of stove over medium-low heat 15 minutes.

• Place shiitake mushrooms, enoki mushrooms and tofu in separate piles over rice, leaving space for seafood. Cover and bake at 450 degrees 10 minutes. Remove from oven and arrange seafood over rice. Cover and bake until fish flakes with fork, about 8 minutes.

• Sprinkle green onions over casserole and let sit, covered, 1 minute.

CONTINUED☞

•   Spoon into bowls, being sure each portion gets some of seafood, mushrooms and tofu. Sprinkle with Mongolian Sauce.

■ MONGOLIAN SAUCE

3/4 cup soy sauce
3 1/2 tablespoons rice wine or sake
3 1/2 tablespoons Chinese black vinegar or Worcestershire sauce
3 tablespoons minced green onions
2 tablespoons minced ginger root
2 tablespoons minced garlic
2 tablespoons sugar
1 teaspoon hot chile paste, optional

•   Combine soy sauce, rice wine, vinegar, green onions, ginger, garlic, sugar and chile paste if using.

6 servings. Each serving: 450 calories; 3,142 mg sodium; 58 mg cholesterol; 4 grams fat; 76 grams carbohydrates; 25 grams protein; 2.06 grams fiber.

SQUID *with* RICE

CHRIS LISICA'S RECIPE TURNED UP in a story on the large Croatian community in San Pedro.

1/4 cup oil
1 large onion, chopped
3 pounds squid, cleaned and cut into rings
4 cloves garlic, chopped
1 green bell pepper, seeded and chopped
1/2 cup parsley, chopped
2 (8-ounce) cans tomato sauce
Salt, pepper
1 3/4 cups rice

•   Heat oil in heavy-bottomed pot over high heat. Add onion and saute until lightly browned. Add squid rings and tentacles and saute together. Add garlic, bell pepper, parsley, tomato sauce and salt and pepper to taste. Squid will release liquid. Cover and simmer over low heat until squid is tender, 1 to 1 1/2 hours, adding rice last 30 minutes. Stir regularly.

8 servings. Each serving: 302 calories; 425 mg sodium; 222 mg cholesterol; 9 grams fat; 37 grams carbohydrates; 18 grams protein; 0.59 gram fiber.

SALMON IN SWEET RED CURRY
(*Panang Pla Salmon*)

TIMOTHY M. EVANS HAS TWO GREAT PASSIONS: Thai food and wine. He founded the Amador County winery Clos du Lac Cellars with the mission of encouraging wine-lovers to think beyond the usual choices for matching wine with Thai food. Look for kaffir lime leaves, red curry paste, fish sauce and Thai basil at Asian markets.

1 (19-ounce) can coconut milk
4 to 5 tablespoons red curry paste
1 tablespoon fish sauce, plus more if needed
1 tablespoon sugar, plus more if needed
4 Thai (kaffir) lime leaves, torn into small pieces
2 (4- to 6-inch) center-cut salmon fillets, about 1 1/2 pounds
Olive oil
1 tablespoon Cognac
8 to 10 Thai basil leaves

• Remove thick layer of cream from top of unshaken coconut milk can and set aside half. Heat remaining half of coconut cream in skillet and stir in curry paste. Saute until fragrant, 2 to 3 minutes. Add 1/4 of coconut milk (thinner layer) to mixture, heat to boiling and stir until red oil appears at edges. Add another 1/4 of coconut milk and repeat boiling until oil appears. Repeat with another 1/4 of coconut milk. When red oil appears, add 2 tablespoons coconut milk, reserving rest to add later.

• Add fish sauce, sugar and lime leaves. Taste and adjust fish sauce and sugar if needed. Boil until little red-colored oil appears. Remove from heat and strain through coarse sieve. Push as much of solids through as possible. Discard residue. Return strained mixture to skillet and set aside.

• Remove any bones from salmon with fish pliers or tweezers and coat fish with olive oil. If grilling outdoors, place in oiled fish basket. Grill, skin side up, over high heat, ideally over smoking alder wood chips, or on stove-top grill pan, 3 to 4 minutes on flesh side. Turn and grill 5 minutes more. Remove from fish basket if using and keep warm.

• Add remaining coconut milk to sauce and heat, stirring, over medium to medium-high heat, until smooth sauce consistency, 1 to 3 minutes. Add Cognac and boil to evaporate alcohol, about 2 minutes.

• Pour sauce onto heated platter. Place basil around edges, then place grilled salmon on top and sprinkle with basil leaves. Place reserved coconut cream in small plastic bag with tip of 1 corner cut off and pipe onto salmon and sauce in decorative manner, or spoon over fish.

4 servings. Each serving: 559 calories; 523 mg sodium; 53 mg cholesterol; 44 grams fat; 10 grams carbohydrates; 33 grams protein; 2.94 grams fiber.

STEAMED SALMON *with* ASPARAGUS *and* SOBA NOODLES

THIS RECIPE FROM TEST KITCHEN INTERN Charity Ferreira may sound incredibly complex, but it can be prepared in less than 30 minutes.

1 1/2 tablespoons sesame oil
1 tablespoon rice vinegar
1 tablespoon soy sauce
1 (1/2-inch) piece ginger root, minced
1/2 teaspoon red or yellow miso
1 (4- to 6-ounce) salmon filet, skin removed
Salt
6 ounces (about 1/3 bunch) asparagus, cut diagonally into 1-inch pieces
1/4 pound (1/2 package) dried Japanese buckwheat noodles (soba)
2 green onions, white parts chopped, greens reserved

• Whisk together oil, vinegar, soy sauce, ginger and miso. Coat salmon lightly with about 1 teaspoon of mixture. Set aside.

• Blanch asparagus pieces in boiling salted water until crisp-tender, 1 to 2 minutes. Remove from pot using slotted spoon and set aside. Return water to boil and cook soba noodles according to package directions, about 6 minutes.

• In another pot fitted with steaming rack, bring several inches of water to boil. Line rack with reserved green onion tops. Place salmon on rack and cover pot tightly. Steam over medium heat until salmon flakes with fork, 8 to 10 minutes.

• Drain soba noodles and toss with asparagus pieces and remaining dressing. Top with steamed salmon and sprinkle with chopped green onions.

1 serving: 755 calories; 2,410 mg sodium; 82 mg cholesterol; 26 grams fat; 94 grams carbohydrates; 46 grams protein; 3.02 grams fiber.

TROUT MOUSSE

THIS RECIPE FROM FOOD EDITOR Russ Parsons is one of those great dinner party appetizers. It can be mixed ahead and baked at the last minute, and it adapts to a wide variety of sauces and accompaniments.

1 pound boned, skinned trout
2 egg whites
1 egg yolk
1/3 cup half-and-half
1 1/2 teaspoons salt
Pepper
1/4 teaspoon freshly grated nutmeg
1/2 cup (1 stick) butter, room temperature, plus more for greasing
2 cups very cold whipping cream

• In food processor, puree fish, egg whites and egg yolk with half-and-half until smooth. For perfectly smooth mousse, push puree through strainer into bowl set in larger bowl containing crushed ice. Cover tightly and refrigerate at least 2 hours.

• Combine salt, pepper, nutmeg and butter in food processor and puree 15 seconds. Gradually add fish meat, processing to homogeneous consistency. Then add 1 1/2 cups of cream through feed tube. As soon as all cream has been absorbed, stop processor.

• Remove mousse to bowl placed in ice. With large rubber spatula, fold remaining 1/2 cup cream into mousse. Refrigerate until ready to use, as long as 24 hours.

• Pack puree into 8 heavily buttered glass or ceramic ramekins. Place ramekins in large baking dish. Place baking dish on oven shelf and add boiling water to halfway up ramekins. Lay sheet of parchment paper over top and bake at 325 degrees until skewer inserted in center of 1 of ramekins comes out clean and feeling burning hot to bottom lip, about 15 to 17 minutes.

• When ready to serve, whether warm or at room temperature, carefully run thin knife around outside of mousse, place plate over top and invert with quick, forceful thrust. Garnish as desired.

8 servings. Each serving: 382 calories; 610 mg sodium; 174 mg cholesterol; 37 grams fat; 2 grams carbohydrates; 11 grams protein; 0 fiber.

SEVEN

Vegetables

ASPARAGUS *with* SESAME OIL MAYONNAISE DRESSING

THE SESAME OIL IN THIS RECIPE from longtime columnist and cookbook author Marion Cunningham gives the mayonnaise a rich, nutty taste that enhances the flavor of the asparagus.

1/2 cup mayonnaise
1/2 teaspoon sesame oil
2 pounds asparagus
Salt

• Combine mayonnaise and sesame oil and refrigerate until ready to use.

• Cut stems off asparagus where stems begin to look green.

• Bring enough water to cover asparagus to boil in large skillet. Add salt to taste and stir. Put asparagus in skillet and let boil 1 to 2 minutes. Remove 1 spear and cut off piece of thickest bottom part and taste; if tender but not soft, asparagus is done.

• Remove asparagus from skillet and spread on wax paper to cool. When cool, wrap and refrigerate.

• Remove asparagus from refrigerator several hours before serving to bring to room temperature. Place asparagus on plates with spoonful of dressing on the side.

4 to 6 servings. Each of 6 servings: 112 calories; 189 mg sodium; 6 mg cholesterol; 7 grams fat; 10 grams carbohydrates; 5 grams protein; 1.24 grams fiber.

CANDIED YAMS

TRUE YAMS ARE RARELY FOUND in this country; it's more of a nickname given to certain varieties of sweet potatoes. Aunt Kizzy's Back Porch, the landmark Marina del Rey soul food restaurant, advises picking sweet potatoes "with moist, dark orange flesh and skin ranging in color from almost purple to copper."

3 sweet potatoes (about 2 1/2 pounds)
1/4 cup (1/2 stick) butter, plus more for greasing
1 cup sugar
1 1/2 cups water
1/2 teaspoon nutmeg
Zest of 1/4 lemon
2 tablespoons lemon juice
1 teaspoon vanilla extract

a   Scrub sweet potatoes and place in large pot. Cover with boiling water and cook, covered, over medium heat 25 to 30 minutes, until potatoes are tender but firm. Drain and cool potatoes. Peel potatoes and slice into thick pieces.

•   Grease shallow baking dish and arrange sweet potato slices in single layer in dish.

•   Heat sugar, water, nutmeg and lemon zest in saucepan. Add butter and lemon juice. When butter melts, remove from heat and add vanilla. Stir syrup and pour over potatoes in dish. Bake at 425 degrees until bubbly, 30 minutes.

4 to 6 servings. Each of 6 servings: 387 calories; 93 mg sodium; 21 mg cholesterol; 8 grams fat; 79 grams carbohydrates; 3 grams protein; 1.6 grams fiber.

BEANS THORAN

1995

THIS RECIPE COOKS IN LESS THAN 15 minutes, it has almost no fat, and it tastes really wonderful. What's the catch? We're still looking for one. It is from Nirmala Kripanarayanan, who was born in Southern India. It's an example of Hindu vegetarian cooking at its best. You can sometimes find it on the menu at India's Tandoori, a restaurant in West Los Angeles that Kripanarayanan and her family run. Look for urad dal at Indian markets.

2 1/4 teaspoons oil
1/2 teaspoon mustard seeds
1/2 teaspoon cumin seeds
1 tablespoon split, peeled urad dal
1 onion, chopped
4 jalapenos, chopped
1 stalk curry leaves
1 teaspoon turmeric
1 pound green beans, cut crosswise in thin slices
1/4 coconut, grated
2 teaspoons salt
Chopped cilantro

• Heat oil in skillet. Add mustard and cumin seeds. When mustard seeds pop, add dal, onion and jalapenos. Cook until onion is tender-crisp. Add curry leaves and turmeric and cook briefly. Add green beans and stir to mix with seasonings. Add coconut and continue to stir.

• Add salt and cook 5 to 7 minutes, stirring. Beans should be slightly crisp. Check seasoning. Serve garnished with cilantro.

8 servings. Each serving: 49 calories; 594 mg sodium; 0 cholesterol; 2 grams fat; 7 grams carbohydrates; 2 grams protein; 1 gram fiber.

BRUSSELS SPROUTS *and* BACON

THAT STINKY MUSTARD SMELL? You won't find it developing when cooking these Brussels sprouts. That's because they cook quickly. Even people who don't normally like sprouts will love this recipe from Food Editor Russ Parsons.

1999

2 pounds Brussels sprouts
3 strips bacon
1/2 cup red wine vinegar
Salt
1/4 cup pine nuts, toasted

• Trim Brussels sprouts, removing any outer leaves that are too dark or are damaged. Trim dried-out base of sprouts and cut an "X" 1/4 to 1/2 inch deep in each.

• Steam sprouts over rapidly boiling water just until tender, about 5 minutes, no longer than 7 minutes. Cool and cut into lengthwise quarters. Set aside.

• While sprouts steam, cut bacon into thin strips. Cook in skillet over medium-low heat until crisp. Raise heat to high and add red wine vinegar. Cook until vinegar loses raw smell, about 3 minutes.

• Reduce heat and add sprouts. Heat through, season to taste with salt and 1 to 2 tablespoons additional red wine vinegar, if necessary. Add pine nuts, stir and serve.

6 servings. Each serving: 120 calories; 138 mg sodium; 3 mg cholesterol; 5 grams fat; 16 grams carbohydrates; 8 grams protein; 2.34 grams fiber.

ONION RINGS

ONE OF THE HALLMARKS OF CAMPANILE restaurant in Los Angeles is doing simple things extremely well. These onion rings are a perfect example. Chef Nancy Silverton says the key is keeping the batter iced until frying, as you would with tempura.

3 or 4 red onions, sliced 1/2 inch thick
3 tablespoons balsamic vinegar
2 cups flour
1 cup cornstarch
1 tablespoon baking soda
1 tablespoon baking powder
1/2 tablespoon salt, plus more for serving
1 (12-ounce) bottle dark beer, ice cold
Soda water, ice cold
Oil, for frying

• Marinate onions in balsamic vinegar 1 hour.

• Meanwhile, prepare batter, mixing flour, cornstarch, baking soda, baking powder and salt in large bowl placed on top of larger bowl filled with ice. Whisk in beer, then enough soda water to thin batter to point that it just coats spoon.

• Heat oil for frying to 375 degrees. Keeping batter on ice, dredge onions in batter and fry until light brown, about 1 minute. Remove and drain on paper towels, salt lightly and serve immediately.

8 to 10 servings. Each of 10 servings: 271 calories; 608 mg sodium; 0 cholesterol; 2 grams fat; 42 grams carbohydrates; 4 grams protein; 0.28 gram fiber.

CARAWAY POTATOES DUCHESSE

POTATOES DUCHESSE IS ONE OF THOSE classic dishes that few people take the time to make any more. Times Test Kitchen intern Phil Andres does, and the addition of caraway seeds and bacon gives this recipe a neat twist.

1 1/2 pounds baking potatoes, quartered
1 tablespoon butter, melted
2 tablespoons caraway seeds
8 slices bacon, cooked and chopped into small pieces
Salt
White pepper
2 egg yolks

• Place potatoes in cold salted water and simmer until tender. Drain, then dry potatoes in oven several minutes.

• Mash potatoes, add butter, caraway seeds, bacon and salt and pepper to taste. Mix to uniform consistency. Mixture should be fairly stiff. Add egg yolks and mix until smooth. Using pastry bag with large star tip, pipe mixture into conical spirals.

• Just before serving, place potatoes in 400-degree oven to brown lightly, about 5 to 8 minutes.

6 servings. Each serving: 171 calories; 180 mg sodium; 101 mg cholesterol; 7 grams fat; 22 grams carbohydrates; 6 grams protein; 0.76 gram fiber.

SAAG

1994

THE SECRET OF GREAT INDIAN SAAG is simmering mustard greens for hours to bring out the full flavor. Hari B. Alipuria, owner of Chameli restaurant in Rosemead, gave us this relatively quick recipe for his restaurant's saag, an adaptation of his family's traditional slow-cooked greens. The mustard greens cook in about 40 minutes, and they don't ooze with as much butter as they would in India because Alipuria tries to reduce some of the fat that normally is so much a part of traditional Indian cooking. Fenugreek leaves can be found at Indian markets.

1 1/2 pounds mustard greens
3/4 pound spinach
1 (7-inch) piece ginger root, peeled and chopped
1 jalapeno, chopped
Salt
4 cups water
3/4 cup oil
3 onions, finely chopped
4 teaspoons ground coriander
1 tablespoon ground cumin
1 teaspoon ground turmeric
3 small juicy tomatoes, chopped
1 tablespoon chopped garlic
1 teaspoon dried fenugreek (methi) leaves
1 tablespoon butter

• Rinse mustard greens and spinach thoroughly. Remove only coarsest bottom portion of stems. Chop roughly. Place in Dutch oven and add 1 1/2 tablespoons chopped ginger root, jalapeno, salt to taste and water. Boil, uncovered, about 30 minutes.

• Heat 1/2 cup oil in large pot. Add onions and fry until tender but not browned. Add 1 tablespoon chopped ginger root, then coriander, cumin and turmeric. Fry 1 to 2 minutes. Add tomatoes, garlic and 1 tablespoon salt, or salt to taste, and cook until tomatoes are tender. Add fenugreek.

• Drain any liquid remaining with greens and reserve. Place greens in food processor or blender and blend until finely chopped but not pureed.

• Add greens to onion mixture with reserved cooking liquid. Boil, uncovered, 40 minutes, until well combined and liquid is reduced but mixture is still moist.

• Meanwhile, in skillet fry remaining ginger root in 1/4 cup oil until lightly browned. Turn cooked saag into serving bowl. Place butter in center. Sprinkle with fried ginger, or serve ginger on side to add as desired.

8 to 10 servings. Each of 10 servings: 258 calories; 150 mg sodium; 4 mg cholesterol; 23 grams fat; 13 grams carbohydrates; 5 grams protein; 2.02 grams fiber.

KOHLRABI PANCAKES

KOHLRABI IS ONE OF THOSE ROOT vegetables that most people don't know how to use. This recipe from novelist and frequent contributor Michelle Huneven is kind of a Midwestern turn on latkes. It's delicious.

2 cups grated kohlrabi, peeled, leaves removed
1/2 cup grated or finely chopped onion
2 eggs lightly beaten
1/4 cup bread crumbs
1/4 teaspoon salt
Freshly ground pepper
Oil

• Combine kohlrabi, onion, eggs, bread crumbs, salt and pepper to taste in bowl.

• Heat oil in large skillet. Pat kohlrabi mixture into 3-inch patties in palm of hand and lower gently into hot oil. Fry over medium-low heat, flipping when firmed up and nicely browned, about 2 minutes per side.

• Drain on paper towels. Can be kept warm in oven. Serve with applesauce or grilled pear slices.

12 pancakes or 4 servings. Each serving: 97 calories; 239 mg sodium; 107 mg cholesterol; 4 grams fat; 11 grams carbohydrates; 5 grams protein; 0.83 gram fiber.

EGGPLANT *alla* PARMIGIANA

1988

WHO'D EXPECT TO FIND a nearly 100-year-old working winery in downtown Los Angeles? While San Antonio Winery might not be mentioned in the same breath as Caymus or Joseph Phelps Vineyards, it does make a rough and ready sort of hearty red wine. And it does have a restaurant as well, serving homey Italian food that pairs nicely with the wine. This recipe comes from Maddalena Riboli, the matriarch of the family that owns the winery.

■ MARINARA SAUCE

1/2 cup finely grated or ground carrot
1/2 cup minced or ground celery
1/2 onion, minced
2 tablespoons olive oil
2 (28-ounce) cans tomato puree
1/2 tomato puree can water
1/2 teaspoon dried basil
2 or 3 bay leaves
2 teaspoons beef stock base
2 teaspoons sugar
1/2 teaspoon Worcestershire sauce
Garlic powder
Salt
White pepper

• Carrot, celery and onion can be ground in food processor or minced by hand. Heat olive oil in Dutch oven. Add vegetables and cook until lightly browned. Add tomato puree, water, basil, bay leaves, stock base, sugar, Worcestershire and dash garlic powder. Season to taste with salt and pepper.

• Simmer, uncovered, 20 to 25 minutes. Makes 6 cups.

■ EGGPLANT PARMIGIANA

3 medium-large eggplants, peeled
1 egg
1 cup milk
1/8 teaspoon garlic powder
1/2 teaspoon dried parsley leaves
1/2 teaspoon dried basil leaves
1/2 teaspoon salt
1/8 teaspoon white pepper
Flour
Olive oil

CONTINUED☞

1 1/2 pounds mozzarella cheese, thinly sliced
1 cup grated Romano cheese

• Cut eggplant into 1/2-inch-thick rounds. Pile eggplant in colander and let stand 45 minutes. Beat egg with milk, then add garlic powder, parsley, basil, salt and pepper. Place flour in shallow bowl or on plate.

• Heat small amount olive oil in heavy skillet. Flour each slice eggplant, then dip in egg mixture and place in single layer in skillet. Saute until lightly browned. Remove and set aside.

• To assemble, line 14x11-inch baking dish with 1 cup Maddalena's Marinara Sauce. Place layer of eggplant on sauce. Cover with mozzarella slices. Add 1/3 cup Romano cheese. Cover with 1 1/2 cups marinara sauce.

• Top with layer of eggplant, then cheeses. Make 1 more layer in this fashion, ending with cheeses. Cover with foil, supporting with wood picks so foil does not touch cheese.

• Bake at 375 degrees until heated through and cheese is melted, 20 to 25 minutes. Cut into squares to serve. Spoon additional marinara sauce over each serving.

12 servings. Each serving: 75 calories; 488 mg sodium; 0 cholesterol; 2 grams fat; 13 grams carbohydrates; 2 grams protein; 1.07 grams fiber.

GOAT CHEESE-STUFFED CHILES

THIS WONDERFUL APPETIZER from Test Kitchen Director Donna Deane goes together easily and can be prepared in advance up to the point of the final baking.

6 small poblano chiles
1 ear corn
Freshly ground pepper
1/2 pound goat cheese
Chopped tomato

• Roast chiles and corn on rack over gas burner placed on stove top or under broiler until peppers are charred and corn is lightly charred, about 10 minutes. Put chiles in paper bag and close. Let chiles cool, about 15 to 20 minutes, then remove from bag and peel. Make a slit on one side of each chile and remove seeds. Pat dry. When corn is cool enough to handle, cut kernels from cob to make about 1 cup.

• Crumble goat cheese into bowl. Stir in 1/2 cup of grilled corn and season to taste with pepper. Spoon cheese mixture into peppers. Place peppers in shallow glass baking dish seam side up and bake at 350 degrees until cheese is heated through, 10 to 15 minutes.

• Place chiles on serving plates and sprinkle with tomatoes and remaining corn.

6 servings. Each serving: 164 calories; 196 mg sodium; 17 mg cholesterol; 10 grams fat; 13 grams carbohydrates; 9 grams protein; 3.95 grams fiber.

MUSHROOM POT PIE

THIS WONDERFUL WINTERY DISH was proposed by Test Kitchen intern Charity Ferreira, who went on to cook at the renowned San Francisco vegetarian restaurant Greens. Use a mixture of flavorful wild and domestic mushrooms such as brown criminis, porcinis and shiitakes. Avoid portabello mushrooms; they will turn the filling black unless you trim off the gills.

■ CRUST

1 1/2 cups flour
1/2 teaspoon salt
1/2 cup (1 stick) butter, chilled and cut into small pieces
1 egg yolk
5 tablespoons ice water

* Combine flour and salt in food processor or mixing bowl.

* Process or cut in butter with pastry blender until mixture resembles coarse crumbs.

* Beat egg yolk with water and add to flour and salt. Pulse or mix just until dough starts to come together, being careful not to overwork. Turn out onto work surface and gather dough into ball. Flatten into disk and wrap in plastic wrap and chill 1 hour.

■ FILLING

2 tablespoons olive oil
1 onion, sliced
2 shallots, chopped
Salt, pepper
1 3/4 pounds mixed mushrooms
4 cloves garlic, minced
2/3 cup red wine
1 tablespoon butter
1 tablespoon flour
1 1/2 cups low-salt vegetable broth, heated
8 to 10 sprigs thyme
1 tablespoon chopped parsley
1 egg yolk beaten with 1 tablespoon milk

* Heat 1 tablespoon olive oil in skillet over medium heat. Cook onion and shallots until soft and just starting to brown, 10 to 15 minutes.

CONTINUED☛

• Season with salt and pepper and put in mixing bowl. Heat another tablespoon oil over high heat in same skillet. Saute mushrooms until tender, about 5 minutes. Add garlic and cook 1 to 2 minutes. Season with salt and pepper. Add wine and cook, stirring frequently, until liquid has cooked away. As mushrooms cook, use wooden spoon or spatula to scrape up any browned bits of mushroom stuck to skillet. Add mushrooms to onions and combine.

• Make roux by melting 1 tablespoon butter and stirring in 1 tablespoon flour. Cook over medium heat, stirring constantly, for 2 minutes. Slowly whisk in hot vegetable broth. Bring to simmer and cook until slightly thickened, about 2 minutes. Stir sauce into mushroom mixture, adding thyme leaves and parsley. Taste for seasoning and cool to room temperature.

• Roll out pastry on lightly floured board into 11-inch circle. Spoon mushroom mixture into 9-inch shallow ceramic casserole or pie dish. Top with pastry, pinching edges to seal and trim away extra crust, leaving slight overhang around edge of dish. Cut few vents in crust for steam to escape. Brush with beaten egg yolk and 1 tablespoon milk. Bake at 375 degrees until crust is golden brown, about 45 minutes.

4 to 6 servings. Each of 6 servings: 389 calories; 685 mg sodium; 138 mg cholesterol; 25 grams fat; 32 grams carbohydrates; 7 grams protein; 1.11 grams fiber.

BALSAMIC SQUASH PUREE

ROASTING WINTER SQUASH concentrates the flavor and turns what looks like a hard, clumsy weapon into a silky smooth, sweet puree. Cut the squash in half and scoop out the seeds, and roast about 40 minutes at 400 degrees. Then, use the result in a variety of ways.

1995

2 tablespoons minced shallots
1/4 cup (1/2 stick) butter
3 tablespoons balsamic vinegar
2 cups roast squash pulp
1 teaspoon salt
Freshly grated nutmeg

• Cook shallots in medium saucepan with 1 tablespoon butter over medium heat until soft, about 3 to 5 minutes.

• Add vinegar, increase heat to high and cook until vinegar is reduced to syrup, another 3 to 5 minutes. Add squash pulp and salt and stir to combine.

• Reduce heat to low and cook until heated through, about 5 minutes.

• Cut remaining butter into small cubes, add to squash and beat in until fairly smooth. Serve immediately, dusted with freshly grated nutmeg.

4 servings. Each serving: 159 calories; 708 mg sodium; 31 mg cholesterol; 12 grams fat; 13 grams carbohydrates; 1 gram protein; 0.83 gram fiber.

TOFU STEAK

THIS IS A MUCH-REQUESTED RECIPE from the Sherman Oaks restaurant Mako Sushi. Using more than one pan at a time allows you to juggle the cooking so that everything is done at once.

1/2 cup olive oil
2 pounds sliced mushrooms
1/2 white onion, sliced
2 (13-ounce) cartons extra-firm tofu, drained
1 1/2 cups cream Sherry
3 tablespoons butter
1 teaspoon garlic powder mixed with 1 teaspoon water
3 tablespoons soy sauce

• Heat 1/4 cup olive oil in 12-inch skillet over medium-high heat. Add mushrooms and onion, and saute until onion is tender, 15 minutes.

• Cut tofu into "steaks" by slicing each block into 3 lengthwise slabs. Heat 1/4 cup olive oil in a second skillet over medium-high heat and saute tofu steaks until cooked on both sides, 4 to 5 minutes a side. You may need to cook tofu in batches. Remove tofu and set steaks in skillet on top of cooked mushroom mixture.

• Add Sherry to pan that held tofu and heat. Tilt pan away from you and with a long-handled match, ignite Sherry (keep face and loose clothing away from flames; do not allow children near flames).

• When flames burn down, add butter and garlic-water mixture to skillet. Heat until butter melts. Add soy sauce and simmer over medium heat until sauce thickens slightly, 3 to 4 minutes. Return tofu to pan and saute until light brown on both sides, 2 to 4 minutes a side.

• Divide tofu among 6 serving plates and top with mushroom mixture and sauce. Serve hot.

6 servings. Each serving: 496 calories; 589 mg sodium; 16 mg cholesterol; 35 grams fat; 17 grams carbohydrates; 24 grams protein; 1.48 grams fiber.

RATATOUILLE NICOISE

SOUTHERN CALIFORNIAN CLAUDIE CES hails from Aix-en-Provence in the south of France. This version of the Provencal classic is intended to be served with her Gigot d'Agneau Roti a la Provencale (page 90).

1992

2 tablespoons olive oil
1 large onion, chopped
3 cloves garlic, chopped
3 Japanese eggplants, peeled and cubed
4 zucchini, peeled and cubed
2 green bell peppers, cut into thin strips
3 large tomatoes, peeled, seeded and diced
1 tablespoon herbes de Provence or combination of 3/4 teaspoon thyme,
3/4 teaspoon basil, 3/4 teaspoon marjoram, 3/4 teaspoon rosemary
1/2 cup canned Greek olives, pitted
Salt, pepper

• Heat olive oil in heavy skillet. Add onion, garlic, eggplants, zucchini and green pepper strips and saute. Add tomatoes, herbes de Provence and olives, and season to taste with salt and pepper.

• Cook over medium heat, covered, 45 minutes. If vegetables yield too much liquid, cook partially covered to reduce juices.

6 servings. Each serving: 93 calories; 121 mg sodium; 0 cholesterol; 5 grams fat; 9 grams carbohydrates; 2 grams protein; 1 gram fiber.

PAUL BOCUSE'S STUFFED CABBAGE

———

YOU DON'T NORMALLY ASSOCIATE Paul Bocuse with Southern California or with humble dishes like this. But when we tried this cool-weather main course, we loved it so much it became one of our favorite recipes.

———

1 sheet caul fat, optional
5 or 6 slices country-style bread
2/3 cup milk
3/4 pound boned shoulder of veal
3/4 pound pork loin
3/4 pound smoked slab bacon
2 1/2 tablespoons butter
2 onions, chopped
1 bunch Italian parsley, finely chopped
1 egg
1 egg yolk
1/2 teaspoon ground allspice
Salt
Freshly ground pepper
2 carrots, peeled and finely diced
2 turnips, peeled and finely diced
2 onions, finely diced
1 large head savoy cabbage
2 chicken bouillon cubes
2 tablespoons oil

• If using caul fat, soak in cold water. Drain and rinse several times.

• Remove crusts from bread slices and crumble into bowl. Add milk and let soak 5 minutes. Gently squeeze bread to remove excess liquid. Place bread in large mixing bowl and set aside.

• Finely chop veal, pork and bacon separately, or ask butcher to grind them. Melt 1 tablespoon butter in skillet over medium heat. Add chopped onions and saute until tender. Add to bread with veal, pork and bacon.

• Add parsley, egg, egg yolk and allspice. Season to taste with salt and pepper. Blend thoroughly.

• Bring saucepan of lightly salted water to boil. Add carrots, turnips and finely diced onions. Blanch several minutes. Drain and refresh vegetables under cold water. Drain and pat dry.

CONTINUED ☛

- Trim cabbage, removing tough outer leaves and stem. Rinse. Blanch in large pot boiling salted water about 10 minutes, turning halfway through to cook all sides. Remove cabbage and rinse under cold water. Drain, stem-side up. Place cabbage, stem down, on work surface. Gently fan out leaves, 1 at time, being careful not to detach from core. Using sharp knife, remove inner core or heart.

- Form 2/3 meat stuffing mixture into ball size of cabbage heart and place in center of cabbage. Fold up inner leaves of cabbage, wrapping firmly around stuffing. Continue to fold cabbage leaves around core, sprinkling diced vegetables and remaining stuffing mixture between layers of leaves.

- Spread caul fat on work surface. Place stuffed cabbage in center and wrap fat around, using kitchen string to tie firmly but gently in place. If not using caul fat, use string to gently truss cabbage.

- Dissolve bouillon cubes in 1 3/4 cups boiling water. Heat remaining 1 1/2 tablespoons butter with oil in large Dutch oven. Add cabbage and saute, turning until lightly browned on all sides. Drain fat. Pour bouillon over cabbage. Cover and bake at 400 degrees 30 minutes. Lower temperature to 300 degrees and bake 1 hour 30 minutes, basting occasionally.

8 servings. Each serving: 455 calories; 720 mg sodium; 141 mg cholesterol; 31 grams fat; 22 grams carbohydrates; 21 grams protein; 0.92 gram fiber.

SCALLOPED GARLIC POTATOES

THIS VERSION OF ONE OF THE ALL-TIME GREAT potato dishes comes from longtime Food section columnist and cookbook author Marion Cunningham.

5 baking potatoes, peeled and sliced
Butter, for greasing
Salt
4 large cloves garlic, finely chopped
1 1/2 cups milk
1/3 cup whipping cream

- Place potatoes in 1 layer over bottom of buttered 8-inch-square baking dish. Salt lightly and sprinkle with garlic. Repeat in layers until all potatoes are used. Pour milk evenly over potatoes.

- Bake uncovered at 325 degrees 45 minutes. Remove from oven and drizzle cream over potatoes. Return to oven and bake 45 minutes. Serve hot. If not serving right away, cool potatoes, cover tightly with foil and freeze until needed.

4 to 6 servings. Each of 6 servings: 152 calories; 91 mg sodium; 23 mg cholesterol; 6 grams fat; 21 grams carbohydrates; 4 grams protein; 0.44 gram fiber.

STIR-FRIED BABY BOK CHOY
with MUSHROOMS

TIMES STAFF WRITER BARBARA HANSEN contributed this recipe in a story on cooking for one. If you want to serve this dish with rice instead of pasta, add 1 more tablespoon mushroom soaking liquid to the seasoning mixture. Then you will have more sauce to mix with the rice. Look for baby bok choy in Asian markets, where it's sold in bunches of 3 heads, and in some supermarkets.

1 dried shiitake mushroom
1/3 cup warm water
2 teaspoons soy sauce
1 teaspoon oyster sauce
1 teaspoon cornstarch
1/4 teaspoon sesame oil
1/8 teaspoon sugar
1 head baby bok choy (about 5 ounces)
2 teaspoons oil
2 fresh mushrooms, sliced

• Combine shiitake and water in small bowl and let stand until completely soft, 15 to 20 minutes. Spoon 3 tablespoons soaking liquid into custard cup. Add soy sauce, oyster sauce, cornstarch, sesame oil and sugar. Set aside.

• Slice softened shiitake. Cut off root end of bok choy and separate into stalks. Wash well. Cut crosswise into 1-inch slices.

• Heat oil in nonstick wok over high heat. Add fresh mushrooms and saute until softened, about 1 minute. Add shiitake and bok choy and stir-fry 3 minutes. Stir cornstarch mixture until evenly blended, add to wok and cook until mixture boils, thickens and coats vegetables, about 2 minutes longer.

1 serving: 152 calories; 1,095 mg sodium; 0 cholesterol; 11 grams fat; 12 grams carbohydrates; 4 grams protein; 1.44 grams fiber.

SWEDISH POTATO *and* LOX CASSEROLE

SOUTHERN CALIFORNIAN KERSTIN MARSH is a great cook. She serves this family specialty as a first course, but it is a perfect addition to a Yom Kippur break-the-fast meal.

8 white or red boiling potatoes (about 1 3/4 pounds), peeled
2 tablespoons butter, cut into pieces, plus more for greasing
8 large slices smoked salmon
1/2 small red onion, thinly sliced
2 tablespoons snipped dill
Salt, pepper
1 1/2 cups whipping cream
3 tablespoons bread crumbs

• Steam potatoes over rapidly boiling water just until tender, about 20 minutes. Remove from steamer and, when cool enough to handle, slice thin.

• Arrange half of potatoes in bottom of buttered 8-inch square baking dish. Arrange slices of salmon on top of potatoes. Sprinkle with onion, dill and salt and pepper to taste. Repeat with top layer of remaining sliced potatoes. Season with salt and pepper to taste.

• Pour cream over potato mixture. Sprinkle with bread crumbs and dot with pieces of butter. Bake at 400 degrees until golden brown and cooked through, about 25 minutes. Serve hot or cold.

6 servings. Each serving: 382 calories; 516 mg sodium; 97 mg cholesterol; 27 grams fat; 28 grams carbohydrates; 8 grams protein; 0.61 gram fiber.

VEGETARIAN MOUSSAKA

THIS RECIPE COMES FROM SANTA BARBARA Greek restaurant Zeus and Co. chef Gloria Menedes. She says you can shuffle the vegetable selection pretty much at will.

■ BECHAMEL SAUCE

1/2 cup flour
Ground cinnamon
Ground nutmeg
1/2 cup (1 stick) butter
4 cups milk
1/3 cup grated Parmesan cheese

• Mix flour with cinnamon and nutmeg to taste. Melt butter in saucepan.

• Stir in flour mixture and cook 2 to 3 minutes, then add milk and cook, stirring, until thickened. Stir in cheese and keep warm until ready to use.

■ MOUSSAKA

2 large baking potatoes, peeled and sliced 1/4-inch thick
1 large eggplant, sliced 1/4-inch thick
3 zucchini, sliced 1/4-inch thick
Olive oil
1 onion, chopped
1 cup cooked garbanzo beans
1 (15-ounce) can tomato sauce
Salt, pepper
Ground cinnamon
Ground nutmeg
1/4 cup bread crumbs, preferably from pita bread
1/3 cup grated Parmesan cheese

• Brush potatoes, eggplant and zucchini with olive oil and grill until soft. Set aside.

• Cook onion in 2 tablespoons olive oil until soft. Add garbanzo beans and tomato sauce and cook, stirring. Add salt, pepper, cinnamon and nutmeg to taste. Heat through.

• Layer potato slices in bottom of greased 13x9-inch baking pan and sprinkle with bread crumbs. Spoon layer of tomato mixture over potatoes.

• Place layer of eggplant, then layer of tomato sauce, followed by layer of zucchini slices, then remaining tomato sauce. Spread top with Bechamel Sauce. Sprinkle with Parmesan cheese. Bake at 375 degrees 1 hour.

6 to 8 servings. Each of 8 servings: 432 calories; 775 mg sodium; 56 mg cholesterol; 25 grams fat; 38 grams carbohydrates; 17 grams protein; 1.51 grams fiber.

TRANSYLVANIAN STACKED POTATOES
(*Erdelyi Rakottkrumpli*)

1994

STACKED POTATOES IS A SUBSTANTIAL and filling regional dish from Transylvania. Ask 10 different Transylvanian cooks to make it and you'll probably end up with 10 slightly different versions. This version comes from Southern Californian Gabriella Rado, a Hungarian who was born in Nagyvarad, Transylvania.

Butter
1/2 cup fresh bread crumbs
4 large baking potatoes, cooked and peeled
Salt, pepper
3 cups shredded mozzarella cheese
6 hard-boiled eggs, peeled and sliced
3/4 pound smoked sausage, cut into 1/2-inch slices
2 cups sour cream
1/2 cup milk

• Butter 13x9-inch baking dish. Sprinkle with 2 tablespoons bread crumbs.

• Cut potatoes into 1/2-inch slices. Arrange 1/3 of potatoes in bottom of baking pan. Season to taste with salt and pepper. Sprinkle with 2 tablespoons bread crumbs. Sprinkle with 2 cups cheese.

• Arrange sliced eggs in single layer over potatoes. Season to taste with salt. Sprinkle with 2 tablespoons bread crumbs, then 1/2 cup cheese.

• Top with another layer of sliced potatoes. Arrange sliced sausage in single layer over potatoes. Top with remaining potatoes in single layer.

• Season to taste with salt. Sprinkle with remaining bread crumbs and remaining cheese.

• Blend together sour cream and milk in bowl. Pour over top of casserole. Shake casserole to settle sour cream mixture. Bake at 350 degrees until hot throughout, 45 minutes to 1 hour.

6 to 8 servings. Each of 8 servings: 600 calories; 815 mg sodium; 313 mg cholesterol; 44 grams fat; 27 grams carbohydrates; 25 grams protein; 0.3 gram fiber.

VEGETABLE CARPACCIO

THIS SIMPLE RECIPE COMES FROM Viana la Place, a noted cookbook author who lived for many years in Southern California. Be sure to slice the artichoke hearts very thinly.

■ DRESSING

3 tablespoons extra-virgin olive oil
3 tablespoons lemon juice
1 teaspoon Dijon mustard
Salt
Freshly ground pepper

• Combine oil, lemon juice, mustard and salt and pepper to taste in small bowl. Beat with fork to blend.

■ VEGETABLE CARPACCIO

1 artichoke
1/2 lemon
4 to 5 small, firm red radishes, trimmed and sliced paper-thin
1 small carrot, peeled and thinly sliced on diagonal
1 tender leek, small portion of white base cut into thin rings
1 small fennel bulb, trimmed and sliced into paper-thin strips
Dressing
1 heaping tablespoon capers
1 (1-ounce) piece Parmesan cheese, thinly shaved
Freshly ground black pepper

• Completely trim artichoke, snapping off all leaves and cutting away dark green portions around heart. Cut away choke. Rub cut portions of artichoke with lemon half to prevent flesh from darkening. Very thinly slice artichoke heart.

• Combine artichoke, radishes, carrot, leek and fennel in large serving platter. Toss immediately with Dressing. Adjust seasonings, adding more oil, lemon juice, salt, or pepper as needed to taste.

• Spread vegetables out so that they form thin layer over platter. Sprinkle with capers. Cover top of vegetables with cheese and season to taste with pepper.

4 servings. Each serving: 174 calories; 245 mg sodium; 5 mg cholesterol; 12 grams fat; 14 grams carbohydrates; 5 grams protein; 1.06 grams fiber.

VEGETABLES
in CHESTNUT CREAM SAUCE

THIS IS AN UNUSUAL SOUNDING DISH, but the rich earthiness of the chestnuts pairs perfectly with the taste of the winter vegetables.

2 tablespoons chopped onion
1 1/4 cups chopped roasted chestnuts
1/4 cup (1/2 stick) plus 2 tablespoons butter
3 tablespoons flour
1 cup chicken broth
1 cup milk
Salt
White pepper
2 cups broccoli florets
2 cups cauliflower florets
2 cups sliced carrots
1 teaspoon minced fresh rosemary
1/2 cup fresh bread crumbs

• Saute onion and 1 cup chestnuts in 1/4 cup butter. Stir in flour and cook, stirring, about 2 minutes. Remove from heat and gradually add chicken broth and milk. Return to heat and cook, stirring, until thickened. Season to taste with salt and white pepper.

• Cook broccoli, cauliflower and carrots in boiling water until tender-crisp. Drain. Combine with cream sauce and spoon into casserole.

• Saute remaining 1/4 cup chestnuts, rosemary and bread crumbs in remaining 2 tablespoons butter. Sprinkle over top of casserole. Bake at 350 degrees 30 minutes or until heated through.

8 servings. Each serving: 174 calories; 273 mg sodium; 26 mg cholesterol; 10 grams fat; 18 grams carbohydrates; 4 grams protein; 1.04 grams fiber.

Note: If prepared ahead, sprinkle casserole with bread crumbs just before baking. Increase baking time if vegetables have been refrigerated.

FRESH CORN CAKES

WINE COUNTRY COOK JOHN ASH is one of California's pioneers in cooking with great produce from farmers markets. This summertime dish will go well with any kind of grilled meat.

1/2 cup minced green onions
2 tablespoons butter
1/4 cup dry white wine
4 eggs
3/4 cup half-and-half
1/3 cup yellow cornmeal
1/2 cup flour
1 teaspoon salt
1/2 teaspoon minced seeded serrano chile
1 teaspoon minced fresh basil or 1/2 teaspoon dried
1 tablespoon honey
1/2 teaspoon baking powder
Salt
Freshly ground pepper
2 1/2 cups freshly cut corn kernels
Clarified butter or light vegetable oil

• Saute green onions in 2 tablespoons butter until tender. Add wine and cook over high heat to evaporate. Cool to room temperature. Beat onion mixture, eggs, half-and-half, cornmeal, flour, salt, serrano chile, basil, honey and baking powder together until smooth. Season to taste with salt and pepper. Add corn kernels.

• Heat clarified butter in skillet over medium heat. For each corn cake, add 2 tablespoons batter. Cook until very lightly browned on each side.

• Place on warm plates.

2 dozen corn cakes. Each corn cake: 75 calories; 146 mg sodium; 41 mg cholesterol; 4 grams fat; 8 grams carbohydrates; 2 grams protein; 0.16 grams fiber.

EIGHT

Pastas, Rice and Beans

BARLEY RISOTTO

THIS RECIPE FROM PATINA CHEF Joachim Splichal is neither low-fat nor fast. But one taste and you'll understand why—despite the winds of fashion—this kind of cooking is still in favor. After completing the cooking process, including 4 1/2 hours of cooking the oxtail, you may also understand why a meal in a fine restaurant costs so much.

■ OXTAIL MEAT AND BRAISING JUICE

2 1/4 pounds oxtail, cut up
1 large onion, sliced
2 heads garlic, sliced in half
6 sprigs thyme, tied in bundle
4 bay leaves
8 cups chicken stock

• Combine oxtail, onion, garlic, thyme, bay leaves and chicken stock in large casserole. Cover tightly with foil. Bake at 325 degrees about 4 1/2 hours, until beef is tender and just about falling off bone.

• Strain meat juices and reserve. (Should have about 4 cups.) Pick meat off bones and, if cooking ahead, refrigerate. (Oxtail can be prepared 1 day ahead.)

■ RISOTTO

1 large onion, diced
3/4 cup (1 1/2 sticks) butter
1 cup dry white wine, preferably Chardonnay
1/2 pound pearl barley
About 3 cups chicken stock
1 carrot, diced
1 leek, white part only, diced
5 shallots, minced
Cloves from 1/2 head garlic, diced
Salt, pepper
1 cup finely chopped parsley
1/2 cup freshly grated Parmesan cheese

• Cut oxtail meat into small pieces and reserve. Reduce braising juice to about 2 cups. Strain and reserve.

• Place onion in saucepan with 2 tablespoons butter and saute until caramelized. Deglaze with wine until liquid evaporates. Add barley and roast 2 minutes, stirring. Add chicken stock and simmer until barley is al dente, about 30 minutes. If barley doesn't cook through, add bit more chicken stock than called for. Repeat until barley is cooked.

CONTINUED ☞

- Saute carrot, leek, shallots and garlic separately, using 1 1/2 tablespoons butter for each vegetable. Combine vegetables in bowl and refrigerate.

- Combine cooked barley, sauteed vegetables and 1/2 cup reduced braising juice in large saucepan. Cook over medium-high heat until liquid is absorbed. Add another 1/2 cup reduced juice, stirring until additional liquid is completely absorbed. Repeat process until all reduced juices are absorbed. Add reserved chopped oxtail. Whisk in remaining 1/4 cup butter, little at time, until it emulsifies into risotto. Season to taste with salt and pepper. Place in serving dish and top with parsley and Parmesan cheese.

8 servings. Each serving: 470 calories; 1,430 mg sodium; 77 mg cholesterol; 28 grams fat; 32 grams carbohydrates; 19 grams protein; 0.8 grams fiber.

SANTA MARIA-STYLE BARBECUE BEANS

BARBECUED TRI-TIP AND BOILED PINQUITO beans are the classic dishes of California's Central Coast. This recipe comes from former Times cooking columnist Merle Ellis.

1 pound small pink beans (pinquito)
1 strip bacon, diced
1/2 cup diced ham
1 small clove garlic, minced
3/4 cup tomato puree
1/4 cup red chile sauce
1 teaspoon dry mustard
1 tablespoon sugar
1 teaspoon salt

- Pick over beans to remove dirt and small stones. Place in large container, cover with water and let soak overnight.

- Drain beans, cover with fresh water and simmer 2 hours or until tender. Saute bacon and ham until lightly browned. Add garlic, saute 1 to 2 minutes longer, then add tomato puree, chile sauce, sugar, mustard and salt. Drain most liquid off beans and stir in sauce. Keep hot over low heat until ready to serve.

6 to 8 servings. Each of 8 servings: 230 calories; 569 mg sodium; 5 mg cholesterol; 2 grams fat; 41 grams carbohydrates; 14 grams protein; 2 grams fiber.

CHOLENT

1997

THIS VERSION OF THE SLOW-COOKING Sabbath stew cholent reminded a few tasters in the Times Test Kitchen of the French bean-and-meat stew cassoulet. One difference: This stew calls for barley, which adds a nice textural contrast to the softer beans. The recipe was adapted by cookbook writer Joan Nathan from one by Sara Brizdle Dickman and Dassi Stern. After we printed the recipe, a couple of readers called asking about the addition of 10 to 12 eggs in the stew. The eggs are put into the cholent with their shells left on. The slow, long heat cooks the eggs, which are then peeled before serving or at the table. The stew may also be made without the eggs.

1 cup mixed dried beans, such as cranberry, kidney, large and small navy beans, black or lentils
Water
1/4 cup olive or vegetable oil
2 large onions, chopped, plus 1 whole onion with skin
3 pounds flanken (short ribs) or chuck in 1 piece
2 tablespoons honey
3/4 cup barley
6 potatoes, peeled
2 whole cloves garlic or as much as 1/2 head
2 teaspoons salt
1/2 teaspoon freshly ground pepper
2 teaspoons paprika
Neck bones or marrow bones, about 1 pound
10 to 12 eggs, in shells, washed

• Day before cooking, soak beans 6 hours in water to cover. Rinse and drain.

• Heat oil in large skillet and cook chopped onions until soft, 3 to 5 minutes. Add meat and brown on both sides.

• Heat honey in bottom of 8-quart casserole over low heat until it darkens and caramelizes, 3 to 5 minutes, stirring constantly to prevent burning. Add beans, barley, potatoes, meat and cooked onions. Scatter garlic around meat.

• Night before serving, dissolve salt, pepper and paprika in small amount of water and pour over meat, adding enough water just to cover.

• Add meat bones, whole onion (skin adds color) and eggs (in shells) to pot. Bring to boil. Cover pot with foil and lid and simmer 30 minutes on stove top. Remove to 200-degree oven and cook overnight.

• Next morning, remove lid and check water. If water covers meat, uncover and bake 2 more hours so that water evaporates to make thick sauce. If there is no water, add some.

• Serve each ingredient separately on serving plates or on very large platter with ingredients separated.

CONTINUED

- **Variations**:
  Alsatian Cholent: Use lima beans instead of other beans.
  Vegetarian Cholent: Omit meat and add 1 (15-ounce) can tomatoes.
  Indian Vegetarian Cholent: Omit canned tomatoes and add 2 teaspoons each ground cumin, tarragon and turmeric, and 1/2 teaspoon each ground ginger, cinnamon and curry powder.

10 servings. Each serving: 380 calories; 548 mg sodium; 61 mg cholesterol; 10 grams fat; 42 grams carbohydrates; 30 grams protein; 1.19 grams fiber.

LEMON PASTA *with* SHRIMP

WHEN STAFF WRITER BARBARA HANSEN first explored the fledgling wine growing region just north of Santa Barbara in 1987, there weren't many wineries. She did manage to come back with this recipe from Jeri Mosby, of the Mosby Winery.

6 tablespoons lemon juice
1/4 cup (1/2 stick) butter
1 teaspoon grated lemon zest
White pepper
1 cup whipping cream
Salt
12 large shrimp, peeled and deveined
6 ounces penne pasta, cooked
Grated Parmesan cheese
Chopped fresh basil

- Combine lemon juice, butter, lemon zest and generous dash pepper in saucepan. Bring to simmer. Add whipping cream. Bring to boil and cook until slightly reduced. Season to taste with salt. Add shrimp and cook just until shrimp turn pink. Combine mixture with penne. Serve at once topped with Parmesan cheese and basil.

4 servings. Each serving: 487 calories; 244 mg sodium; 145 mg cholesterol; 35 grams fat; 33 grams carbohydrates; 11 grams protein; 0 fiber.

CORNMEAL PASTA *with* LEEKS

THE PIEDMONT IS A MOUNTAINOUS region in Northwestern Italy that just happens to produce some of that country's greatest red wines (Barolo, Barbaresco, Barbera and Dolcetto) and is also the source of white truffles. And if that's not enough, the region's Cesare Giaccone—one of the finest chefs in the world—also makes wonderful dishes from the simplest ingredients, as in this dish.

■ CORNMEAL PASTA

1 cup finely ground cornmeal, organic if possible
1 1/2 cups flour, plus more for kneading
Salt
1 tablespoon olive oil
5 eggs

• Mix cornmeal, flour and dash salt together and mound on work surface. Make well in center, add oil and break eggs into well. Beat eggs with fork, gradually incorporating flour from sides of well to form soft dough. Knead in more flour as needed. Scrape up any scraps and knead into dough. Flour work table and knead dough by hand until dough is smooth and elastic and no longer sticky, 10 or more minutes.

• Divide dough into 4 parts. Flatten 1 part on lightly floured surface and roll out by hand (cornmeal makes dough easy to work, but it's a little too soft for pasta machine). Repeat with remaining dough.

• Lay pasta strips out on work table or wooden surface to dry. When pasta is no longer tacky, roll up strips and cut by hand into 1/2- to 3/4-inch noodles.

■ LEEK SAUCE

1/4 cup (1/2 stick) butter
1 pound slender leeks, white parts only, finely sliced
1/2 cup whipping cream
2/3 cup or more rich homemade broth
Salt, pepper

• Heat butter in skillet and gently stew leeks until slightly brown, about 15 minutes. Add cream to cover, then broth. Cook over medium heat until sauce is bubbling, about 10 minutes. Season to taste with salt and pepper.

• Cook pasta until al dente, about 5 minutes. Top with little leek sauce.

4 servings. Each serving: 604 calories; 599 mg sodium; 263 mg cholesterol; 34 grams fat; 60 grams carbohydrates; 15 grams protein; 2.23 grams fiber.

DONA JUANA'S
SPANISH RICE CASSEROLE

COOKBOOK AUTHOR AND MAGAZINE EDITOR Colman Andrews turned up this hearty casserole of rice and potatoes during a search through Spain's Catalan region. Not surprisingly, perhaps, it comes not from Spain itself, but from a Southern California Spanish expatriate, Juana Gimeno de Faraone (originally from Valencia), owner of La Espanola Meats in Lomita.

6 tablespoons olive oil
1 head garlic, unpeeled
2 boiling potatoes, cut in 1/2-inch thick slices
2 cups rice
1 tablespoon Spanish paprika, hot or mild
1 pound Spanish chorizos, cut in 2-inch pieces
4 to 6 ounces morcilla (blood sausage), sliced in 1-inch pieces
1 (15-ounce) can garbanzo beans, drained
2 small tomatoes, sliced in thick wedges or rings
4 cups boiling chicken broth
Salt
Saffron threads

• Heat olive oil in oven-proof shallow casserole over medium heat. Add garlic head and saute a few minutes. Add potatoes and rice and cook about 3 minutes, stirring occasionally. Stir in paprika and remove from heat.

• Gently mix in chorizos, morcilla, garbanzo beans and tomatoes.

• Rearrange garlic head in middle, alternately surrounding with some tomato and potato slices. Add boiling chicken broth to casserole and lightly season to taste with salt and dash saffron. Cover and bake at 425 degrees 10 minutes. Uncover and bake 10 to 15 minutes longer.

6 servings. Each serving: 812 calories; 1,581 mg sodium; 68 mg cholesterol; 42 grams fat; 78 grams carbohydrates; 28 grams protein; 1.57 grams fiber.

MEXICAN PAELLA

1996

THIS RECIPE FROM ROSARITO BEACH'S Hosteria Derby restaurant wasn't just one of the best recipes of the year—it was a landslide winner. Though preparing the dish is a long, involved process, it makes enough to feed a crowd, and the results are certainly worth the effort.

24 medium shrimp
3 to 4 quarts fish or chicken stock
1/2 cup plus 2 tablespoons olive oil
1/2 cup vegetable oil
6 cloves garlic, sliced
1 sprig rosemary, chopped
12 pork ribs
12 Catalonian sausages (Spanish sausage) or any pork sausage, thickly sliced
12 small chicken drumsticks or thighs or 12 chicken breasts, cut up
1 rabbit, cut up, optional
1/4 cup tequila, rum or brandy
5 tablespoons chopped onion
3 poblano chiles, roasted, peeled, deveined and chopped
6 red bell peppers, cut in thin strips
8 small hot chiles (gueros or serranos), deveined, optional
12 small artichokes, trimmed of tough outer leaves, stems peeled
Juice of 2 lemons or vinegar
3 dried ancho chiles, roasted, deveined and soaked in hot water
1 (2-inch) stick cinnamon, toasted
Salt or 1 tablespoon chicken bouillon powder
1 pound tomatoes, peeled, seeded and chopped
36 small squid, cleaned
12 large shrimp or prawns with heads intact
36 clams
4 1/2 cups converted rice
1/2 pound pea pods, shelled (1/2 cup frozen peas)
2 tablespoons chopped parsley

• Peel medium shrimp, reserving meat in covered container in refrigerator. Cook shells in simmering stock until they turn color, about 10 minutes. Strain stock, discarding shells. Return stock to pan and keep hot.

• Heat 1/2 cup olive oil and vegetable oil in paella pan. Add 4 cloves garlic and rosemary and cook over medium-high heat until garlic browns, about 5 minutes. Remove garlic and rosemary.

CONTINUED➤

- Add ribs and sausages and brown over medium-high heat, about 10 minutes. Remove to platter.

- Add chicken and rabbit to pan and brown, about 10 minutes. Remove to platter.

- Deglaze pan by adding 3 tablespoons tequila, placing pan over high heat until sauce bubbles and reduces, and scraping up solids stuck to bottom of pan. Carefully light remaining tablespoon tequila in ladle and immediately add to tequila in pan. Flame until all alcohol burns off.

- Add onion, poblanos, 1/2 of bell peppers and small hot chiles to pan. Cook until tender, about 8 minutes.

- In separate saucepan, cook artichokes in simmering water and lemon juice until tender, about 15 minutes. Drain and cut in half. Add to paella pan and cook until golden, about 5 minutes. Remove to platter.

- Grind ancho chiles with remaining 2 garlic cloves, 2 tablespoons olive oil, cinnamon and salt to taste. Add to paella pan along with tomatoes. Cook 5 minutes. Add squid, peeled medium and head-on large shrimp and clams to pan, cover tightly, and cook just until shrimp are done and clams open, about 5 minutes. Remove seafood to platter.

- Add rice to pan and cook, stirring, 3 to 4 minutes. Add 14 cups strained hot stock to pan and cook over medium-high heat, stirring occasionally, about 20 minutes.

- Return chicken, ribs and sausage to pan, cover and cook 15 more minutes, adding more stock if necessary. Return artichokes, medium shrimp, squid and clams to pan (reserving large shrimp for garnish) and cook 5 more minutes.

- Add peas and 1/2 to 1 cup more hot stock to paella, cover and remove from heat. Set aside 5 minutes until ready to serve. Garnish with remaining strips of bell pepper, large shrimp and sprinkling of parsley.

---

12 to 14 servings. Each of 14 servings: 824 calories; 1,407 mg sodium; 202 mg cholesterol; 42 grams fat; 64 grams carbohydrates; 44 grams protein; 1.27 grams fiber.

CHELO KEBAB

1995

THE RICE IS WHAT EVERYONE WENT crazy for in this Persian dish. Chelo starts as a plain rice pilaf, but it's very buttery and it's made so that a crunchy golden crust forms on the bottom of the pot. Everyone wants a bite of the crust, but it's traditional in Iran to offer the crust to your guest. Sour ground sumac berries, available in most of Southern California's Near Eastern markets, are sprinkled over the dish. Fresh onion juice is used to give the meat marinade a richer aroma than that of chopped onions. Saffron makes the kebab elegant, but if you're unable to find saffron, substitute 2 teaspoons ground cumin and 2 tablespoons ground coriander.

◼ CHELO

1 3/4 cups fragrant long-grain white rice, such as basmati
Water
Salt
1/3 cup melted butter

• Rinse rice in three changes of lukewarm water. Soak rice in cold water to cover with 1 1/2 tablespoons salt 1 hour.

• Put 8 cups water in pot, add 1 tablespoon salt and bring to boil. Drain soaked rice and add to boiling water. Boil until rice is nearly done but not soft, 5 to 10 minutes, stirring twice to keep grains from sticking together. Drain rice in colander and rinse with luke-warm water.

• Put 1/3 of melted butter and 2 tablespoons water in bottom of pot. Using large spoon, sprinkle rice grains into pot, distributing evenly. Allow rice to form cone shape. Pour remaining melted butter over rice, distributing evenly. With handle of wooden spoon, punch 2 to 3 holes from top of rice mound to bottom of pot.

• Put dish towel or paper towels over pot, then cover with pot lid. Set pot on medium heat 10 to 15 minutes, then reduce heat to low 35 to 40 minutes. Can be kept in warm oven 1 hour.

CONTINUED ☛

■ KEBAB

5 large onions
1/8 teaspoon saffron threads
2 pounds boneless lamb or beef, in kebab pieces
Salt, pepper
1/4 cup (1/2 stick) butter, melted, optional
Cilantro
4 onions, quartered, optional
1 to 2 teaspoons ground sumac, optional

• Quarter 1 onion and reduce to fine puree in food processor (leave kitchen windows open because of fumes). Push puree through fine strainer.

• Grind saffron to powder in mortar, or on plate using back of spoon, and dissolve in onion juice.

• Clean meat and trim excess fat. Mix meat with onion juice marinade, cover with plastic wrap and marinate 1 hour at room temperature.

• When ready to cook meat, season with salt and pepper to taste and thread onto skewers. Grill until done. Brush with melted butter.

• To serve, set Chelo pot in sink of cold water 1 minute to loosen crust on bottom of pot. Remove pot lid. Turn large serving plate upside-down and cover pot with it. Holding pot and plate tightly together, turn both upside down. Rice should come out on plate.

• Remove pot. Divide crust among diners and serve rice with Kebab.

• Quarter remaining onions. Garnish with cilantro and raw onions, and sprinkle kebab with sumac.

4 to 6 servings. Each of 6 servings: 434 calories; 515 mg sodium; 100 mg cholesterol; 16 grams fat; 11 grams carbohydrates; 26 grams protein; 0.19 gram fiber.

VEGETABLE CHILI

1985

GELSON'S, A LONG-TIME UPSCALE Southern California grocery store chain, has a popular take-out department featuring items such as this chili.

1/2 cup kidney beans
1/4 cup bulgur
1/2 cup olive oil
1 small red onion, diced
1 small white onion, diced
1 1/2 tablespoons minced garlic
1/2 cup diced celery
1/2 cup diced carrots
2 tablespoons chili powder
2 tablespoons ground cumin
1/2 teaspoon cayenne pepper
4 teaspoons chopped fresh basil
1 tablespoon chopped fresh oregano
1 yellow squash, diced
1 zucchini, diced
1 green bell pepper, diced
1 red bell pepper, diced
1 cup mushrooms
1/2 cup diced tomatoes
1/2 cup tomato paste
3/4 cup white wine
Salt, pepper

• Soak beans in cold water to cover overnight. Drain off water. Add 3 cups fresh water to beans and cook over medium heat until tender, about 45 minutes. Drain beans, reserving cooking liquid.

• Bring 1/2 cup water to boil. Pour over bulgur in bowl. Let stand 30 minutes to soften wheat (water will be absorbed).

• Heat oil in large saucepan. Add red and sweet onions. Saute until tender. Add garlic, celery and carrots. Saute until glazed. Add chili powder, cumin, cayenne, basil and oregano. Cook over low heat until carrots are almost tender. Add squash, zucchini, green and red peppers and mushrooms. Cook 4 minutes. Add bulgur, kidney beans, tomatoes and reserved liquid from cooking beans. Cook 30 minutes or until vegetables are tender.

• Mix tomato paste with white wine until smooth. Stir into vegetable mixture.

• Season to taste with salt and pepper.

8 servings. Each serving: 215 calories; 193 mg sodium; 0 cholesterol; 15 grams fat; 17 grams carbohydrates; 4 grams protein; 1.89 grams fiber.

LEMON LENTILS
(*Nimbu Masoor Dal*)

FILM PRODUCER ISMAIL MERCHANT is also an accomplished cook. There is nothing he loves more than lentils, dal in Indian cooking. "I can't live without dal," he wrote. "I am a dal junkie. Every household in India has its own version. Dal is a rich man's food, a middle-class man's food and a poor man's food." This recipe is one delicious way Merchant feeds his obsession.

1994

1/2 cup plus 2 tablespoons oil
1 onion, halved and thinly sliced
2 (2-inch) cinnamon sticks
1 pound masoor dal (orange lentils), picked over and rinsed
1 1/2 teaspoons chopped ginger root
2 1/2 cups chicken stock
Water
1/2 teaspoon ground red pepper
Salt
1/2 lemon
1/2 small onion, chopped
1 small clove garlic, chopped
1/2 serrano or jalapeno chile, chopped, with seeds
2 bay leaves
1 tablespoon chopped cilantro

• Heat 6 tablespoons oil in large, deep saucepan over medium-low heat.

• Add sliced onion and cook, stirring, until tender. Add cinnamon sticks, dal and ginger. Cook, stirring often, 10 minutes. Add stock, 2 cups water, red pepper and salt to taste. Bring to boil, reduce heat and simmer 10 minutes. Squeeze juice from lemon, straining seeds, and add lemon juice and lemon to lentils. Cook 50 minutes, stirring often. Add up to 1 cup more water, if dal dries out too much.

• Heat remaining 1/4 cup oil in small pan. Add chopped onion, garlic, chile and bay leaves. Cook, stirring, until onion is browned. Add mixture to lentils and stir. Remove bay leaves. Turn into serving bowl and sprinkle with cilantro. Serve hot.

4 to 6 servings. Each of 6 servings: 487 calories; 382 mg sodium; 0 cholesterol; 25 grams fat; 47 grams carbohydrates; 24 grams protein; 4.23 grams fiber.

LASGNA ALLA PINA

PINA DE GASPARDIS IS THE CHEF-OWNER of Al Fogher in Rome. It's hard to believe today, but when we first printed this recipe in 1987, we had to explain where to find Parmigiano Reggiano.

3 leeks, sliced 1/4 inch thick
1/4 cup (1/2 stick) butter, plus more for greasing
Pepper
1/4 cup red wine
2 radicchio, sliced 1/4 inch thick
Bechamel Sauce
4 (13x9-inch) sheets fresh Lasagna Noodle Dough, or 12 packaged lasagna noodles, cooked
1 to 1 1/2 cups grated Parmesan cheese, preferably Reggiano
4 small or 3 medium tomatoes, sliced
Parsley

• Saute leeks in 2 tablespoons butter over medium-low heat until tender, about 5 minutes. Season lightly with pepper. Add 2 tablespoons red wine and cook until wine evaporates. Set aside.

• Saute radicchio in remaining 2 tablespoons butter until tender, about 3 minutes. Season lightly with pepper. Add remaining 2 tablespoons red wine and cook until wine evaporates. Set aside.

• Add 1/2 to 3/4 cup Bechamel Sauce to leeks and mix lightly. Add 1/2 to 3/4 cup Bechamel Sauce to radicchio and mix lightly.

• Place 1 sheet Lasagna Noodle Dough rolled wide enough to fit pan (or 4 packaged lasagna noodles) in bottom of well-buttered 13x9-inch baking pan. Spread half leek mixture over noodle layer. Sprinkle with some Parmesan cheese. Top with 1/3 remaining Bechamel Sauce. Add half radicchio mixture, spreading evenly. Dust with more cheese and cover with another Lasagna Noodle Dough layer.

• Repeat layering. Cover with dough and spread remaining 1/3 Bechamel Sauce over dough. Sprinkle with remaining cheese. Garnish with tomato slices and parsley. Bake at 350 degrees 45 minute or until lasagna is pale golden in color. Let stand 10 minutes before cutting into squares.

CONTINUED ☞

■ BECHAMEL SAUCE

1/2 cup (1 stick) butter
3/4 cup flour
About 6 cups milk
Salt
1/2 to 3/4 cup grated Parmesan cheese

• Melt butter in saucepan. Stir in flour until smooth. Gradually add milk, stirring constantly until well blended. Bring to boil, then reduce heat and continue to simmer, stirring, until creamy and smooth. Stir in salt to taste and 1/2 cup cheese and cook, stirring, until sauce is smooth and slightly thickened. If too thick, add more milk. If too thin, stir in more cheese.

■ LASAGNA NOODLE DOUGH

2 eggs
1/4 cup water
1/2 pound semolina flour (about 2 cups)

• Beat eggs and water lightly. Place flour on board and make well in center. Add egg-water mixture and incorporate into flour until soft, pliable dough is formed. Roll dough out on pasta machine or by hand until too large to handle. Cut in half and roll each half 1/4 inch thick. Cut into 4 (13x9-inch) rectangles.

6 servings. Each serving: 762 calories; 894 mg sodium; 170 mg cholesterol; 38 grams fat; 74 grams carbohydrates; 30 grams protein; 1.31 grams fiber.

LITTLE RAGS *with* CABBAGE

THIS IS A CLASSIC DISH FROM THE Croatian community in San Pedro. The little rags in this version from Regina Herceg are homemade pasta squares, which are combined with cabbage cooked until browned. Bow tie pasta from the supermarket can be substituted, Herceg says.

1 1/2 cups bread flour
Salt
2 to 4 tablespoons milk
2 eggs
1 large cabbage
4 tablespoons oil
2 tablespoons water
Pepper

• Combine flour and dash salt in bowl of food processor. Add 2 tablespoons milk and eggs and pulse to combine, adding more milk if necessary so dough forms. It should resemble couscous and come together when pressed with fingers. Let stand 10 minutes.

• Divide dough into 4 portions and roll out each into a thin square about the thickness of lasagna noodles. Let stand 30 minutes to dry slightly. (This prevents pasta from sticking when boiled.)

• Cut in 3/4-inch-wide strips, then cut crosswise in 3/4-inch strips to form squares.

• Cut cabbage in quarters, then cut each quarter in 3/4-inch strips lengthwise and crosswise to make squares similar in size to pasta. Heat oil over medium-high heat in large pot. Add cabbage and water and cook, stirring, until cabbage begins to fry. Reduce heat to low and cover, stirring occasionally and cooking until cabbage is browned, about 1 hour. Stir in 1/2 teaspoon salt.

• When cabbage is almost done, cook pasta in boiling salted water until al dente, 5 minutes. Drain, add to cabbage and mix gently. Serve with pepper to taste.

6 servings. Each serving: 267 calories; 641 mg sodium; 71 mg cholesterol; 12 grams fat; 33 grams carbohydrates; 8 grams protein; 1.31 grams fiber.

PAN-FRIED TRI-SHREDDED YEE-FU NOODLES

1992

ROWLAND HEIGHTS' LUK YUE restaurant gave us this recipe, which shows the brilliance of simple, flavorful food. The noodles come together in no time and are delicious. Whenever they appeared in the Times Test Kitchen, a line formed for samples. Yee-fu noodles (also spelled e-fu) are dried noodles processed so they cook quickly. Many Chinese markets carry them, packaged in loose clumps. The cooked meats may be purchased at Chinese delis.

1/2 ounce dried shiitake mushrooms
1 (8-ounce) package yee-fu noodles
3 tablespoons peanut oil
1 cup thinly sliced steamed chicken
1 cup thinly sliced barbecued pork
1 cup thinly sliced roast duck
1/2 cup water
1 teaspoon sugar
4 to 5 tablespoons soy sauce
1/4 teaspoon white pepper
1 teaspoon cornstarch dissolved in 2 tablespoons water
1/2 teaspoon salt or to taste
15 stalks yellow chives, cut in 2-inch lengths
1 teaspoon sesame oil

• Soak mushrooms in warm water until tender. Drain and cut into thin strips.

• Cook noodles in boiling water until tender, about 45 seconds. Drain and set aside.

• Heat wok until hot. Add peanut oil and saute chicken, pork and duck meats. Stir in mushrooms. Add water and simmer 3 to 5 minutes. Add sugar, soy sauce and white pepper. Stir in cornstarch paste and cook just until thickened, about 1 minute. Season to taste with salt and adjust other seasonings to taste.

• Gently mix in noodles, chives and sesame oil. Cook over medium-low heat just to heat. Do not overmix. Serve hot.

4 to 6 servings. Each of 6 servings: 497 calories; 1,362 mg sodium; 76 mg cholesterol; 18 grams fat; 49 grams carbohydrates; 33 grams protein; 0.79 gram fiber.

MACARONI *and* CHEESE
with GREEN ONIONS *and* HAM

MAKE THIS RECIPE BY FOOD EDITOR Russ Parsons fancy by using a combination of different cheeses—Fontina with a little fresh goat cheese and some Parmigiano-Reggiano is nice (they're not very strong, so add the mustard to the white sauce). But the classic cheese, of course, is good old American Cheddar.

6 tablespoons butter, plus more for greasing pan
1/4 cup flour
3 cups milk
1 tablespoon Dijon mustard, optional
Salt
White pepper
1 pound dried short noodles, such as elbow macaroni
3/4 pound grated cheese
1/2 pound cooked ham, cubed
1 bunch green onions, sliced
1 1/2 cups fresh bread crumbs

• Make white sauce by melting 4 tablespoons butter in medium saucepan over medium-low heat. Add flour and whisk until smooth. Cook 5 minutes, stirring occasionally, to remove raw taste of flour.

• Add 1 cup milk and whisk until smooth. Raise heat to medium and add remaining milk, whisking occasionally to prevent lumping. Cook until sauce has thickened, about 10 minutes.

• Add mustard, if desired, and season to taste with salt and white pepper.

• Meanwhile, cook noodles in plenty of rapidly boiling, lightly salted water until barely tender, about 8 minutes. Drain, remove to large mixing bowl and toss with 1 tablespoon butter to prevent sticking.

• Add cheese to white sauce and stir to mix. Add cooked ham and green onions and mix again. Add white sauce mixture to cooked noodles and combine thoroughly. Turn noodles out into well-buttered 2-quart gratin dish.

• In small skillet, melt 1 tablespoon butter. Add bread crumbs and fry, stirring constantly, until lightly toasted, about 5 minutes. Scatter bread crumbs over top of noodles and bake at 350 degrees until top is browned and bubbling, about 30 minutes.

6 to 8 servings. Each of 8 servings: 589 calories; 1,401 mg sodium; 73 mg cholesterol; 24 grams fat; 57 grams carbohydrates; 35 grams protein; 0.25 gram fiber.

SPAGHETTI *with* CHERRY TOMATOES

THIS SPAGHETTI RECIPE from chef Rosaria Martufi of Villa Hernicus restaurant in the town of Fiugi, near Rome, is so simple and so good you won't believe it.

1 1/4 pounds cherry tomatoes, halved
1 teaspoon salt
1/4 cup chopped basil
3 cloves garlic, finely chopped
1/4 pound Pecorino Romano cheese, grated
1/3 cup fresh bread crumbs
Extra-virgin olive oil
1 pound spaghetti

• Place tomatoes on baking sheet and sprinkle with salt, 3 tablespoons basil, garlic, 3 tablespoons cheese and bread crumbs. Lightly drizzle with olive oil. Bake at 350 degrees 10 to 15 minutes, until bread starts to toast and tomatoes become soft.

• In large pot, bring water to boil. Cook spaghetti until al dente.

• Drain. In large bowl toss spaghetti with tomatoes. Top with remaining cheese and 1 tablespoon basil.

6 pasta-course or 4-main course servings. Each of 4 servings: 626 calories; 921 mg sodium; 23 mg cholesterol; 15 grams fat; 100 grams carbohydrates; 23 grams protein; 1.3 grams fiber.

RAGU *with* SOFT POLENTA

POLENTA USUALLY REQUIRES a lot of attention and even more stirring. This version doesn't. To someone who loves the Italian cornmeal mush, this is a revelation. The technique originated on the back of a bag of Golden Pheasant brand polenta from San Francisco. This polenta is so good it could be served by itself, with maybe a little butter and grated Parmigiano-Reggiano beaten in at the last minute. But it is also a wonderful sponge to serve under juicy stews or ragus, like this one using spareribs. If you're feeding a crowd, double the polenta recipe, but cook it in two separate pans. Then add whole sausages to the ragu for the last 20 minutes of cooking. This makes a lot of sauce, so you'll probably have some left over—serve it the next day with some lightly buttered boiled noodles.

■ RAGU

2 tablespoons olive oil

6 meaty pork spareribs (sometimes called country-style)

Salt, pepper

3 Italian sausages

2 onions, diced

2 carrots, diced

1 stalk celery, diced

4 cloves garlic, minced

2 teaspoons minced rosemary

1 cup dry red wine

1 (28-ounce) can crushed tomatoes

1/4 cup tomato paste

• Heat oil in bottom of Dutch oven over medium-high heat. Season spareribs with salt and pepper to taste. When oil is hot, almost smoking, add spareribs to pot and brown quickly on all sides, about 15 minutes.

• Leave spareribs in pan and crumble sausages over top. Reduce heat to medium, stir and cook until sausage is no longer raw, about 5 minutes.

• Add onions, carrots and celery to pan and cook, stirring, until lightly browned, about 5 more minutes. Add garlic and rosemary and cook until fragrant, 2 to 3 minutes. Pour wine over top, increase heat to high and cook until wine reduces, about 5 minutes. Add tomatoes and tomato paste. Stir to combine well, cover and bake at 300 degrees until pork is fork-tender, about 2 hours.

CONTINUED ☞

■ SOFT POLENTA

8 cups water
2 teaspoons salt
2 cups coarse-ground cornmeal
2 tablespoons butter
2 tablespoons minced parsley

• Combine water, salt, cornmeal and butter in 3- to 4-quart oven-proof saucepan. Bake at 350 degrees 1 hour 20 minutes. Stir polenta and bake 10 more minutes. Remove from oven and set aside 5 minutes to rest before serving.

• To serve, spoon polenta into each of 6 warmed shallow pasta bowls. Place 1 rib on each and spoon ragu over top. Garnish with parsley. Serve immediately.

6 servings. Each serving: 623 calories; 1,327 mg sodium; 82 mg cholesterol; 35 grams fat; 50 grams carbohydrates; 21 grams protein; 1.58 grams fiber.

WISCONSIN OVEN-BAKED BEANS

IN TEST KITCHEN DIRECTOR Donna Deane's family, this is one of the favorite party dishes. It's based on canned beans, and it includes great bean seasonings that you're likely to have on hand—brown sugar, bacon, horseradish and mustard.

1 (15-ounce) can butter beans with liquid
1 (15-ounce) can Great Northern beans with liquid
1 (15 1/4-ounce) can kidney beans, drained
3/4 pound thick-sliced bacon, cut crosswise into 1/2-inch pieces
1 cup diced onions
3/4 cup brown sugar, packed
1 tablespoon prepared mustard
1 tablespoon prepared horseradish

• Combine butter beans, great northern beans and kidney beans in 3-quart baking dish. Stir in sliced bacon, onions, brown sugar, mustard and horseradish.

• Cover and bake at 325 degrees 2 1/2 to 3 hours. Uncover during last hour of baking to brown top. Add water to beans during cooking if necessary.

8 servings. Each serving: 461 calories; 670 mg sodium; 21 mg cholesterol; 19 grams fat; 57 grams carbohydrates; 17 grams protein; 4.88 grams fiber.

WHITE BEAN SOUP
with CHIPOTLE AIOLI

THIS RECIPE IS FROM JOHN ASH, a celebrated wine country caterer, chef and cookbook author.

■ WHITE BEAN SOUP

1 1/2 cups dry white navy or Great Northern beans
3 tablespoons olive oil
3 cups thinly sliced yellow onions
3 cloves garlic, thinly slivered
2 tablespoons minced parsley
2 teaspoons chopped fresh oregano leaves or 1 teaspoon dried
1 bay leaf
1 teaspoon fennel seeds
1/4 teaspoon dried red pepper flakes
6 cups chicken or vegetable stock
1 cup dry white wine
1 1/2 pounds plum tomatoes, quartered and seeded
1 cup diced carrots
1 cup thinly sliced celery
Salt
Freshly ground pepper
1/2 cup diced fennel bulb

• Rinse beans well and place in pot. Cover with at least 3 inches cold water. Bring to boil and cook 2 minutes. Take off heat. Let stand 1 hour. Drain and set aside. (This optional step shortens cooking time.)

• In separate soup pot, add olive oil along with onions and garlic.

• Saute until just beginning to brown. Add parsley, oregano, bay leaf, fennel seeds, red pepper flakes, stock, wine and beans. Bring to simmer. Cook 20 minutes and then add tomatoes, carrots and celery. Cook until beans are just tender, 15 to 20 minutes longer. For unsoaked beans, cook another 30 to 45 minutes. Season to taste with salt and pepper. Add fresh fennel to pot just before serving.

CONTINUED ☞

■ CHIPOTLE AIOLI

1 egg
1 tablespoon fresh lemon juice
1 tablespoon chopped garlic
1 tablespoon chopped canned chipotle chiles in adobo
3 tablespoons chopped green onions
2/3 cup olive oil
Salt, pepper
6 to 8 basil leaves

•   Combine egg, lemon juice, garlic, chipotles and green onions in food processor or blender. Process until smooth. With motor running, slowly add olive oil to form emulsion. Aioli should have heavy sauce consistency. Season to taste with salt and pepper. Store, covered and refrigerated, up to 7 days. Makes about 1 cup.

•   Ladle soup into warm bowls and stir in 1 tablespoon or to taste of Aioli into each bowl. Garnish with 1 basil leaf.

6 to 8 servings. Each of 8 servings: 457 calories; 884 mg sodium; 14 mg cholesterol; 19 grams fat; 50 grams carbohydrates; 20 grams protein; 4.59 grams fiber.

PASTA *with* TOMATO CONFIT

CHEZ PANISSE'S ALICE WATERS IS one of the most important culinary figures in California. This recipe is a good example of her way of bringing depth of flavor to simple ingredients. The tomatoes can be served whole as a side dish with meat, poultry or fish. They can be used in sauces. And they can be served on top of pasta as described below. The recipe adjusts easily up or down—figure on two tomatoes and 3 to 4 ounces of pasta per person. You might also try throwing in a few cloves of garlic to roast with the tomatoes.

8 tomatoes
1 to 2 bunches basil leaves
Salt
Freshly ground black pepper
Extra-virgin olive oil
About 1 pound pasta, shape of choice

• Make bed of basil leaves in bottom of oven-proof dish that will hold tomatoes snugly in 1 layer.

• Peel and core tomatoes and place core-side down on basil. Lightly season with salt and pepper to taste. Pour in enough olive oil to come halfway up sides of tomatoes. Bake at 350 degrees until tomatoes are soft and lightly caramelized and have infused oil with their perfume, about 1 1/2 hours.

• When tomatoes are nearly done, cook pasta in boiling, salted water just until tender, 8 to 10 minutes for most shapes. Drain pasta and place in serving bowl.

• Remove tomatoes from oven, season with salt and pepper to taste and serve spooned over cooked and drained fresh noodles.

4 servings. Each serving: 592 calories; 98 mg sodium; 0 cholesterol; 16 grams fat; 97 grams carbohydrates; 17 grams protein; 1.94 grams fiber.

RISI *e* BISI

RISI E BISI IS A CROSS BETWEEN a soup and a risotto that is one of the treasured dishes of Venice. This version was developed by novelist and food writer Michelle Huneven.

2 tablespoons butter
2 tablespoons olive oil
1/2 large onion, finely chopped
1 thick slice prosciutto (approximately 1/8-inch thick), cut into small cubes
1 cup Arborio rice
Vegetable Stock, boiling
1 1/2 cups freshly shelled peas
Freshly grated Parmigiano-Reggiano cheese
2 tablespoons chopped Italian parsley
Freshly ground pepper

• Melt butter and olive oil in heavy saute pan over medium heat. When butter starts to foam, add onion and prosciutto. Saute until onion is translucent. Add rice. Saute until rice turns opaque, about 2 to 3 minutes.

• Pour 2 ladles (approximately 1 cup) boiling Vegetable Stock into rice and stir. Stir constantly, allowing stock to be absorbed, and adding more stock when none is pooling up in pan. Keep adding boiling stock and stirring, about 15 minutes. Add peas and start tasting.

• Add more boiling Vegetable Stock. Keep stirring. When peas brighten in color and rice is chewy without being chalky and has thick sauce, stir in 1/2 cup Parmigiano-Reggiano cheese. Serve immediately, sprinkled with chopped parsley. Pass additional freshly grated cheese and pepper.

▪ VEGETABLE STOCK

2 carrots, halved and cut into 1-inch chunks
1 leek, white part and 6 inches of green part, quartered
2 stalks celery, cut into 1-inch chunks
2 large potatoes, unpeeled and quartered
Several large handfuls of pea pod shells from shelled peas
1/2 teaspoon salt
1 gallon cold water

• Place carrots, leek, celery, potatoes, pea pod shells and salt in large pot with water. Bring to boil. Boil gently, uncovered, 45 minutes.

• Strain. Broth should be clear and fragrant. Return to stove. Makes about 5 cups.

4 servings. Each serving: 424 calories; 587 mg sodium; 24 mg cholesterol; 16 grams fat; 58 grams carbohydrates; 12 grams protein; 2.05 grams fiber.

SPICY COLD SOBA NOODLES

THIS IS AN ADAPTATION OF A RECIPE served at City Restaurant. City was owned by Mary Sue Milliken and Susan Feniger and was one of the first places in Southern California to present sophisticated food from cuisines other than French and Italian.

1/3 cup soy sauce
1/2 teaspoon molasses
1/4 cup sesame oil
1/4 cup tahini (sesame seed paste)
1/4 cup brown sugar, packed
1 tablespoon chile oil
3 tablespoons balsamic or red wine vinegar
1/2 bunch green onions (white and green parts), thinly sliced
Salt
1/2 pound soba (Japanese buckwheat noodles)

• Place soy sauce in saucepan over high heat and reduce by half. Turn heat to low. Stir in molasses and warm briefly. Transfer to mixing bowl.

• Add sesame oil, tahini, brown sugar, chile oil, vinegar and green onions. Whisk to combine. Season to taste with salt, if desired. Set aside.

• Bring large pot salted water to rapid boil. Add noodles, bring back to boil. Cook, stirring occasionally, about 3 minutes or until al dente.

• Drain noodles and plunge in ice water. Drain again. Rinse well under cold running water. Combine noodles and sauce, toss well and chill.

2 to 4 servings. Each of 4 servings: 496 calories; 1866 mg sodium; 0 cholesterol; 25 grams fat; 62 grams carbohydrates; 13 grams protein; 1.50 grams fiber.

STEW *of* CHARRED TOMATOES *and* CRANBERRY BEANS

1995

IS THIS A STEW, A SOUP OR A PASTA? Who cares? This recipe from Food Editor Russ Parsons is a perfect meal for a fall day when made with fresh cranberry beans, and it works well in winter when made with dried beans. In a pinch, you could even substitute well-drained canned beans. Charring the tomatoes gives a slight smoky quality to this stew and intensifies the tomato flavor as well. You don't need to push the idea too far, just let the tomatoes scorch enough to flavor them.

3 plum tomatoes
2 ounces prosciutto, minced
1 tablespoon olive oil
1 carrot, diced
1/2 onion, diced
1 clove garlic, minced
1 small sprig sage
1 pound cranberry beans, shelled (about 1 1/2 cups)
1 1/2 cups water
1 teaspoon salt
1/2 pound dried pasta shapes, such as gnocchi or medium shells
2 tablespoons torn basil leaves

• Slice tomatoes in half lengthwise and place cut-side-down on hot griddle. Cook until tomatoes begin to blacken and char, about 5 minutes. Turn over and repeat on opposite side, another 3 minutes. Cool, squeeze out seeds, chop and reserve.

• In large saute pan over medium heat, cook prosciutto in oil until lightly browned, about 5 minutes. Add carrot, onion and garlic, reduce heat and cook, covered, until vegetables soften, about 10 minutes.

• Add sage, cranberry beans, tomatoes, water and salt. Bring to boil, reduce to simmer and cook, covered, until beans are soft, about 30 minutes.

• When beans are done, cook pasta in plenty of rapidly boiling salted water. Drain well and add to beans. Raise heat to high and cook, stirring, 2 to 3 minutes to meld flavors. Divide among 4 pasta plates and garnish with torn basil.

4 servings. Each serving: 299 calories; 782 mg sodium; 8 mg cholesterol; 5 grams fat; 52 grams carbohydrates; 10 grams protein; 1.05 grams fiber.

SQUASH RAVIOLI *in* SAGE BUTTER

STUFFED PASTAS FILLED WITH SQUASH puree are popular around the Parma area of Italy, but they usually emphasize the flavors of the spices that are used to flavor them—cinnamon, clove and ginger. This version by Times Food Editor Russ Parsons goes a different direction, pointing up the earthy flavors of the squash by pairing it with a light sage butter. To make the roast squash pulp, cut a winter squash in half and remove the seeds. Roast it cut side down on a jellyroll pan in a 400-degree oven until soft, about 40 to 60 minutes. Then scoop the pulp away from the peel.

■ SQUASH FILLING

2 cups roast squash pulp
5 slices prosciutto, chopped
1/4 cup fresh bread crumbs
1/2 cup grated Parmigiano-Reggiano cheese
1 teaspoon salt
1 teaspoon freshly ground pepper
1 egg

• Mix squash, prosciutto, bread crumbs, Parmigiano-Reggiano, salt and pepper in bowl. Taste and adjust seasoning; there should be definite pepper bite. Add egg and mix well.

■ PASTA DOUGH

2 1/4 cups flour, plus more for dusting
1 teaspoon salt
1 tablespoon olive oil
3 eggs

• Place flour, salt and olive oil in work bowl of food processor fitted with metal blade and pulse once or twice to combine. Add eggs and run until dough forms ball that rides around on top of blade. Remove from machine, wrap in plastic and set aside for 1/2 hour.

• Divide dough in quarters and run 1 piece through manual pasta maker at widest setting to flatten. Dust lightly with flour, fold into thirds and run through machine again. Repeat, re-folding, until dough is satiny to touch, 4 or 5 times.

• Dust dough lightly with flour and run through machine on middle setting. Dust again and run through machine on next-to-thinnest setting.

• Lay pasta sheet on counter, cover with damp tea towel and repeat using rest of dough.

CONTINUED ☛

• Using 1 sheet at a time, place 2-teaspoon mounds of filling along sheet about 2 inches apart and about 1 inch from edge. Brush other half of sheet lightly with water and fold evenly over top of other half, covering mounds of filling. Press firmly around each filling mound, squeezing out as much air as possible and creating tight seal. Cut into individual ravioli with pasta cutter or knife. Repeat, using rest of pasta sheets.

• Bring large pot of lightly salted water to rolling boil. Add ravioli, a few at a time, making sure they don't stick together. Cook until ravioli float to surface, about 5 minutes. Ravioli may be cooked in 2 batches to prevent crowding.

■ SAGE BUTTER

1/2 cup (1 stick) butter
2 teaspoons minced fresh sage
Freshly grated Parmigiano-Reggiano cheese

• While ravioli are cooking, melt butter with sage in large skillet over medium heat. As soon as butter is melted, remove pan from heat. Drain ravioli and add to skillet. Toss to coat well with butter and divide among 6 plates. Dust lightly with grated Parmigiano-Reggiano and serve immediately.

---

6 servings. Each serving: 457 calories; 1,262 mg sodium; 192 mg cholesterol; 25 grams fat; 43 grams carbohydrates; 15 grams protein; 0.69 grams fiber.

SOUTHERN CALIFORNIA CASSOULET

1998

HOW FANCY CAN BAKED BEANS GET? Pretty danged fancy, judging by this cassoulet. And pretty delicious as well. It comes from David Checchini, chef at the Wine Cask in Santa Barbara.

3 pounds dry navy beans
1/2 cup olive oil
1/4 pound smoked bacon, diced
1 cup diced pancetta
3 white onions, minced
2 tablespoons minced garlic
2 tablespoons finely diced shallots
1 cup diced celery
2 carrots, diced
4 tomatoes, chopped
1/4 pound Italian sausage or other pork sausage, cooked and diced
3 pounds duck legs, browned and drained
16 cups veal stock or chicken or vegetable stock
1 1/2 teaspoons salt
1/2 teaspoon pepper
1/2 cup fresh thyme, whole leaves
1/2 cup minced parsley
2 bay leaves
1/2 loaf day-old Italian or French bread, cut into pieces
1/2 cup (1 stick) butter, melted
1 cup mixed fresh herbs (parsley, basil, thyme), chopped

• Soak beans 8 hours or overnight in water to cover. Drain. Cook beans in large pot with plenty of fresh water until al dente, 35 to 40 minutes. Strain and set aside.

• Heat olive oil in Dutch oven or soup pot. Add bacon, pancetta, onions, garlic, shallots, celery, carrots and tomatoes and saute until vegetables are softened, about 15 minutes. Add sausage and duck legs and stir to mix. Add stock and simmer 15 to 20 minutes. Add salt, pepper, thyme, parsley and bay leaves.

• Place half of beans in 8-quart roasting pan. With slotted spoon, distribute meat-and-vegetable mixture evenly over beans. Reserve stock and skim fat from surface. Cover meats and vegetables with remaining beans. Add just enough stock to barely cover beans. Cover and bake at 350 degrees 2 hours.

• Place bread in food processor and process to fine meal. Add butter and mixed herbs. Process to mix. Uncover cassoulet and sprinkle evenly with prepared crumbs. Bake uncovered until well-browned and bubbling, 1 1/2 hours longer. (Check after 1 hour of cooking and add more stock if needed.)

16 servings. Each serving: 678 calories; 1,530 mg sodium; 54 mg cholesterol; 34 grams fat; 64 grams carbohydrates; 28 grams protein; 5.26 grams fiber.

BLACK BEAN-BROWN RICE ENCHILADA CASSEROLE

ANNE BUNCH WAS ONE OF THE BEST COOKS in Southern California's wine country. When she owned the Side Street Café in Los Olivos, this was one of her favorite recipes. It is a big casserole, great for a party. But even if you are cooking for just a few, make the full amount because it freezes well.

2 cups cooked brown basmati rice (about 1 cup raw rice)
2 (15-ounce) cans black beans, drained and rinsed
4 cups sour cream
4 cups grated Jack cheese
1 bunch cilantro, chopped
4 green onions, chopped
2 tablespoons hot chili powder
1 tablespoon ground cumin
3 large jalapenos, seeded and chopped
Salt
Oil
18 blue or regular corn tortillas
Nonstick cooking spray
2 (19-ounce) cans red enchilada sauce

• Mix rice, beans, sour cream, 2 cups cheese, cilantro, green onions, chili powder, cumin, jalapenos and salt to taste in large bowl.

• Heat 1/4 inch oil in skillet until very hot. Quickly fry each tortilla, turning to cook on both sides. Tortillas should remain soft. Drain on paper towels.

• Spray bottom of 13x9-inch baking pan with nonstick cooking spray. Add light coat of enchilada sauce. Arrange 6 tortillas in pan. Top with 1/3 rice-bean mixture and more enchilada sauce. Top with another 6 tortillas, more filling and sauce. Repeat, making third layer topped with remaining 6 tortillas. Pour layer of enchilada sauce over all. There will be sauce left over, which can be served separately or refrigerated or frozen for another use. Sprinkle remaining cheese on top. Bake at 350 degrees until heated through, 45 to 55 minutes.

9 large servings. Each serving: 749 calories; 738 mg sodium; 79 mg cholesterol; 42 grams fat; 67 grams carbohydrates; 26 grams protein; 4.52 grams fiber.

LENTILS *and* WILD GREENS
(*Lenticchie con Verdura Selvatica*)

1991

VIANA LA PLACE AND HER WRITING PARTNER Evan Kleiman wrote some of the first cookbooks that captured the new Italian spirit of California cooking.

1 bunch mustard greens or other tender bitter greens, stems trimmed,
leaves stripped from ribs
Salt
Extra-virgin olive oil
1 small onion, finely diced
2 cloves garlic, finely chopped
1 stalk celery, finely diced
1 small carrot, finely chopped
1 teaspoon chopped fresh oregano leaves
1 teaspoon finely chopped fresh rosemary leaves
2 tablespoons chopped Italian parsley
2 tablespoons chopped fresh basil leaves
2 cups lentils
Freshly ground pepper
3 small tomatoes, roasted, peeled, seeded and diced
3 tablespoons lemon juice
4 lemon wedges

• Blanch mustard greens in water that clings to leaves after washing. Add salt to taste. Drain in colander. Chop very coarsely and set aside. Combine 3 tablespoons oil, onion, garlic, celery and carrot in medium skillet. Cook, covered, over medium heat until vegetables are tender.

• Stir in oregano, rosemary, Italian parsley, basil and lentils. Allow lentils to absorb flavor for few minutes. Add 4 cups water. Season to taste with salt and pepper. Bring to boil, then simmer, partially covered, until lentils are just tender, about 35 minutes. About 10 minutes before lentils are cooked, add tomatoes.

• Saute greens very briefly in 1 tablespoon oil. Just before serving, stir greens and lemon juice into lentil-tomato mixture.

• Ladle mixture into shallow soup bowls. Grind coarse pepper to taste over top and add few drops of olive oil. Serve with lemon wedges.

4 servings. Each serving: 278 calories; 109 mg sodium; 0 cholesterol; 14 grams fat; 30 grams carbohydrates; 11 grams protein; 4.11 grams fiber.

BUTTER RICE BALLS
(*Arancine con Burro*)

PLENTY OF PEOPLE SEEM TO HAVE a version of this recipe, whether they call it arancine (from the Italian for orange, which they resemble) or suppli al telefono (from the way the cheese strings like telephone lines when pulled apart). This version comes from Southern California cookbook writer Clifford Wright.

Saffron
Water
2 cups milk
2 cups Arborio rice
1/2 cup (1 stick) butter, softened
1 1/2 teaspoons salt
4 eggs, lightly beaten
1/2 teaspoon pepper
1/2 pound fresh mozzarella, finely diced
1/3 cup small fresh or frozen peas
Bread crumbs
Olive oil

• Dissolve dash saffron in 1 tablespoon tepid water. Let stand while cooking rice.

• Bring milk and 2 cups water to boil in heavy pot with heavy lid. Stir in rice, 2 tablespoons butter and salt. Cover and reduce heat to low and cook 15 minutes. Check rice and if soft but liquid is left, strain. It rice is still al dente, continue cooking until liquid is absorbed, about 5 minutes, being careful that rice does not get too mushy. When rice is ready, gently stir in dissolved saffron and half of eggs until rice turns yellow. Spread rice on platter or marble surface and let cool completely.

• Mix together remaining 6 tablespoons butter, pepper, mozzarella and uncooked peas.

• To form rice balls, spread about 1/2 cup rice flat in palm of your hand, then cup your hand slightly, using thumb of other hand to make indentation. To keep rice from becoming sticky, have plate of cold water nearby to dip your hand into each time you form new rice ball. Place about 1 tablespoon cheese mixture into indentation and fold edges over.

• Cover with more rice and shape into large balls.

• Pour remaining eggs into shallow bowl. Spread enough bread crumbs for coating on wax paper. Dip each ball into eggs then roll in bread crumbs.

• Deep-fry rice balls, 3 or 4 at a time, in enough oil to cover at 360 degrees until orange-brown, about 5 minutes. When all balls are fried, place in baking pan at bake at 450 degrees 10 minutes. Serve hot.

---

14 to 20 arancine. Each of 20 arancine: 184 calories; 300 mg sodium; 66 mg cholesterol; 10 grams fat; 18 grams carbohydrates; 6 grams protein; 0.06 gram fiber.

VEGETARIAN RED BEAN STEW

THIS RECIPE IS BASED ON A DISH Border Grill chefs Mary Sue Milliken and Susan Feniger were served at a taco stand. They left out the meat and came up with this winner.

1990

2 cups dry red beans
Salt
2 carrots, peeled and cut in chunks
2 stalks celery, sliced
2 turnips, peeled and cut in chunks
2 parsnips, peeled and cut in chunks
1 zucchini, cut in chunks
1 yellow squash, cut in chunks
4 red boiling potatoes, cut in chunks
Extra-virgin olive oil
6 cups diced onions
Pepper
1 tablespoon garlic puree
6 tablespoons ground roasted ancho chiles
1 habanero chile, seeds removed and diced, optional
Ancho Chile Salsa

• Rinse beans and place in saucepan with 6 cups salted water. Bring to boil over high heat. Boil 3 minutes. Soak beans overnight in salted water. Rinse again. Add 6 cups water and simmer over medium heat until beans are plump but still firm. Rinse again.

• Blanch carrots, celery, turnips and parsnips. Grill zucchini and squash. Cook potatoes in boiling salted water and drain.

• Heat 1/4 cup oil in soup pot. Add onions and season to taste with salt and pepper. Cook until caramelized, stirring over medium heat until dark golden brown. Add garlic puree and continue to stir until garlic is heated and aroma rises. Stir in ground ancho and diced habanero chile. Add cooked beans, vegetables and 4 cups water. Cover and cook until beans are tender, about 1 hour.

CONTINUED☞

■ ANCHO CHILE SALSA

2 ancho chiles, stems and seeds removed
1 cup orange juice
1/2 cup lime juice
1/2 cup grapefruit juice
Salt, pepper

• Roast chiles, being careful not to scorch them. Cool, peel, then chop and mix with orange, lime and grapefruit juices. Season to taste with salt and pepper.

• Serve vegetables and beans in large bowl topped with Ancho Chile Salsa and drizzle with extra olive oil.

6 to 8 servings. Each of 8 servings: 323 calories; 152 mg sodium; 0 cholesterol; 7 grams fat; 53 grams carbohydrates; 15 grams protein; 4.49 grams fiber.

SALVADORAN-STYLE FRIJOLES

TIMES TEST KITCHEN WORKER Ana Oviedo combines black and red beans to come up with a dish that is the same distinctive color that she remembers from her home in El Salvador.

★
1993

1 onion
1 cup dried black beans
1 cup dried red beans
15 cups water
3 cloves garlic
1 tablespoon salt
1/2 cup plus 1 tablespoon oil

• Slice onion into 2 pieces. Reserve 1 piece for refrying beans next day. Cut remaining piece in 1/2.

• Rinse beans. Place in large clay pot or soup pot. Add 6 cups water and bring to boil. Reduce heat, add 2 onion quarters and garlic and simmer 2 hours or until tender. Stir beans occasionally so those on bottom do not burn. Add remaining water in stages as needed. When beans are done, remove from heat, cool and refrigerate in pot overnight.

• Next day, remove beans and wash pot. Cut reserved 1/2 onion into 2 pieces. Reserve 1 piece for another use. Slice remaining piece into strips and separate. Heat oil in pot. Add onion strips and cook until well browned. Remove onion and discard, leaving oil. Add beans and simmer 45 minutes, stirring occasionally.

6 to 8 servings. Each serving: 402 calories; 1,190 mg sodium; 0 cholesterol; 22 grams fat; 41 grams carbohydrates; 15 grams protein; 3.76 grams fiber.

STIR-FRIED BEEF *with* STEWED TOMATOES *and* NOODLES

TIMES TEST KITCHEN INTERN Shoshona Goldberg contributed this recipe, which can be made in less than 30 minutes.

1 (1/2-pound) flank steak
4 teaspoons cornstarch
Water
1/4 teaspoon sugar
Soy sauce
2 tomatoes, each sliced into 8 wedges
Sesame oil
1 tablespoon vegetable oil
1 clove garlic, minced
1 green onion, chopped
2 tablespoons oyster sauce
1 tablespoon salt
1/2 pound fresh wheat-flour (Shanghai) noodles

• Slice steak into 3 strips lengthwise, then into 1/8-inch-thick slices.

• Combine cornstarch, 4 teaspoons water, sugar and 1 tablespoon soy sauce in nonreactive shallow bowl or pan. Add beef and let marinate at least 10 minutes.

• Cook tomatoes and 1/4 cup soy sauce in saucepan over high heat until soy sauce comes to boil. Reduce heat and simmer, covered, 5 to 7 minutes.

• Do not stir or tomatoes will fall apart. Remove from heat and add several drops sesame oil to taste.

• While tomatoes simmer, add salt to pot of boiling water and let water return to boil. Add noodles and cook until just tender, 5 to 7 minutes. Add vegetable oil to heated wok or skillet and heat about 30 seconds over high heat. Add garlic, green onion and marinated beef strips, tossing rapidly until beef turns deep brown, 3 to 4 minutes. Add oyster sauce and toss.

• Drain noodles and place on serving bowl. Top with beef, then tomatoes. Toss at table just before serving.

2 servings. Each serving: 691 calories; 4,344 mg sodium; 43 mg cholesterol; 15 grams fat; 103 grams carbohydrates; 36 grams protein; 4.85 grams fiber.

NINE

Cakes

ANNE BUNCH'S COCONUT CAKE

1996

THE COCONUT CAKE IS ONE OF the all-time classic West Coast desserts. This version, from Los Olivos chef Anne Bunch, is very special. It's more convenient to make the pastry cream the day before so it will be completely cooled and ready to fill the cake.

■ CAKE

4 eggs
2 cups sugar
2 1/2 cups unbleached flour, plus more for dusting
2 teaspoons baking powder
1 teaspoon salt
1 cup oil
1 cup dry white wine
1 tablespoon vanilla extract
Grated zest of 1/2 lemon
Nonstick cooking spray

• Beat eggs and sugar in mixer at high speed until pale and frothy. Turn off mixer and add 2 1/2 cups flour, baking powder, salt, oil, wine, vanilla and lemon zest. Beat 2 minutes at high speed.

• Divide batter between 2 (9-inch) layer cake pans that have been sprayed with nonstick cooking spray and dusted inside with extra flour.

• Bake at 350 degrees until toothpick inserted in center comes out clean, about 40 minutes. Cool cakes in pans on rack 5 minutes. Turn out and cool completely.

■ PASTRY CREAM

1 1/3 cups milk
1 tablespoon vanilla extract
1 cup sugar
6 egg yolks
1/4 cup cornstarch
1 pound mascarpone cheese or cream cheese

• Heat milk and vanilla to boiling and keep hot.

• Beat sugar and egg yolks in mixer until fluffy and pale in color. Reduce speed, add cornstarch and beat until blended. Add hot milk, beating continuously. When well blended, return to saucepan and heat slowly, stirring constantly to keep mixture from sticking to bottom of pan. Cook until very thick. Pour into bowl, cover with plastic wrap and set aside to cool.

• When completely cooled, combine cream mixture with mascarpone cheese to form thick filling.

CONTINUED ☞

■ ASSEMBLY

2 cups whipping cream, whipped
3 cups sweetened flake coconut

• Spread all of Pastry Cream in thick, even layer on bottom cake layer.

• Cover with top cake layer. Frost top and sides of cake with whipped cream and cover with coconut.

12 to 16 servings. Each of 16 servings: 668 calories; 362 mg sodium; 229 mg cholesterol; 43 grams fat; 63 grams carbohydrates; 8 grams protein; 0.34 gram fiber.

THE NEXT BEST THING
to ROBERT REDFORD (*The '90s Version*)

LORD KNOWS WHAT THEY CALLED this cake before Robert Redford became a star, but after we published it, the phone rang off the hook from people wanting it again.

1 cup flour
1/2 cup (1 stick) butter, softened, plus more for greasing
1 cup finely chopped pecans
1 (8-ounce) package cream cheese
1 cup sugar
1 (8-ounce) carton frozen nondairy whipped topping, thawed
1 (5.1-ounce) package instant vanilla pudding mix
1 (5.9-ounce) package instant chocolate pudding mix
3 cups cold milk
Grated chocolate candy bar, optional

• Prepare bottom crust by mixing together flour, butter and pecans until crumb-like. Press mixture into greased 13x9-inch baking pan. Bake at 350 degrees until lightly golden, 15 to 20 minutes. Cool.

• Beat cream cheese with sugar until smooth. Fold in half whipped topping. Spread mixture over cooled crust.

• Combine vanilla and chocolate pudding mixes. Beat in milk until mixture is smooth and thickened. Spread over cream cheese layer. Spread remaining whipped topping over top. Sprinkle with grated chocolate candy bar, if desired. Cover and refrigerate overnight.

16 servings. Each serving: 333 calories; 222 mg sodium; 34 mg cholesterol; 19 grams fat; 42 grams carbohydrates; 4 grams protein; 0.11 gram fiber.

CARAMEL APPLE CAKE,
TARTE-TATIN STYLE

★
1992

♥

YOU WON'T BELIEVE THIS CAKE by Times Test Kitchen Director Donna Deane. It is rich and satisfying, yet it only contains about 2 grams of fat per serving. Incredible.

1 3/4 cups sugar
2 tablespoons water
2 tablespoons butter
1 1/2 teaspoons almond extract
3 pounds apples, preferably Fuji or Golden Delicious
1 cup cake flour
1 1/2 teaspoons baking powder
1/4 cup thawed frozen nonfat egg substitute (equivalent to 1 egg)
1/2 cup apple juice
2 tablespoons amaretto
2 egg whites
1 cup low-fat whipped topping, optional

• Combine 1 cup sugar and water in heavy, deep, oven-proof 10-inch skillet. Bring to boil over medium heat, stirring occasionally. Cook to light caramel stage or pale amber color, stirring occasionally. Remove from heat. Swirl in butter and 1/2 teaspoon almond extract. Set aside.

• Peel, core and cut each apple into 4 wedges. Arrange about 3/4 of apple wedges in tight single layer over caramel. Cut remaining apple wedges in halves and place atop first apple layer. Cover skillet and cook over medium-low heat until apples exude juices, about 10 minutes.

• Uncover skillet, increase heat to medium and continue cooking about 25 to 30 minutes, or until caramel syrup is thick, but not burnt (adjust heat to low if caramel starts cooking too fast). Baste apples occasionally with caramel syrup, using baster or spoon. Remove from heat and cool.

• Sift cake flour with baking powder and 1/2 cup plus 2 tablespoons sugar in bowl. Make well in center. In another bowl whisk egg substitute, apple juice, remaining 1 teaspoon almond extract and amaretto. Add to well in flour mixture, slowly stirring in dry ingredients just to blend.

• Beat egg whites until foamy. Add remaining 2 tablespoons sugar, then beat until stiff but not dry. Fold small amount of batter into egg whites, then fold mixture back into remaining batter.

• Pour over apples in skillet. Bake at 350 degrees until wood pick inserted in center of cake comes out clean, 25 to 30 minutes.

• Cool 5 minutes. Loosen cake around edges. Place platter over skillet and carefully invert pan, shaking gently to release cake onto platter. Spoon any remaining glaze over cake. Serve with low-fat whipped topping.

12 servings. Each serving, without whipped topping: 232 calories; 88 mg sodium; 5 mg cholesterol; 2 grams fat; 52 grams carbohydrates; 2 grams protein; 0.56 gram fiber.

CHARLENE'S AVOCADO CAKE

THIS IS AN OLD CALIFORNIA RECIPE (the original appeared in the Los Angeles Times at least 25 years ago), that talented home cook Cathi Gilmore resurrected and adapted to enter in the Los Angeles County Fair in 1992. It won a blue ribbon.

1 1/3 cups sugar
1/2 cup (1 stick) butter
2 eggs
1 cup mashed avocado (about 1 1/2 medium)
1/2 teaspoon cinnamon
1/2 teaspoon ground allspice
1/2 teaspoon ground nutmeg
1/2 teaspoon salt
1 1/2 teaspoons baking soda
1/3 cup buttermilk
1/2 cup chopped dates
1/4 cup raisins
1/2 cup chopped walnuts
1 1/2 cups flour
Whipped cream, lightly sweetened

- Cream together sugar, butter, eggs and avocado until light and fluffy.

- Beat in cinnamon, allspice, nutmeg, salt and baking soda. Add buttermilk, dates, raisins and nuts. Mix well. Stir in flour until thoroughly mixed. (Mixture will be quite stiff.)

- Spread in greased 9-inch square glass baking dish or metal baking pan. Bake at 300 degrees (for glass dish) or 325 degrees (for metal pan) 50 minutes to 1 hour, or until cake tester inserted in center comes out clean. Cool.

- Serve plain, frost or top with whipped cream.

10 servings. Each serving: 389 calories; 238 mg sodium; 68 mg cholesterol; 19 grams fat; 53 grams carbohydrates; 5 grams protein; 1.21 grams fiber.

WALNUT CAKE

MARK CARTER, NOW CHEF AND OWNER at the well-known Carter House Hotel in Eureka, Calif., got his start at a restaurant called Duplex in the then-unfashionable neighborhood of Los Feliz.

1/2 pound walnuts
2 teaspoons flour
1/2 teaspoon baking powder
8 eggs, separated
1 cup granulated sugar
Grated zest of 1 lemon
1/2 cup cake crumbs
Butter, for greasing
Powdered sugar, for dusting

- Grind walnuts into fine meal using food processor or meat grinder.
- Sift together flour and baking powder.
- Beat egg yolks, granulated sugar and lemon zest until light, 5 minutes. Add walnuts and beat until well combined. Whip egg whites until stiff. Alternately fold in whites, flour mixture and cake crumbs, beginning and ending with whites.
- Pour into greased 9-inch cake pan. Bake at 350 degrees until cake pulls away from sides of pan, 35 to 40 minutes. Invert onto rack to cool. Dust with powdered sugar just before serving.

8 servings. Each serving: 190 calories; 57 mg sodium; 109 mg cholesterol; 12 grams fat; 18 grams carbohydrates; 5 grams protein; 0.66 gram fiber.

BOURBON-CHOCOLATE-PECAN CAKE

1991

JIM DODGE IS A DESSERT WIZARD. This is one of his greatest cakes, a flourless torte that is topped with a sheer, glistening glaze.

2 cups pecans
1 cup (2 sticks) butter, plus more for greasing
8 ounces bittersweet or semisweet chocolate
1 1/2 cups sugar
1 cup unsweetened cocoa powder
6 eggs
1/3 cup Bourbon

• Spread pecans on baking sheet and toast in 350-degree oven until fragrant, about 10 minutes. Cool.

• Cut circle of parchment to fit bottom of 9-inch round cake pan. Grease pan well and line with parchment circle.

• Melt 1 cup butter and chocolate in top of double boiler set over, but not touching, simmering water. Stir until very smooth. Cool.

• Mix sugar, cocoa powder and eggs just until well combined. Add melted chocolate, stirring to combine. Coarsely chop 1 1/2 cups pecans and stir into chocolate mixture. Stir in Bourbon.

• Pour batter into prepared pan. Place pan inside larger pan and pour hot water to level of 1 inch in outer pan. Bake at 350 degrees until cake is firm to touch, about 45 minutes. (Cake surface may crack slightly.)

• Cool cake on wire rack, then remove from pan, leaving parchment paper attached. Wrap cake in plastic wrap and refrigerate overnight.

■ GLAZE

4 ounces bittersweet or semisweet chocolate
1/2 cup (1 stick) butter

• Melt chocolate and butter in top of double boiler set over, but not touching, simmering water. Stir until completely smooth. Cool about 5 minutes.

• Remove cake from refrigerator and place upside down on wire rack with sheet of wax paper underneath to catch drips. Peel off parchment circle, then drizzle spoonfuls of glaze along sides of cake. When sides are completely covered, spoon remaining glaze on top of cake and smooth with icing spatula.

• Cover sides of cake with remaining 1/2 cup pecans, chopped if desired, pressing gently against glaze. Refrigerate cake until 30 minutes before serving.

12 servings. Each serving: 633 calories; 36 mg sodium; 168 mg cholesterol; 49 grams fat; 48 grams carbohydrates; 7 grams protein; 0.88 grams fiber.

CARAMEL-GLAZED APPLE-PECAN POUND CAKE

TIMES RECIPE TESTER Mayi Brady developed this dessert based on the childhood flavors of caramel apples. The drizzled caramel sauce works as frosting. It's a perfect homey cake for cool weather.

■ APPLE-PECAN POUND CAKE

2 1/2 cups chopped green apples
1 cup (2 sticks) butter, softened
1 1/2 cups sugar
1 1/2 teaspoons vanilla extract
5 eggs
2 cups flour
1 tablespoon baking powder
1 tablespoon cinnamon
3/4 cup chopped pecans

• In skillet, lightly saute apple chunks in 2 tablespoons butter. Set aside.

• In bowl, cream remaining butter with sugar until light and fluffy. Beat in vanilla. Beat in eggs 1 at time. In bowl sift together flour, baking powder and cinnamon. Stir into butter mixture until blended. Fold in apples and pecans. Spoon into greased and floured bundt pan. Bake at 325 degrees 1 hour, or until wood pick inserted near center comes out clean.

■ CARAMEL SAUCE

1/2 cup brown sugar, packed
1/2 cup granulated sugar
1/2 cup whipping cream
1 tablespoon butter

• Combine brown sugar, sugar and whipping cream in medium saucepan. Bring to boil. Cook and stir, about 2 minutes. Remove from heat. Stir in butter until melted. Cool, then drizzle over cake.

12 servings. Each serving: 495 calories; 306 mg sodium; 146 mg cholesterol; 26 grams fat; 62 grams carbohydrates; 6 grams protein; 0.28 gram fiber.

HOLIDAY FRUITCAKE

FORMER TIMES STAFF WRITER Kathie Jenkins contributed this recipe for a fruit cake with a decidedly California spin—it's rich in dried fruits like raisins, dates and apricots, and nuts such as almonds and pecans. The longer the fruitcake sits, the better it tastes.

1990

1 pound dried apricots, chopped
1 pound dates, chopped
1 pound golden raisins
1 pound red and green candied cherries
1 pound red and green candied pineapple
1 pound almonds, blanched, toasted and chopped
1 pound pecans, broken into pieces
4 cups flour
2 cups (4 sticks) butter, softened
1 1/2 cups brown sugar, packed
1 1/2 cups granulated sugar
12 eggs
1 teaspoon ground cloves
2 teaspoons cinnamon
1 teaspoon ground mace
1 1/2 teaspoons baking soda
1 teaspoon salt
1/4 cup rum
1/4 cup brandy
Grand Marnier
Juice and zest of 2 oranges
Juice and zest of 2 lemons

• Thoroughly grease 4 (8x5-inch) loaf pans. Combine apricots, dates, raisins, candied cherries and pineapple, almonds and pecans in large bowl. Mix in 1 cup flour to dredge mixture. Set aside.

• Cream butter and sugars until light and fluffy. Add eggs, 1 at time, beating after each addition.

• Sift remaining flour with cloves, cinnamon, mace, baking soda and salt. Add to creamed mixture alternately with rum, brandy, 1/4 cup Grand Marnier and fruit juices and zests. Fold into fruit-nut mixture. Pour into loaf pans. Bake until wood pick inserted in center of cake comes out clean, 2 1/2 to 3 hours.

• Cool in pans 15 minutes. Remove from pans onto wire rack and let cool to room temperature. Moisten 4 pieces cheesecloth, large enough to cover each loaf, with Grand Marnier and wrap around each loaf. Wrap Grand Marnier-soaked loaves in foil and refrigerate or store in cool place.

4 (8x4-inch) loaves, 32 servings. Each serving: 591 calories; 264 mg sodium; 111 mg cholesterol; 30 grams fat; 77 grams carbohydrates; 9 grams protein; 1.95 grams fiber.

FROM SCRATCH
TUNNEL *of* FUDGE CAKE

1986

THE TUNNEL OF FUDGE CAKE is one of those Pillsbury Bake-Off winners that become a standard recipe for families across the country. Nuts are essential to this recipe. And since this cake has a soft tunnel of fudge, an ordinary doneness test cannot be used. Accurate oven temperature and baking time are critical. In altitudes above 3,500 feet, increase flour to 2 1/4 cups plus 3 tablespoons.

1 3/4 cups (3 1/2 sticks) butter, softened, plus more for greasing
1 3/4 cups granulated sugar
6 eggs
2 cups powdered sugar
2 1/4 cups flour, plus more for preparing pan
3/4 cup cocoa powder
2 cups chopped walnuts

• Beat butter and granulated sugar in large bowl until light and fluffy. Add eggs, 1 at a time, beating well after each addition. Gradually add powdered sugar, blending well. By hand, stir in flour, cocoa and walnuts until well blended.

• Spoon batter into greased and floured 12-cup bundt pan or 10-inch tube pan. Bake at 350 degrees 1 hour. Cool upright in pan on cooling rack 1 hour. Invert onto serving plate. Cool completely.

■ GLAZE

3/4 cup powdered sugar
1/4 cup cocoa powder
1 1/2 to 2 tablespoons milk

• Combine sugar, cocoa and milk in small bowl until well blended. Spoon Glaze over top of cake, allowing some to run down sides.

16 servings. Each serving: 536 calories; 233 mg sodium; 134 mg cholesterol; 32 grams fat; 60 grams carbohydrates; 7 grams protein; 1.04 grams fiber.

LAZY DAISY OATMEAL CAKE

Nobody knows home baking better than Marion Cunningham, longtime Times Food Section columnist and author of many cookbooks including "The Fannie Farmer Baking Book."

■ OATMEAL CAKE

1 1/4 cups water
1/2 teaspoon salt
1 cup uncooked rolled oats
1/2 cup (1 stick) butter, room temperature
1 cup granulated sugar
1 cup light brown sugar, packed
2 teaspoons vanilla extract
2 eggs
1 1/2 cups flour
1 teaspoon baking soda
1/4 teaspoon nutmeg

• Bring water and 1/4 teaspoon salt to boil and add oats. Remove pan from heat, stir well, cover and let stand 30 minutes.

• Beat butter until creamy. Gradually add granulated and brown sugars and beat until light and well mixed. Stir in vanilla extract and eggs. Add cooked oatmeal and beat well.

• Sift flour, baking soda, remaining 1/4 teaspoon salt and nutmeg onto piece of wax paper. Gradually add sifted ingredients to creamed butter mixture, beating well. Spoon batter either into 14 greased cupcake cups or greased 13x9-inch baking pan.

• Bake at 350 degrees until toothpick inserted in center of cake comes out clean, about 15 minutes for cupcakes, about 35 to 45 minutes for cake. Cool cupcakes 5 minutes and cake 10 minutes before removing from pan.

■ DAISY FROSTING

1/4 cup (1/2 stick) butter
1/2 cup light brown sugar, packed
3 tablespoons half-and-half
1/3 cup chopped walnuts
3/4 cup shredded coconut

• Melt butter in small pan over low heat. Stir in sugar until melted. Remove from heat and stir in half-and-half, walnuts and coconut. Spread over cupcakes or cake. Place frosted cupcakes or cake under broiler, watching constantly, until frosting bubbles, 2 or 3 minutes. Serve warm or cold.

12 to 14 servings. Each of 14 servings: 382 calories; 240 mg sodium; 69 mg cholesterol; 18 grams fat; 53 grams carbohydrates; 4 grams protein; 0.40 grams fiber.

CHOCOLATE CHESTNUT GATEAU

1988

MARGARET CLARK, FORMER CHEF AT Guenoc Winery in Northern California, came up with this recipe. If chestnut puree is not available, 1 (8 3/4-ounce) can chestnut spread (sweetened) may be substituted for the puree and the honey in the cake batter.

1/4 cup (1/2 stick) butter, plus more for greasing
2 cups crumbled canned chestnut puree
1/4 cup honey
1/4 cup brandy
1/3 cup whipping cream
1/2 pound bittersweet or semisweet chocolate, chopped
3 eggs, well beaten
2 tablespoons flour

• Line bottom of 8-inch cake pan with parchment paper. Grease pan sides and parchment paper.

• Melt 1/4 cup butter in small saucepan. Slowly incorporate well into chestnut puree in medium bowl. Add honey, brandy and cream and continue mixing until thoroughly blended.

• Melt chocolate in top of double boiler over simmering water. When melted, but only lukewarm, add 1/2 at time to chestnut mixture, mixing well at low speed. Add eggs and blend well, still at low speed. Stir in flour, mixing well.

• Pour into prepared pan and bake at 300 degrees until just set in center, 35 minutes. Remove from oven and cool completely in pan on rack.

■ HONEY SAUCE

1 cup milk
3 tablespoons honey
3 egg yolks, well beaten
1 teaspoon orange flower water

• Warm milk over medium heat until small bubbles appear around edge. Whisk honey into egg yolks, then continuing to whisk, add milk slowly until thoroughly mixed.

• Return mixture to saucepan and cook over medium-low heat, stirring constantly with wooden spoon, until slightly thickened. Do not boil. Cooked sauce should coat spoon.

• Remove from heat and strain into small bowl. Stir in orange flower water, cover and chill thoroughly before serving (sauce will thicken somewhat during cooling). Makes about 1 1/3 cups.

• Unmold onto plate just before serving. Serve with Honey Sauce.

16 servings. Each serving: 227 calories; 53 mg sodium; 107 mg cholesterol; 13 grams fat; 25 grams carbohydrates; 4 grams protein; 0.60 gram fiber.

CORN CHIFFON CAKE

CORN CAKE? IT MIGHT SOUND SURPRISING, but it's a favorite dessert in the Philippines, says former Test Kitchen Director Minnie Bernardino. This can be made without the frosting, if desired.

1 (16-ounce) can whole-kernel corn
2 1/4 cups cake flour
1 1/2 cups sugar
1 tablespoon baking powder
1 teaspoon salt
7 egg yolks
1/2 cup oil
2 teaspoons vanilla extract
8 egg whites
1/2 teaspoon cream of tartar
2 tablespoons melted butter
Butter Icing or sweetened whipped cream, optional

• Drain corn kernels well. Add water to liquid to make 3/4 cup.

• Sift together cake flour, 3/4 cup sugar, baking powder and salt into small mixer bowl. Make well in center and drop in egg yolks, oil, vanilla and corn liquid. Starting from center, beat slowly until smooth.

• Beat egg whites with cream of tartar in large mixer bowl until foamy and opaque white. Gradually add remaining 3/4 cup sugar, beating until stiff but not dry. Pour yolk batter in slow steady stream into whites, folding until just blended. Gently fold in drained corn. Fold in melted butter. Turn into ungreased tube pan.

• Bake at 325 until top springs back when touched lightly, 55 minutes to 1 hour. Invert pan on heat-proof funnel or wine bottle and let hang until cake is completely cool. Remove from pan. Wrap airtight or frost with Butter Icing, if desired.

■ BUTTER ICING
1 cup (2 sticks) butter, room temperature
2/3 cup evaporated milk
1/3 cup whipping cream, room temperature
3/4 cup sugar
1 teaspoon vanilla extract or grated lime zest

• Cream butter until light. Combine evaporated milk, whipping cream and sugar until smooth. Slowly add to creamed butter, and continue to beat at medium speed until smooth and creamy. Beat in vanilla. If mixture curdles (caused by cold temperature), blend in food processor until smooth.

Variation: Omit corn. In place of corn liquid, use 3/4 cup fruit juice such as orange or pineapple, or for coffee chiffon cake, use strong coffee, cooled.

12 servings. Each serving: 578 calories; 651 mg sodium; 222 mg cholesterol; 35 grams fat; 62 grams carbohydrates; 8 grams protein; 0.23 gram fiber.

OLD-FASHIONED
MILK CHOCOLATE CAKE
with MILK CHOCOLATE FROSTING

THIS MODEL BUTTER CAKE recipe by gifted Southern California cookbook writer Sylvia Thompson is perhaps the best you'll ever eat—three sumptuous chocolate layers. If you'd rather mix a non-chocolate butter cake, simply leave out the chocolate. For a two-layer cake, just use two-thirds of the ingredients. Remember that butter cakes should be served within 12 hours of baking.

■ CAKE

3 1/2 cups sifted cake flour
1/2 tablespoon baking soda
1/2 teaspoon baking powder
1/2 tablespoon salt
6 ounces unsweetened chocolate, chopped into 1- to 2-inch pieces
1 cup water
1 cup (2 sticks) butter, softened to consistency of mayonnaise, plus more for greasing
2 cups granulated sugar
1/2 cup light brown sugar, packed
1 1/2 tablespoons vanilla extract
6 extra-large eggs, warmed in shells
1 cup buttermilk
Unsprayed or silk leaves, such as rose, geranium or strawberry, optional

• Sift flour, baking soda, baking powder and salt together in bowl.

• In medium heat-proof bowl set over, but not touching, barely simmering water, melt chocolate in water, stirring occasionally until perfectly smooth. Remove from heat.

• In large mixing bowl, beat 1 cup butter on medium speed until creamy.

• Continue beating while sprinkling in granulated and brown sugars, 1 tablespoon at time. Add vanilla and beat until very light. Add eggs singly, beating until thoroughly blended after each, then beat until very light and creamy. Blend in chocolate. Add flour in 3 parts by sprinkling over bowl. Alternate with buttermilk in 2 parts. Beat on lowest speed manageable just until each addition disappears. Fold batter with large flexible rubber spatula just until thoroughly blended.

CONTINUED ☞

• Divide batter among greased 9-inch round cake pans with bottoms lined with wax paper. Smooth tops, then push batter slightly up against sides. Bake 2 layers on middle oven rack and 1 layer on lower oven rack, staggering so top pans are not directly over bottom pan. Bake at 350 degrees until wood pick emerges clean from center of cake, 30 to 35 minutes.

• Cool in pans on racks 15 minutes. Then turn out onto racks, top sides up, to cool completely.

■ MILK CHOCOLATE FROSTING

14 ounces milk chocolate
5 cups powdered sugar, sifted if lumpy
3/4 cup unsweetened cocoa (not Dutch-processed)
3/4 cup plus 2 tablespoons butter
7 to 8 tablespoons milk
2 tablespoons vanilla extract

• In medium heat-proof bowl set over, but not touching, barely simmering water, melt chocolate, stirring occasionally until perfectly smooth. Be careful not to let steam or water touch chocolate. Remove from heat.

• In food processor or mixing bowl, blend sugar and cocoa. Melt butter with 7 tablespoons milk at half power in microwave or over low heat. Add hot butter to sugar with chocolate and vanilla. Process or beat until smooth. Do not overprocess. If too thick, beat in remaining tablespoon hot milk. If too thin, add sugar. Spread at once.

• Up to 6 hours before serving, set thickest cake layer on platter, bottom up. Spread with 2/3 cup frosting. Repeat with second layer. Place last layer top side up. Frost top and sides, making decorative sweeps in frosting with knife. Keep cool. Do not refrigerate. Just before serving, wreathe leaves around bottom of platter.

16 servings. Each serving: 776 calories; 317 mg sodium; 145 mg cholesterol; 37 grams fat; 108 grams carbohydrates; 8 grams protein; 1.72 grams fiber.

DOUBLE CHOCOLATE CAKE

1985

YOU CAN'T HAVE TOO MANY chocolate cakes. This one is from the Royal Sonesta Hotel in Massachusetts.

1/2 cup (1 stick) plus 2 tablespoons butter, plus more for greasing
1 cup sugar
1/2 cup cocoa powder
1/2 cup water
1/2 cup plus 2 tablespoons flour, plus more for preparing pan
1/2 teaspoon salt
1 1/2 teaspoons baking powder
3/4 teaspoon baking soda
4 eggs
Orange-flavored liqueur

• Cream butter with sugar until light and creamy. Stir in cocoa and water. Beat 7 minutes on electric mixer. Add flour, salt, baking powder and baking soda. Beat 2 minutes longer. Add eggs. Mix 5 minutes longer.

• Pour batter into greased and floured 9-inch round cake pan. Bake at 350 degrees or until cake center springs back when lightly touched, 30 to 40 minutes. Invert onto wire rack to cool completely.

■ GANACHE

18 ounces semisweet chocolate (squares or chips)
1 1/2 cups whipping cream

• Melt chocolate in top of double boiler set over, but not touching, simmering water. Add whipping cream. Remove from heat. Remove 2 cups chocolate mixture and set aside. Refrigerate remaining chocolate mixture until thick and creamy.

• Use refrigerated portion for spreading between layers. Use unrefrigerated portion for glazing top layer of cake.

• Split cake into 3 horizontal layers. Drizzle orange-flavored liqueur lightly over each layer. Frost layers with refrigerated ganache. Pour remaining unrefrigerated ganache over top layer to glaze.

10 to 12 servings. Each of 12 servings: 449 calories; 242 mg sodium; 118 mg cholesterol; 33 grams fat; 41 grams carbohydrates; 5 grams protein; 0.55 gram fiber.

Cookies

BASEBALL BARS

READER CINDY GUTTENPLAN submitted these to the old *My Best Recipe* column.

★
1986

■ COOKIE

2/3 cup butter
1 cup brown sugar, packed
1/4 cup light corn syrup
1/4 cup chunky peanut butter
1 teaspoon vanilla extract
4 cups instant oatmeal

• Melt butter, brown sugar and corn syrup together. Add peanut butter and vanilla. Mix well. Stir in oats. Press mixture into greased 9-inch baking pan. Bake at 375 degrees 15 minutes.

■ TOPPING

1 (12-ounce) package semisweet chocolate pieces
1 (12-ounce) package butterscotch pieces
2/3 cup chunky peanut butter
1 cup chopped unsalted nuts

• Mix chocolate and butterscotch pieces, peanut butter and nuts in saucepan. Heat over medium heat, stirring until blended. Spread over bars. Sprinkle with nuts. Refrigerate. If too cold, let stand about 15 minutes for ease in cutting. Cut into bars.

16 to 20 bars. Each of 20 bars: 412 calories; 129 mg sodium; 16 mg cholesterol; 25 grams fat; 44 grams carbohydrates; 7 grams protein; 0.70 gram fiber.

BRANDY SNAPS

THESE COOKIES FROM LONGTIME COLUMNIST Marion Cunningham are thin caramel wafers rolled round as a fat cigar, about 2 1/2 to 3 inches long, often filled with sweetened brandy-flavored whipped cream. Traditionally, the brandy is added to the batter, but the flavor of the brandy dissipates during baking. It is better to add it to the whipped cream. These keep indefinitely in an airtight container. You can eat brandy snaps as is, without filling, or mix a little brandy into whipped cream and fill them after the rolled cookies have cooled.

1/3 cup dark corn syrup
1/2 cup (1 stick) butter, cut into pieces, plus more for greasing
1/2 cup sugar
1/2 cup flour

• Put corn syrup, butter and sugar into heavy-bottomed pan. Heat mixture over low heat, stirring, until butter has melted and mixture is smooth. Don't let mixture boil.

• Remove from heat and vigorously stir in flour, beating until smooth. (Rotary beater will do this easily.)

• Drop batter by 1/2 teaspoons on greased baking sheets. Try making only 5 cookies at a time, until you see how much they spread. Bake at 350 degrees until cookies turn nice medium caramel color, about 5 to 7 minutes. Cookies should spread into about 2 1/2-inch rounds, or little larger, and bubble.

• Remove from oven and cool until cookies are firm enough to lift off baking sheet with spatula. Roll with fingers or around clean broom handle into tubes about 3/4 inch around.

• If cookies get too firm to manage, return to oven 1 to 2 minutes to soften. If batter in pan gets too stiff to use, heat, stirring, until melted enough to drop from teaspoon.

About 3 dozen (4-inch) cookies. Each cookie: 37 calories; 15 mg sodium; 3 mg cholesterol; 1 gram fat; 6 grams carbohydrates; 0 protein; 0 fiber.

OATMEAL COOKIES

THESE COOKIES ARE SERVED at Disneyland. No wonder it is the happiest place on Earth.

2 cups flour
1/2 teaspoon salt
1/2 teaspoon baking soda
1 teaspoon baking powder
3/4 teaspoon cinnamon
1 1/3 cups butter
1 1/4 cups granulated sugar
3/4 cup brown sugar, packed
2 eggs
2 tablespoons water
1/2 teaspoon vanilla extract
2 1/2 cups uncooked oatmeal (not instant)
1 1/4 cups raisins

• Combine flour, salt, baking soda, baking powder and cinnamon in medium bowl. Set aside.

• Cream butter in very large bowl. Beat in granulated sugar and brown sugar. Beat in eggs, 1 at time. Add water and vanilla. Mix until well blended, about 4 minutes.

• Mix oats, raisins and flour mixture into sugar mixture. Stir until thoroughly blended. Drop by large tablespoons onto ungreased baking sheet. Bake at 350 degrees until light-brown in color, 9 to 14 minutes. Cool on baking sheet before removing from pan.

4 dozen cookies. Each cookie: 128 calories; 90 mg sodium; 23 mg cholesterol; 6 grams fat; 18 grams carbohydrates; 2 grams protein; 0.12 grams fiber.

JUMBLE COOKIES

THESE COOKIES COME FROM Julienne, a stylish little luncheon room and take-out store in San Marino.

1 cup plus 2 tablespoons flour
1 teaspoon baking soda
1/4 teaspoon salt
1/2 cup (1 stick) butter, softened
1/2 cup granulated sugar
1/4 cup light brown sugar, packed
1 egg
3/4 teaspoon vanilla extract
1 1/2 cups semisweet chocolate chips
1 1/4 cups unblanched whole almonds, toasted
1/4 cup chopped pecans, toasted
1 cup currants

• Sift together flour, baking soda and salt in large bowl. Cream butter, granulated sugar and brown sugar in separate mixing bowl until light and fluffy. Beat in egg and vanilla until well blended. Beat in flour mixture until incorporated.

• Stir together chocolate chips, almonds, pecans and currants in large bowl. Empty batter into nut mixture and mix evenly.

• Drop batter by rounded tablespoons onto ungreased baking sheet 2 inches apart. Press down lightly. Bake at 375 degrees until light golden brown, 10 to 12 minutes. Do not overbake.

30 cookies. Each cookie: 154 calories; 55 mg sodium; 15 mg cholesterol; 10 grams fat; 10 grams carbohydrates; 2 grams protein; 0.32 gram fiber.

HELLO DOLLIES

THESE BAR COOKIES ARE Times Food Editor Russ Parsons' wife's contribution to Christmas every year. They always get more requests than almost anything he cooks.

1 cup (2 sticks) butter
22 graham crackers (3/4 pound), crushed
2 cups shredded coconut
2 cups chocolate chips
2 cups chopped pecans
2 (14-ounce) cans sweetened condensed milk

• Melt butter in bottom of 13x9-inch baking pan in 325-degree oven. When melted, add graham cracker crumbs, mix thoroughly to moisten and spread evenly across bottom of pan. Distribute coconut evenly across graham cracker crust. Distribute chocolate chips evenly over coconut. Top with pecans, distributed evenly. Pour sweetened condensed milk over all, being careful to coat top evenly without stirring, which will disturb layers below.

• Bake at 325 degrees until center is bubbly and light brown, about 45 minutes. Cool and cut in squares.

50 cookies. Each cookie: 303 calories; 319 mg sodium; 15 mg cholesterol; 13 grams fat; 38 grams carbohydrates; 4 grams protein; 0.69 gram fiber.

POTATO CHIP COOKIES

THIS DELIGHTFULLY OLD-FASHIONED treat came from reader Frances Dewar.

1 cup (2 sticks) butter
Sugar
1 teaspoon vanilla extract
1/2 cup crushed potato chips
1/2 cup chopped mixed nuts
2 cups flour

• Cream butter and 1/2 cup sugar. Add vanilla, potato chips, nuts and flour and mix well. Form into small balls and place on ungreased baking sheets. Dip glass in sugar and flatten cookies.

• Bake at 350 degrees until firm and lightly browned, 16 to 18 minutes.

80 cookies. Each cookie: 45 calories; 34 mg sodium; 6 mg cholesterol; 3 grams fat; 3 grams carbohydrates; 1 gram protein; 0.07 gram fiber.

PISTACHIO MADELEINES

MADELEINES ARE SUCH DAINTY little cookies, but when they're done right, they pack one delicious buttery wallop. And these are done very right, indeed. They come from Keswick Hall at Monticello in Keswick, Va.

1999

1 1/2 cups (3 sticks) butter, plus more for greasing
1 1/3 cups sugar
4 eggs
1/2 teaspoon vanilla extract
Salt
1/2 cup chopped pistachios
2 cups flour

• Heat 1 1/2 cups butter in small saucepan over low heat until it melts and separates. Spoon off any foam on top. Spoon off clear clarified butter and reserve (you'll need 1 1/4 cups), leaving milky residue in pan. Discard residue. Cool clarified butter and refrigerate 2 hours until firm but not hard.

• Mix clarified butter and sugar until fluffy. Add eggs 1 at a time. Add vanilla and dash salt. Fold in pistachios and flour.

• Pipe or spoon batter into greased madeleine molds. Bake at 350 degrees until light brown, 10 to 15 minutes. Cool 10 minutes before removing from molds.

3 1/2 dozen madeleines. Each madeleine: 118 calories; 79 mg sodium; 38 mg cholesterol; 8 grams fat; 11 grams carbohydrates; 2 grams protein; 0.04 gram fiber.

LEMON SQUARES

1990

LEMON BARS DON'T GET MUCH EASIER to make than this recipe and they certainly don't get much better.

■ COOKIE

1 cup (2 sticks) butter, plus more for greasing
Powdered sugar
2 cups flour

• Blend together butter and 1/2 cup powdered sugar until pale in color. Mix in flour. Press into lightly greased 13x9-inch baking pan. Bake at 350 degrees until set, 20 to 25 minutes. Set aside.

■ FILLING

4 eggs
2 cups sugar
1/3 cup lemon juice
1/4 cup flour
1/2 teaspoon baking powder

• Combine eggs, sugar, lemon juice, flour and baking powder. Pour filling over cookie layer and bake at 350 degrees 25 to 30 minutes.
• Cool slightly, then cut into squares. Dust lightly with powdered sugar.

3 dozen squares. Each square: 129 calories; 65 mg sodium; 37 mg cholesterol; 6 grams fat; 18 grams carbohydrates; 2 grams protein; 0.02 gram fiber.

PLEASANTVILLE DELUXE DATE SQUARES

THIS IS THE EPITOME OF A California cookie: chewy, nutty and packed with the flavor of dates. All this despite the fact that it comes from Canadian writer Marcy Goldman, a frequent contributor to the Food section.

1999

2 1/2 cups pitted dates (about 1 1/4 pounds)
1 2/3 cups light brown sugar, packed
1 cup water
1 teaspoon vanilla extract
1 tablespoon lemon juice
1/4 teaspoon orange oil, optional
1 1/2 cups flour
1 1/2 cups oatmeal
1/2 teaspoon baking soda
1/4 teaspoon salt
1/8 teaspoon cinnamon
1 cup (2 sticks) cold butter

• Combine dates, 2/3 cup brown sugar, water, vanilla, lemon juice and orange oil in 2-quart saucepan. Bring to simmer over medium heat. Cook until dates are softened, 1 to 3 minutes. Remove from stove and cool. Puree in food processor until smooth

• Place flour, oatmeal, 1 cup brown sugar, baking soda, salt and cinnamon in work bowl of food processor. Pulse to combine, then add chunks of butter until mixture is crumbly.

• Pat 1/2 mixture into lightly greased 9-inch-square baking pan. Cover with date mixture, spreading evenly. Top with remaining crumb mixture as evenly as possible. Press down lightly.

• Place pan on baking sheet. Bake at 350 degrees until top is golden brown, 30 to 40 minutes. Cool 20 minutes then put in freezer 20 minutes before cutting into squares.

12 to 16 squares. Each of 16 squares: 327 calories; 47 mg sodium; 31 mg cholesterol; 12 grams fat; 56 grams carbohydrates; 3 grams protein; 0.73 gram fiber.

SOFT CHOCOLATE CHIP COOKIES

1987

EVERYONE HAS THEIR OWN IDEA about what the ideal chocolate chip cookie tastes like. This is one that we published in 1987 in response to a request for something like the ones that the newly popular Mrs. Fields stores made. Whether it is the best chocolate chip cookie or not is open to debate, but it was voted one of our best recipes of that year.

1 cup (2 sticks) butter
1 cup granulated sugar
1 cup brown sugar, packed
2 eggs
1 teaspoon vanilla extract
2 cups flour
2 1/2 cups oatmeal
1/2 teaspoon salt
1 teaspoon baking powder
1 teaspoon baking soda
1 (12-ounce) package semisweet chocolate pieces
1 (4-ounce) bar milk chocolate, grated
1 1/2 cups chopped nuts

• Cream butter with granulated sugar and brown sugar. Add eggs and vanilla, beating well.

• Mix together flour, oatmeal, salt, baking powder and baking soda. Place small amounts in blender and process until mixture turns into powder.

• Mix butter-egg mixture with flour mixture until just blended. Add chocolate pieces, milk chocolate and chopped nuts. Roll into balls about size of golf balls and place 2 inches apart on ungreased baking sheet.

• Bake at 375 degrees until firm and lightly browned, 12 minutes.

3 to 4 dozen cookies. Each of 4 dozen cookies: 177 calories; 108 mg sodium; 20 mg cholesterol; 10 grams fat; 22 grams carbohydrates; 3 grams protein; 0.17 gram fiber.

SOFT MOLASSES COOKIES

OVER THE YEARS, MANY READERS have requested the recipe for the soft molasses cookies that were sold off the Helm's Bakery trucks that used to roam the Southland. This is the closest we could come, and it's a good one.

1997

1/2 cup (1 stick) butter, softened, plus more for greasing
1/2 cup sugar
3/4 cup molasses
1 egg
2 1/2 cups flour, plus more for preparing baking sheets
1 1/2 teaspoons ground ginger
1 teaspoon cinnamon
1/4 teaspoon salt
2 teaspoons baking soda
1/4 cup water

• Beat _ cup butter with sugar until light and fluffy. Beat in molasses and egg.

• Sift flour with ginger, cinnamon and salt.

• Dissolve baking soda in water. Add flour mixture to butter mixture, then add baking soda mixture, beating well between additions.

• Drop by tablespoons onto greased and floured baking sheets. Bake at 400 degrees until cracked and barely set, about 10 minutes. Remove from baking sheets and cool on wire racks.

3 dozen cookies. Each cookie: 81 calories; 47 mg sodium; 13 mg cholesterol; 3 grams fat; 13 grams carbohydrates; 1 gram protein; 0.03 gram fiber.

KOURAMBIEDES

1995

THESE ARE THE MOST DELICATE little cookies, mostly butter and powdered sugar. They're the ones that are served by the thousands every year by ladies of the St. Nicholas Orthodox Church at the Valley Greek Festival.

2 cups (4 sticks) butter, softened
1/2 cup sifted powdered sugar, plus more for coating
1 egg yolk
1 tablespoon Bourbon
4 cups flour

• Whip butter in electric mixer until white and fluffy, about 25 minutes. Add 1/2 cup sifted powdered sugar, egg yolk and Bourbon. Mix well. Add flour gradually and beat until dough is very soft but can be handled without sticking.

• Shape dough into walnut-size balls. Place on ungreased baking sheets and flatten slightly. With finger tip, make depression in center of each.

• Bake at 325 degrees until lightly browned, about 25 minutes.

• Immediately remove cookies from hot baking sheet and place on another baking sheet thickly coated with sifted powdered sugar. Cover with additional sifted powdered sugar. Cool completely. Place in individual paper cups and store in airtight container.

3 dozen cookies. Each cookie: 146 calories; 2 mg sodium; 35 mg cholesterol; 10 grams fat; 11 grams carbohydrates; 2 grams protein; 0.04 gram fiber.

MACAROONS

SUMI CHANG, THE OWNER OF Europane in Pasadena, gave us the recipe for these amazing sticky, chewy macaroons shaped like little haystacks—or as Chang put it, "witches' hats." The quality and plumpness of the coconut make the cookie. She uses unsweetened shredded organic coconut from health food stores.

1 cup egg whites
4 cups sugar
8 cups unsweetened shredded and preferably organic coconut, divided into 2 equal parts

• Mix egg whites and sugar in double boiler set over, but not touching, simmering water, and slowly bring to 90 degrees on candy thermometer (little hot to the touch). Remove from heat.

• Add half of coconut. Mix thoroughly. Cool few minutes. Add remaining coconut. Refrigerate 1 hour. Shape into pyramid, or cone or "haystack" shapes. After macaroons are shaped, chill 30 minutes or longer.

• Bake at 350 degrees until golden brown, 15 to 20 minutes.

4 dozen cookies. Each cookie: 160 calories; 14 mg sodium; 0 cholesterol; 9 grams fat; 20 grams carbohydrates; 2 grams protein; 0.75 gram fiber.

VACUUM CLEANER COOKIES

1986

REMEMBER THE URBAN LEGEND about the Neiman Marcus cookie recipe? That was a fake story about a cookie that never existed. But these bar cookies have been served at Neiman Marcus cafes for years. Do not use the cake mix with pudding added.

1/2 cup (1 stick) margarine (not butter), melted
1 (18 1/4-ounce) box yellow cake mix
3 eggs
1 (8-ounce) package cream cheese, softened
1 (1-pound) box powdered sugar
1/2 cup flaked coconut
1/2 cup chopped walnuts or pecans

• Combine margarine, cake mix and 1 egg. Stir together until dry ingredients are moistened. Pat mixture into bottom of well-greased 15x10-inch jellyroll pan.

• Beat remaining 2 eggs lightly, then beat in cream cheese and powdered sugar. Stir in coconut and nuts. Pour over mixture in jellyroll pan, spreading evenly. Bake at 325 degrees until golden brown, 45 to 50 minutes. Cool pan on wire rack to room temperature.

4 dozen bars. Each bar: 132 calories; 113 mg sodium; 18 mg cholesterol; 6 grams fat; 19 grams carbohydrates; 1 gram protein; 0.08 gram fiber.

WORLD'S BEST SUGAR COOKIES

WHAT IS IT ABOUT SOMETHING as innocent as a sugar cookie that prompts people to make such extravagant claims? We're not sure, but this recipe from reader Doris Ray certainly deserves its applause.

1989

1 cup (2 sticks) butter
1 cup powdered sugar
Granulated sugar
2 eggs
1 cup oil
2 teaspoons vanilla extract
1 teaspoon baking soda
1 teaspoon cream of tartar
1/2 teaspoon salt
5 cups flour

• Cream butter with powdered sugar and 1 cup granulated sugar in large bowl. Beat in eggs until smooth. Slowly stir in oil, vanilla, baking soda, cream of tartar, salt and flour.

• Chill for easy handling. Shape into walnut-size balls. Dip in sugar.

• Place on baking sheet and press down. Bake at 350 degrees 10 to 12 minutes.

4 dozen cookies. Each cookie: 151 calories; 71 mg sodium; 19 mg cholesterol; 9 grams fat; 17 grams carbohydrates; 2 grams protein; 0.04 gram fiber.

ELEVEN

Pies and Tarts

APPLES *and* CREAM CRUMB PIE

THERE'S NOTHING BETTER THAN apple pie, and there may be no apple pie better than this one. It came from Wonderful Parties, Wonderful Foods, a Culver City catering company.

■ CINNAMON PASTRY SHELL

1 3/4 cups flour, plus more for rolling
1/4 cup sugar
1 teaspoon ground cinnamon
1/2 teaspoon salt
2/3 cup cold butter
2 to 3 tablespoons cold water

• Combine flour, sugar, cinnamon and salt in mixer bowl. Cut in cold butter until particles are size of small peas. Sprinkle in cold water, 1 tablespoon at time, tossing with fork until all flour is moistened and pastry almost cleans side of bowl.

• Gather into ball. On lightly floured board, roll pastry 2 inches larger than inverted 10-inch pie plate. Ease into pie plate and crimp edges decoratively.

■ SOUR CREAM FILLING

1 1/2 cups sour cream
1 egg
1 cup sugar
1/4 cup flour
2 teaspoons vanilla extract
1/2 teaspoon salt
3 pounds apples, peeled, cored and cut in thin wedges

• Combine sour cream, egg, sugar, flour, vanilla and salt in large bowl. Add apples and mix well. Turn into pie shell. Cover crimped edges lightly with foil. Bake at 450 degrees 10 minutes, reduce heat to 350 degrees and continue baking 35 to 40 minutes.

• Remove pie from oven. Stir apple filling, gently but thoroughly.

• Remove foil around edges.

■ STREUSEL TOPPING

1/2 cup flour
1/3 cup granulated sugar
1/3 cup brown sugar, packed
1 tablespoon cinnamon
1/4 teaspoon salt
1/2 cup (1 stick) cold butter
1 cup coarsely chopped walnuts

CONTINUED☞

- Combine flour, granulated sugar, brown sugar, cinnamon and salt in bowl. Cut in cold butter until crumbly. Add walnuts.

- Spoon Streusel Topping evenly on top of filling. Return to oven and bake 15 to 20 minutes longer. Serve warm, at room temperature or cold.

6 to 8 servings. Each of 8 servings: 849 calories; 676 mg sodium; 118 mg cholesterol; 47 grams fat; 106 grams carbohydrates; 9 grams protein; 1.70 grams fiber.

COCONUT CREAM PIE

THIS VERSION OF THE CLASSIC American pie comes from the cafes of the now-defunct Broadway department store chain.

1987

3/4 cup cornstarch
1 1/2 cups sugar
1/2 teaspoon salt
4 cups milk, scalded
2 eggs
1/2 tablespoon vanilla extract
2 tablespoons margarine
1/2 teaspoon coconut extract
1 cup coarsely shredded fresh coconut
1 10-inch pie shell, baked
4 cups whipped topping or whipped cream

- Combine cornstarch, sugar and salt and mix well. Gradually stir scalded milk into cornstarch mixture. Bring to boil, stirring constantly, and boil 2 minutes until thickened and shiny. Add small amount of hot mixture to eggs and beat until blended. Return to pan and whip 2 minutes over medium heat until slightly thickened, being careful not to curdle mixture.

- Remove from heat and add vanilla and margarine, mixing until smooth. Pour through sieve. Place plastic wrap directly over cream. Set aside to cool.

- Add coconut extract and 1/2 cup coconut to cooled pie cream. Pour into pie shell. Chill. Spread whipped topping over pie, mounding in center.

- Sprinkle with remaining 1/2 cup coconut.

6 to 8 servings. Each of 8 servings: 599 calories; 374 mg sodium; 85 mg cholesterol; 29 grams fat; 76 grams carbohydrates; 9 grams protein; 0.50 grams fiber.

ASIAN PEAR TART

1998

CHEF SUZANNE TRACHT, FORMERLY WITH Jozu in West Hollywood, came up with this recipe that shows off the subtle pear taste and the terrific crispness of Asian pears. The recipe can also be made with apples or European pear varieties.

■ SWEET DOUGH

2 cups (4 sticks) butter, ice cold and cut into 1/2-inch pieces
2 cups powdered sugar
3 egg yolks
1/4 cup whipping cream
4 3/4 cups flour

• Beat butter and powdered sugar on medium speed in electric mixer fitted with paddle attachment 5 minutes. Scrape down sides of bowl. Add yolks 1 at a time with mixer on low speed. Add cream and mix at medium speed 1 minute. Turn off mixer and add flour. Mix on low speed until combined. Do not over mix.
• Divide dough in half, wrap in plastic wrap and refrigerate 1 hour.

■ BROWN SUGAR FILLING

1 1/2 cups light brown sugar, packed
1/3 cup flour
1/4 teaspoon cinnamon

• Combine brown sugar, flour and cinnamon in bowl and stir until there are no lumps. Set aside.

■ ASSEMBLY

1/4 cup (1/2 stick) butter, plus more for greasing tart shells
Flour for dusting tart shells
2 1/4 cups whipping cream
3 to 5 Asian pears, cored and cut into 1/4-inch-thick slices

• Butter and flour 12 (4 1/2-inch) or 2 (10-inch) tart shells. Remove 1 piece Sweet Dough from refrigerator and roll out 1/4 inch thick. If making individual tarts, cut dough into 6-inch rounds. Line tart shells with dough, trimming any excess dough even with edge of tart shell. Repeat with remaining piece of dough.
• Fill each tart shell half way with Brown Sugar Filling. For individual tarts, dot each with 1 teaspoon butter in pieces and spoon on 3 tablespoons cream. Arrange 1/4 to 1/2 Asian pear, depending on size of fruit, on each tart. Bake at 325 degrees until golden brown, about 35 minutes.
• For 10-inch tarts, dot each with 2 tablespoons butter in pieces and spoon on 9 tablespoons cream. Arrange Asian pear slices on each tart. Bake at 325 degrees until golden brown, 45 to 50 minutes.

12 servings. Each serving: 869 calories; 379 mg sodium; 230 mg cholesterol; 55 grams fat; 79 grams carbohydrates; 8 grams protein; 0.15 gram fiber.

BUTTERMILK PIE

THIS OLD-FASHIONED PIE from the Los Angeles public schools is one of our most requested recipes.

3/4 cup sugar
1/8 teaspoon salt
2 tablespoons plus 1 teaspoon flour
4 eggs, separated
1 3/4 cups buttermilk
1/2 cup (1 stick) butter, melted
1 3/4 teaspoons vanilla extract
1 unbaked (9-inch) deep-dish pie shell

• Stir sugar, salt and flour together in mixing bowl. Add egg yolks, buttermilk, butter and vanilla. Blend well.

• In separate bowl, whip egg whites until moist peaks form, 1 minute.

• Fold beaten egg whites into buttermilk mixture. Do not over-mix.

• Pour 1 quart (4 cups) buttermilk custard mixture into unbaked pie shell. (Any remaining custard filling may be poured into cups and baked at 350 degrees until set, about 25 to 35 minutes.)

• Bake pie at 300 degrees until knife inserted in center comes out clean and top is crusty and golden brown, about 55 to 60 minutes.

6 servings. Each serving: 579 calories; 421 mg sodium; 186 mg cholesterol; 37 grams fat; 53 grams carbohydrates; 10 grams protein; 0.10 gram fiber.

CHOCOLATE-BUCKWHEAT TART

1992

ON THE FACE OF IT, CHOCOLATE and buckwheat don't sound compatible. But cook-book author Ken Haedrich points out that since both are quite assertive, they actually complement one another, and this tart proves his point. It's rich, sophisticated and delicious.

■ BUCKWHEAT-COCOA TART SHELL

3/4 cup buckwheat flour
1/2 cup unbleached flour
2 1/2 tablespoons sugar
1 tablespoon unsweetened cocoa powder, sifted
1/4 teaspoon salt
1/2 cup (1 stick) cold butter, cut into 1/4-inch pieces
1 1/2 to 2 tablespoons ice-cold water

• Combine buckwheat flour and unbleached flour with sugar, cocoa powder and salt in large bowl. Stir well. Add butter and cut in thoroughly until mixture resembles fine crumbs. Sprinkle on 1 tablespoon water, tossing and compacting mixture with fork. Sprinkle on another 1/2 tablespoon water and continue to toss and compact, adding remaining 1/2 tablespoon water, if needed, to allow dough to be gathered into ball. Knead dough in bowl several times to distribute fat. Gather in ball.

• Place dough on sheet of plastic wrap and flatten with palm into disk about 1/2 inch thick. Wrap in plastic wrap, then refrigerate about 30 minutes. (If dough is refrigerated longer, it will be too cold to roll out easily. If dough is too cold, let pastry stand at room temperature about 10 minutes before rolling.)

• Place dough on lightly floured sheet of wax paper and roll into 11-inch circle. Leave pastry on paper and invert over 9-inch tart pan.

• Center pastry, then peel off paper. Gently tuck pastry into crease of pan. Pastry will be slightly fragile and may develop cracks at this point. Remedy by pushing dough back together. Take any overhanging dough and push against side of pan even with top of pan, to push side up.

• Refrigerate or freeze pastry 30 minutes to firm up.

• Line pastry with foil and weights and bake at 400 degrees 20 minutes.

• Remove foil and weights and bake another 10 to 12 minutes. Shell will be shade or two darker when done and will feel crisp, not soft. Cool. Makes 1 (9-inch) tart pan.

CONTINUED ☛

■ FILLING

3/4 cup whipping cream
1/4 cup milk
1/3 cup plus 2 tablespoons sugar
6 ounces unsweetened chocolate, coarsely chopped
1 1/2 teaspoons vanilla extract
1 egg, lightly beaten
Lightly sweetened whipped cream, optional
Almond extract, optional

• Heat whipping cream, milk and sugar in small saucepan over medium heat until very hot. Add chocolate, turn off heat and whisk until smooth, about 15 seconds. Stir in vanilla. Let mixture stand in saucepan 15 minutes. Whisk egg into chocolate mixture just until smooth.

• Scrape filling into Buckwheat-Cocoa Tart Shell and bake at 350 degrees just until surface looks set and edge looks slightly dry, 20 to 25 minutes. Transfer to rack and cool in pan.

• Slice and serve warm or at room temperature with lightly sweetened whipped cream flavored with drop of almond extract. Store tart in cool spot, covered with plastic wrap.

8 servings. Each serving: 612 calories; 134 mg sodium; 119 mg cholesterol; 44 grams fat; 47 grams carbohydrates; 9 grams protein; 0.34 gram fiber.

CREME BRULEE TART

EVEN IN THE EARLY DAYS OF California cuisine, creme brulee was ubiquitous. In response to the overabundance of burnt sugar, Jimmy Brinkley, the original pastry chef of Michael's restaurant in Santa Monica, came up with this variation when the restaurant opened in 1979. Today, we're still eating too much creme brulée and Brinkley's alternative seems practically new. Note that the Pate Sucree recipe makes much more pastry than you'll need for a single tart; it's designed to make four (10-inch) tart crusts. But the pastry freezes well; you may also divide the recipe in half.

■ PATE SUCREE

5 1/3 cups flour
3/4 cup granulated sugar
2 cups (4 sticks) butter, chilled and cut into 1-inch cubes
3 large egg yolks
3 tablespoons whipping cream

• Put flour and sugar into bowl of mixer fitted with dough hook. With mixer on low, add butter and mix until ingredients resemble cornmeal, about 10 minutes. (Food processor may also be used.)

• In separate bowl, whisk together egg yolks and cream until smooth.

• Increase mixer speed to medium and add yolk-cream mixture. As soon as dough comes together (should just take few seconds), stop mixer. Divide dough into 4 equal pieces. Gather each piece of dough into ball; wrap each in plastic wrap. Chill in refrigerator 30 to 60 minutes before using.

■ FILLING

3 cups whipping cream
7 large egg yolks
6 tablespoons granulated sugar
3/4 cup brown sugar, packed

• Bring cream to boil in heavy saucepan over medium heat. At same time, bring water to boil in bottom of double boiler, then reduce heat to simmer. Combine egg yolks and granulated sugar in top of double boiler set over simmering water. Whisk together until mixture is very thick.

• Whisking continuously, pour hot cream into yolks. Reduce heat to low and let mixture cook 30 minutes, whisking about every 3 minutes.

CONTINUED ☞

- Place cake ring 8 inches in diameter and 2 inches high on baking sheet lined with parchment paper. Roll out pastry to circle about 10 inches in diameter. Roll pastry around rolling pin and unroll onto cake ring. Press pastry into bottom and up sides of ring, raising and pinching edges just barely over rim. Place large flat coffee filter inside and fill with pie weights or beans. Bake pastry at 350 degrees on bottom oven rack until edges are light golden brown, about 20 minutes. Remove pie weights and filter. Slide circle of heavy cardboard under pastry and remove ring.

- Fill pastry shell with thick cream mixture. Using sifter, sift even layer of brown sugar on top. Crimp strip of foil over edge of pastry to prevent burning. Place dessert in heated broiler and broil until sugar is melted, 1 to 1 1/2 minutes, watching carefully to prevent burning.

- Refrigerate tart until filling sets, about 2 hours.

------

6 to 8 servings. Each of 8 servings: 678 calories; 51 mg sodium; 420 mg cholesterol; 51 grams fat; 51 grams carbohydrates; 7 grams protein; 0.06 grams fiber.

JUNE BLUEBERRY PIE

★
1993
♥

THIS LOW-FAT DESSERT is absolutely irresistible and extraordinarily fresh-tasting. It comes from former staff writer Kathie Jenkins' mother, Ardell Kochevar of Aurora, Minn. If you like to experiment, try other fresh fruits in season, such as raspberries or peaches.

■ LOW-FAT PASTRY CRUST

1 cup cake flour, plus more for rolling
2 tablespoons sugar
1/2 teaspoon salt
1/8 teaspoon baking powder
3 tablespoons butter, cut up
2 tablespoon thawed nonfat egg substitute (equivalent to 1/2 egg)
1 to 1 1/2 tablespoons water
1/4 teaspoon vanilla extract

• Combine flour, sugar, salt and baking powder in bowl. Cut in butter until size of small peas. Combine egg substitute, water and vanilla. Stir into flour mixture with fork. Gather dough into small flattened round.

• Chill dough for ease in handling. Roll out on lightly floured board to fit 9-inch pie plate. Gently pierce bottom and sides with fork. Bake at 375 degrees until lightly browned, 12 to 15 minutes. Remove to wire rack to cool. Makes 1 (9-inch) pie shell.

■ FILLING

3 cups blueberries
Water
Juice of 1 lemon
3/4 cup sugar
3 tablespoons cornstarch
Non-fat, non-dairy whipped topping, optional
Blueberries, optional
Mint leaves

• Rinse blueberries and drain. Set aside few blueberries for garnish. Place 1 cup berries, 2 tablespoons water, lemon juice and sugar in medium saucepan. Heat to boiling. Heat and stir 3 minutes. Blend together cornstarch and 3 tablespoons water until smooth. Stir into blueberries.

• Bring to boil. Heat and stir until thickened and clear. Remove from heat. Stir in remaining blueberries. Turn into cooled baked pie shell.

• Chill until set. Pipe with non-fat, non-dairy whipped topping. Garnish with blueberries and mint leaves.

8 servings. Each serving: 216 calories; 181 mg sodium; 12 mg cholesterol; 5 grams fat; 43 grams carbohydrates; 2 grams protein; 0.74 gram fiber.

LAVENDER FIG TART

THIS RECIPE FROM FOOD EDITOR Russ Parsons captures the essence of late summer in Southern California. The figs are sweet and melting, and lavender sugar sprinkled over top accents their slightly herbal flavor.

■ PASTRY SHELL

1 1/4 cups flour, plus more for rolling
1 tablespoon sugar
Salt
1/2 cup (1 stick) butter, plus more for greasing
2 to 3 tablespoons water

• Combine flour, sugar, dash salt and butter in food processor or mixing bowl and cut together until mixture resembles coarse meal. Add water 1 tablespoon at a time, stirring constantly, until mixture just begins to come together. Remove from bowl and knead lightly and briefly to make smooth mass. Wrap in plastic wrap and refrigerate 30 minutes.

• When chilled, remove plastic wrap and place dough on well-floured work surface. Roll out into circle roughly 11 inches in diameter. Fold in quarters and transfer to greased 9-inch tart pan with removable bottom.

• Unfold and gently press into pan. Trim rim 1 inch from pan edge and fold extra dough between pan and dough rim to make taller edge. Refrigerate 30 minutes.

• Bake at 425 degrees until firm and rim begins to brown, about 10 minutes.

■ FIG FILLING

1 pound fresh figs
1 (8-ounce) jar raspberry jam
1 tablespoon water
Juice of 1/2 lemon
3 tablespoons sugar
1 tablespoon minced lavender leaves
Barely sweetened whipped cream

• Trim stems from figs and cut crosses in tops, coming down nearly to bottom, so fig will open like a flower. Heat jam, water and lemon juice over medium-high heat until smooth and flowing. Cook until slightly thickened, about 5 minutes. Pour mixture through strainer into baked tart crust. Spread evenly across bottom.

• Arrange figs in tart, pressing them open first and then arranging to cover as much of bottom as possible. Combine sugar and lavender in small bowl and stir to combine. Strain out chunks of lavender and sprinkle flavored sugar over top of figs. Bake at 425 degrees until figs soften, about 10 minutes. Cool slightly and serve with whipped cream.

6 to 8 servings. Each of 8 servings: 321 calories; 151 mg sodium; 31 mg cholesterol; 12 grams fat; 54 grams carbohydrates; 3 grams protein; 0.73 gram fiber.

LEMON CURD TART

THIS RECIPE BY FOOD EDITOR Russ Parsons is the perfect ending to a heavy winter meal. Tart and sweet with a fine taste of butter, it is even better when made with Meyer lemons, a common backyard fruit in Southern California.

1 (9-inch) prebaked tart shell, cooled
2 whole eggs
2 egg yolks
1/4 teaspoon salt
1/2 cup sugar
1/2 cup lemon juice
Zest of 1 lemon
6 tablespoons cold butter, cut in pieces

• Beat eggs, yolks, salt and sugar in small saucepan until smooth and light colored. Add lemon juice, lemon zest and butter and cook over medium heat, stirring constantly, until butter melts, about 5 minutes.

• Reduce heat to medium-low and continue cooking until curd is thick enough that it coats back of spoon and when you draw your finger across the curd it leaves a definite track, about 5 minutes. Curd should as thick as thick hollandaise. Pour through fine strainer into cooled tart shell.

6 servings. Each serving: 472 calories; 338 mg sodium; 193 mg cholesterol; 32 grams fat; 41 grams carbohydrates; 6 grams protein; 0.09 gram fiber.

FROZEN PEANUT BUTTER PIE

THOUGH THE COMBINATION OF chocolate and peanut butter might make you think of a similarly named candy, this dessert actually comes from Reese's Country Inn in Niagara Falls.

1986

■ COCOA-GRAHAM CRACKER CRUST

2 1/3 cups graham cracker crumbs
3/4 cup (1 1/2 sticks) melted butter
1/3 cup superfine granulated sugar
2/3 cup sifted cocoa powder

• Mix together crumbs, butter, sugar and cocoa until well incorporated. Press firmly into 9-inch pie plate to make solid bottom crust. Freeze until ready to use.

■ FILLING

2 3/4 pints vanilla ice cream
1/2 cup peanut butter
2 ounces semisweet chocolate pieces
Sweetened whipped cream

• Stir vanilla ice cream with peanut butter and chocolate pieces by hand. Spoon into Cocoa-Graham Cracker Crust. Freeze immediately until solid, about 2 hours or overnight. Do not allow ice cream to become too soft before mixing with peanut butter. If using electric mixer, do not over-mix. Mix at slow speed.

■ CHOCOLATE SAUCE

1/2 cup sugar
1/3 cup water
1 tablespoon corn syrup
2 1/4 ounces sweet chocolate, grated
1/4 cup whipping cream

• Combine sugar, water, corn syrup and chocolate in saucepan. Bring to boil. Remove immediately from heat and stir until smooth. In separate saucepan, bring cream to boil. Stir into chocolate mixture until smooth. Serve over top of pie.

16 servings. Each serving: 762 calories; 330 mg sodium; 150 mg cholesterol; 51 grams fat; 73 grams carbohydrates; 10 grams protein; 0.57 gram fiber.

PEACH MARZIPAN STREUSEL PIE

1991

FORMER TEST KITCHEN DIRECTOR Minnie Bernardino and her then-assistant Donna Deane created this recipe for a story on local summer produce. Like everything made with peaches, this one is at its best only when the fruit is at its peak.

■ ALMOND CRUST

1 cup ground almonds
1 1/2 cups flour
1/4 cup sugar
2/3 cup butter, melted
1 teaspoon almond extract
1 egg white, lightly beaten

• Combine almonds, flour and sugar in bowl. Add melted butter, almond extract and egg white. Mix well. Press into 9-inch pie plate. Cover with foil, then pie weights (or rice or beans). Bake at 375 degrees 12 minutes. Cool. Carefully remove foil and pie weights.

■ FILLING

4 cups sliced peeled peaches, about 6 large
1 cup sugar
1/4 cup quick-cooking tapioca

• Combine peaches, sugar and tapioca in bowl. Turn into Almond Crust.

■ MARZIPAN STREUSEL TOPPING

1/2 cup flour
1/2 cup brown sugar, packed
1 teaspoon vanilla extract
1/4 teaspoon salt
1/4 cup (1/2 stick) cold butter, cut up
1/4 cup marzipan or almond paste

• Combine flour, brown sugar, vanilla and salt in bowl. Rub in cold butter and marzipan until crumbly. Sprinkle over filling. Cover crust rim with foil.

• Bake at 325 degrees 45 to 55 minutes, checking after 30 minutes if topping is getting too browned. Cover top with foil if necessary. Cool.

• Serve warm or at room temperature.

8 servings. Each serving: 578 calories; 298 mg sodium; 56 mg cholesterol; 27 grams fat; 80 grams carbohydrates; 7 grams protein; 1.21 grams fiber.

ORANGE-APPLE PIE *with* ALMONDS

JEREMY KISNER, ONLY 18 at the time, submitted this dessert in our My Best Recipe contest. It was not only selected for that, but it was one of our best recipes of the whole year.

1988

■ ORANGE CRUST

2 cups flour
1/4 teaspoon salt
2 tablespoons sugar
3/4 cup shortening
3 to 4 tablespoons orange juice

• Combine flour, salt and sugar in small bowl. Cut in shortening until crumbly. Slowly add orange juice while mixing flour mixture.

• Add just enough juice until dough sticks together. Divide into 2 portions. Chill dough while making filling. Roll each dough portion thinly and use 1 to line bottom of 9-inch pie plate while reserving other for top crust.

■ FILLING

5 to 6 green apples
3 tablespoons cornstarch
1 1/4 cups sugar
1/2 cup golden raisins
1/4 cup orange liqueur
1 tablespoon grated orange zest
1 egg yolk diluted with 2 tablespoons water
1/2 cup finely chopped almonds

• Peel and slice apples into thin wedges. Combine with cornstarch, sugar, raisins, orange liqueur and zest. Turn into bottom of Orange Crust. Cover with top crust and brush top with egg wash.

• Seal and flute edges. Sprinkle top with almonds. Cut vents on top and bake at 375 degrees until golden brown, 1 hour. (If crust seems to brown too fast, cover with foil.)

8 servings. Each serving: 577 calories; 79 mg sodium; 34 mg cholesterol; 25 grams fat; 83 grams carbohydrates; 6 grams protein; 0.86 gram fiber.

ALMOND TART

1996

THIS DESSERT HAS BEEN PART of the menu at Chez Panisse since the day the restaurant opened. Talk about a dish with staying power.

■ TART PASTRY

1/2 cup (1 stick) butter
1 cup flour
1 tablespoon sugar
3 to 4 drops almond extract
3 to 4 drops vanilla extract
1 tablespoon cold water

• Cut butter into bits and let soften slightly. Mix flour and sugar in bowl. Cut butter into flour with pastry blender or 2 knives until mixture resembles coarse meal.

• Combine almond and vanilla extracts with cold water in small bowl, then quickly stir mixture into flour. Gather dough into ball and flatten slightly. Cover with plastic wrap and chill at least 1 hour.

• Allow dough to stand at room temperature briefly until it is malleable. Roll out dough and press into 9-inch tart form with removable ring, reserving small amount. Press dough evenly over bottom and sides of pan, about 1/8-inch thick, and extend dough 1/8 inch above top of ring.

• Prick shell lightly and refrigerate at least 1 hour. Dough may be refrigerated 8 hours or frozen.

• Partly bake tart shell at 400 degrees until shell begins to set and brown, about 10 minutes. Remove shell to cake rack and cool to room temperature. Patch any holes in shell by smoothing very small bit of reserved dough over tears.

CONTINUED☞

■ FILLING

1 cup whipping cream
3/4 cup sugar
Salt
1 tablespoon Grand Marnier
1 tablespoon kirsch
2 drops almond extract
1 cup blanched sliced almonds

• Bring whipping cream, sugar, dash salt, Grand Marnier, kirsch and almond extract to full rolling boil in large, heavy saucepan. Cook until liquid bubbles thickly and has silky texture, about 5 minutes. Remove from heat and add almonds. Set aside 15 minutes to steep, then pour into prepared tart shell.

• Line floor of oven with foil and bake tart on center rack at 350 degrees 20 to 30 minutes. Filling will bubble up and may overflow, then settle and begin to caramelize. Rotate tart frequently during last 15 minutes of baking so top is even deep golden brown. Remove tart to cake rack and let cool to room temperature before cutting.

6 to 8 servings. Each of 8 servings: 450 calories; 160 mg sodium; 72 mg cholesterol; 32 grams fat; 35 grams carbohydrates; 6 grams protein; 0.46 gram fiber.

APPLE TART

NORTH HOLLYWOOD'S PRODUCTION CATERERS, which specialized in cooking for film and television crews, came up with this tart. It was developed by the firm's chef, German Montoya.

■ TART SHELL

1 cup flour
3 1/2 tablespoons sugar
3 1/4 ounces butter
1/2 lightly beaten egg
1/2 teaspoon vanilla extract

• Mix flour and sugar in bowl. Cut butter into small pieces, add to bowl and mix until crumbly. Add egg and vanilla. Form dough into ball, wrap securely and refrigerate 4 hours or overnight. Roll out dough and fit into 9-inch tart pan with removable bottom.

■ FILLING

5 cups peeled, cored, sliced apples
Lemon juice
1/4 cup sugar
1 1/2 tablespoons flour
1 teaspoon cinnamon
1/4 teaspoon ground nutmeg

• Peel apples. Cut into eighths, removing core section. Sprinkle lightly with lemon juice. Add sugar, flour, cinnamon and nutmeg and mix well.

• Place apples in Tart Shell, mounding in center.

■ CRUMB TOPPING

3/4 cup flour
3/4 cup brown sugar, packed
1 teaspoon cinnamon
1/2 cup (1 stick) butter

• Combine flour, sugar and cinnamon in bowl. Cut butter into small pieces, add to bowl and mix until crumbly. Sprinkle evenly over filled tart shell and pack apples securely into shell. Bake at 350 degrees 45 minutes. Remove to rack to cool. Remove outer rim of tart pan to serve.

6 servings. Each serving: 599 calories; 298 mg sodium; 93 mg cholesterol; 29 grams fat; 83 grams carbohydrates; 5 grams protein; 0.81 gram fiber.

FAIRY PIE

1986

GOAT CHEESE HAS BECOME so commonplace in California cooking that it is almost a stereotype. Even goat milk is pretty much of a dairy section staple these days. But back in 1986, goat products were new, and this recipe from baker Gerda Jacobsen was something pretty special. It was one of our best recipes of the year. A variation on an old-time recipe, Fairy Pie is not so much a pie as a cake. Baked with a meringue-nut topping, the "pie" is cut into wedges and served with whipped cream and raspberry sauce.

1/2 cup (1 stick) butter
1 1/4 cups sugar
1/2 cup plus 2 tablespoons flour
1 teaspoon baking powder
Salt
4 eggs, separated
1/4 cup goat milk
1 teaspoon vanilla extract
1 cup chopped walnuts, optional
1 (10-ounce) package frozen raspberries, packed in sugar syrup
1 1/2 teaspoons cornstarch, or less
Whipped Cream

Cream together butter and 1/2 cup sugar. Combine flour, baking powder and dash salt. Beat egg yolks with goat milk. Add flour and egg mixtures alternately to creamed mixture. Pour batter into 2 greased 8-inch round layer cake pans. Spread evenly to edge, forming thin layer. Beat egg whites until stiff. Gradually beat in 3/4 cup sugar. Blend in vanilla. Add nuts.

Spread meringue on batter in layer pans to within 1 inch of edge. Bake at 350 degrees until wood pick comes out clean, 25 minutes. Remove from oven. Cool on racks 10 minutes, then remove from pans and cool completely. Drain syrup from raspberries into saucepan. Blend in cornstarch. Cook and stir until thickened. Add berries.

To serve, cut each layer into 4 to 6 wedges. Top each wedge with spoonful of whipped cream. Drizzle some of raspberry sauce over cream.

8 to 12 servings. Each of 12 servings: 224 calories; 157 mg sodium; 92 mg cholesterol; 10 grams fat; 32 grams carbohydrates; 3 grams protein; 0.54 gram fiber.

TWELVE

Breads

BASIL TWISTS

LONGTIME FOOD SECTION COLUMNIST and cookbook author Abby Mandel comes from the "little things mean a lot" school of entertaining. For an elegant cocktail party, she suggests serving these delicious twists with one or two other things you've made, then filling out the rest of the menu with food from a good grocery.

1 sheet frozen puff pastry, thawed according to package instructions
Flour
1 egg
Salt
2 teaspoons Dijon mustard
16 to 24 large basil leaves, washed and patted dry
Freshly ground pepper

• Roll puff pastry on floured surface into 14x10-inch rectangle. Cut in half lengthwise. Brush off excess flour.

• Whisk egg with 1/2 teaspoon salt to make glaze. Lightly brush each half of puff pastry with glaze. Spread one half with mustard. Arrange basil leaves in single layer to cover (remove tough veins from mature, very large leaves). Sprinkle generously with pepper to taste. Top with second half of puff pastry, egg side down. Roll rectangle to seal.

• Brush off excess flour on both sides. Starting on short side of dough, use kitchen shears or very sharp knife to cut 24 (1/2-inch-wide) strips (use ruler to make job easier). Twist each strip 3 times. Place single layer on greased baking sheets. Lightly brush each with egg mixture.

• Lightly, but evenly, sprinkle twists with salt to taste.

• Bake at 400 degrees until browned, about 10 to 12 minutes. Remove to wire rack to cool. (Twists can be made 2 days ahead and stored at room temperature or frozen for as long as 1 month, wrapped airtight. Reheat to serve. Place in single layer on baking sheet and bake at 300 degrees until sizzling, about 10 minutes. Cool to room temperature.)

24 twists. Each twist: 37 calories; 122 mg sodium; 9 mg cholesterol; 3 grams fat; 4 grams carbohydrates; 1 gram protein; 0 fiber.

ORANGE ROLLS

PEOPLE GOT VERY EMOTIONAL about the closing of Bullock's department stores. These rolls from the tea room at the landmark mid-Wilshire store may be one reason why.

■ ROLLS

2 cups milk
1/4 cup (1/2 stick) butter
1/4 cup sugar
2 teaspoons salt
2 packages dry yeast
1/4 cup lukewarm water
5 1/2 to 6 1/2 cups sifted flour, plus more for kneading
Melted butter or 1 egg, beaten with 1 teaspoon water

• Place milk in saucepan and bring to boil. Add butter, sugar and salt. Set aside to cool to lukewarm.

• Dissolve yeast in warm water. Add to cooled mixture. Add half of flour and mix well. Add enough remaining flour to make soft dough. Turn out onto floured board and let stand 10 minutes. Knead, working in flour until dough no longer sticks to board and is smooth and elastic, about 10 minutes. Place in greased bowl, cover and let rise in warm place until doubled.

• Turn dough out onto floured board and knead lightly until surface is smooth. Shape into rolls 1 1/2 to 2 inches in diameter. Place close together in 13x9-inch baking pan. Cover with kitchen towel and let rise until doubled. Brush with melted butter or egg-water mixture. Bake at 375 degrees until browned, 20 to 25 minutes. Turn out onto rack to cool.

■ ORANGE SAUCE

4 oranges
Water
1 cup sugar
4 teaspoons arrowroot

• Peel oranges with potato peeler. Remove any white pith from peel. Cut peel in fine strips. Place in saucepan and add water just to cover. Bring to boil, then drain under running water. Cover with water and bring to boil. Drain and discard peel, reserving liquid.

• Blend sugar with arrowroot. Squeeze juice from oranges. Add orange juice and reserved liquid to sugar mixture. Bring to boil and cook and stir until thickened and clear, about 5 minutes. Makes 3 cups.

• To serve, place generous tablespoon Orange Sauce on plate. Set warm roll on top. Drizzle with additional tablespoon Orange Sauce.

20 rolls. Each roll: 215 calories; 276 mg sodium; 19 mg cholesterol; 3 grams fat; 41 grams carbohydrates; 5 grams protein; 0.22 gram fiber.

BUTTERMILK-CINNAMON COFFEECAKE

1985

YOU WON'T FIND A BETTER WAY to start a lazy morning than a hot cup of coffee and this delicious cake from Café Beaujolais' Margaret Fox.

2 1/4 cups flour
1 cup brown sugar, packed
3/4 cup granulated sugar
2 teaspoons ground cinnamon
1/2 teaspoon salt
1/4 teaspoon ground ginger
3/4 cup corn oil
1 cup sliced almonds
1 teaspoon baking powder
1 teaspoon baking soda
1 egg
1 cup buttermilk

• Mix flour, brown sugar, granulated sugar, 1 teaspoon cinnamon, salt and ginger. Blend in oil until smooth. Remove 3/4 cup mixture and combine with almonds and remaining 1 teaspoon cinnamon. Mix and set aside. To remaining flour mixture, add baking powder, baking soda, egg and buttermilk. Blend until smooth. Pour into buttered 13x9-inch baking pan.

• Sprinkle reserved nut mixture evenly over surface of batter. Bake at 350 degrees 35 to 40 minutes. Place pan on wire rack to cool. Cut into squares to serve.

8 to 12 servings. Each of 12 servings: 398 calories; 168 mg sodium; 18 mg cholesterol; 20 grams fat; 51 grams carbohydrates; 5 grams protein; 0.64 gram fiber.

BEL-AIR SCONES

THERE MAY BE NO MORE LUXURIOUS experience in all of Southern California than breakfast or brunch at the Bel-Air Hotel. These scones from chef Gary Clauson are an attraction all their own.

3 cups cake flour, plus more for rolling
2 tablespoons baking powder
2 tablespoons sugar
3/4 teaspoon salt
1/2 cup (1 stick) butter, cut into cubes
2 cups whipping cream
1 cup currants
1 egg yolk, beaten
Devonshire cream and preserves, optional

• Sift together flour, baking powder, sugar and salt. Use paddle on electric mixer to work butter into flour mixture until mealy. Add whipping cream and currants. Mix on low until dough is smooth, 1 minute.

• Turn dough onto floured board and roll out to about 3/4-inch thick. Cut into 2 1/4-inch rounds with pastry cutter or biscuit cutter. Place dough rounds 2 inches apart on baking sheet lined with parchment paper. Brush with beaten egg yolk and bake at 375 degrees until golden brown, 18 to 20 minutes. Serve with Devonshire cream and preserves, if desired.

12 to 14 scones. Each of 14 scones: 278 calories; 390 mg sodium; 84 mg cholesterol; 20 grams fat; 22 grams carbohydrates; 3 grams protein; 0.32 gram fiber.

CINNAMON BUNS

ONE OF THE HOTTEST DINING SPOTS in Pasadena used to be the Old Town Bakery. Former owner Amy Pressman gave us this recipe for what likely will be among the best cinnamon rolls you will ever eat.

■ BUN DOUGH

6 cups flour, plus more for kneading
1/2 cup sugar
2 teaspoons salt
1 cup buttermilk
1 1/4 cups orange juice
3 (1/4-ounce) packages dry yeast
2 tablespoons honey
1/2 cup (1 stick) salted butter, room temperature

• Mix flour, sugar and salt in large mixing bowl, using fork to distribute evenly. Set aside.

• Pour buttermilk and orange juice into saucepan and whisk over low heat until lukewarm. Sprinkle yeast over liquid and stir to dissolve.

• Pour liquid onto flour in mixing bowl and add honey and butter. Mix and massage everything with both hands until all dry ingredients are absorbed into dough. Dough will be somewhat lumpy and uneven. Place dough on floured board and knead with heel of hand until somewhat smooth and elastic, 10 to 15 minutes. Warning: If dough is completely smooth, it has been overworked.

• Place dough in clean, lightly greased bowl. Cover with clean dish cloth and let rise in warm, draft-free area until doubled in bulk, about 1 hour.

■ CINNAMON FILLING

3 tablespoons corn syrup
1/4 cup ground cinnamon
1 1/2 cups (3 sticks) salted butter, room temperature
6 tablespoons sugar
1 tablespoon flour

• Place corn syrup, cinnamon, butter, sugar and flour in bowl and whisk until well blended. (If you make filling the day before you're going to bake, do not refrigerate overnight. Cover and leave on counter until needed.)

CONTINUED ☞

■ SUGAR ICING

2 cups powdered sugar
1 tablespoon vanilla extract
1/4 cup water

• Put sugar, vanilla and water in bowl and whisk vigorously until mixture is free of lumps.

■ ASSEMBLY

Flour
Butter

• Flour work surface generously and rolling pin lightly. Divide Bun Dough in half. Roll first half as best you can into 10x12-inch rectangle 1/2-inch thick.

• With spatula or clean hands, spread half Cinnamon Filling over surface of dough rectangle, stopping 1/2 inch from edge of 1 long side. Starting from opposite long side, roll dough up, snugly but not so tightly that you push filling out. When rolled completely, pinch 1/2-inch edge that is free of filling onto rest of length of roll to create sturdy seam.

• With sharp serrated knife, cut roll crosswise into buns 1 1/2 inches thick, using sawing motion to avoid pressing down on roll. Place buns on baking pan lightly greased with butter 1 to 1 1/2 inches from each other.

• Repeat with remaining Dough and Filling. Cover buns and let rise until puffy and half again as large, about 1 hour. They should spring back from a light touch.

• Uncover baking pans and set in oven to bake at 350 degrees until slightly firm and light golden brown, about 15 minutes. Check to see that buns are cooked through to center, but if buns are too brown, they will develop undesirable crust. Cool until warm to the touch and drizzle with generous amount of Sugar Icing.

16 buns. Each bun: 552 calories; 547 mg sodium; 63 mg cholesterol; 24 grams fat; 91 grams carbohydrates; 6 grams protein, 0.55 gram fiber.

DEWY BUNS

—————

Dewy Buns are a Pennsylvania Dutch classic that longtime columnist and cook-book author Marion Cunningham discovered on a trip. She says the person who goes into business making these is guaranteed their fortune. Even if you're not in it for the money, she recommends the bun dough by itself as an ideal yeast dough to use for dinner rolls.

—————

■ BUNS

2 packages dry yeast
1/3 cup warm water
1 1/2 cups milk
1/3 cup shortening
1/4 cup sugar
2 teaspoons salt
2 eggs, lightly beaten
4 1/2 cups flour

• Sprinkle yeast over warm water in bowl and let dissolve 5 minutes.

• Heat milk and shortening in saucepan until shortening melts. Cool to lukewarm.

• Put yeast in large bowl and add milk mixture. Stir in sugar, salt, eggs and 2 cups flour. Beat briskly until well blended. Add remaining flour and beat until smooth. At this point, dough may be covered with plastic wrap and refrigerated overnight, up to 24 hours.

• To rise, cover bowl and place in warm, draft-free spot until doubled in bulk, about 2 hours, 3 or more if dough has been refrigerated.

• When dough has doubled in bulk, flour work board generously and turn dough out. Dough will be soft and needs enough flour on board to prevent sticking. Pat dough in cir-cle for round dewy buns, or into 1/2-inch-thick square for square buns. Cut dough with cir-cular biscuit cutter or use knife and cut into 2 1/2-inch squares.

• Place buns 1 inch apart on greased baking sheet. Let buns rise uncovered on baking sheets 20 minutes. Bake at 425 degrees until golden, about 10 minutes. Do not brown. Remove and cool slightly.

■ CUSTARD FILLING

1 cup milk
1/3 cup sugar
3 tablespoons cornstarch
1/8 teaspoon salt
2 eggs, lightly beaten until uniform yellow color
1 1/2 tablespoons butter
1 teaspoon vanilla extract

CONTINUED☞

- Scald milk in small saucepan over medium heat. While milk is heating, mix sugar, cornstarch and salt together in bowl large enough to contain milk. When milk forms bubbles and develops scalded aroma, slowly pour over sugar mixture. Stir briskly until mixture is smooth.

- Pour mixture back into saucepan and stir over medium heat until thickened, 3 to 5 minutes. Taste. When mixture is smooth, not coarse, remove from heat.

- Add 1 cup of thickened milk to beaten eggs, whisking in rapidly to prevent curdling. Pour egg mixture into thickened milk in saucepan, stir well and return pan to heat. Cook another 2 to 3 minutes, stirring constantly. Remove from heat. Add butter and vanilla extract and stir to blend. Let cool. Cover and refrigerate until needed. Makes about 1 1/4 cups.

- To serve, split as many buns as you are going to serve. Spread each with about 2 tablespoons custard. Freeze leftover buns to be used later. (Ideally, buns should be warm when served.)

20 (2 1/2-inch) square or round buns. Each bun, with 2 tablespoons Custard Filling: 161 calories; 288 mg sodium; 47 mg cholesterol; 3 grams fat; 28 grams carbohydrates; 5 grams protein; 0.08 gram fiber.

≈≈≈

FLANNEL CAKES

In Los Angeles, restaurants come and go with alarming rapidity. One notable exception is Musso & Frank, which has inhabited the same spot on Hollywood Boulevard since 1919. The restaurant's Flannel Cakes are much in demand.

6 eggs
2 cups milk
1 tablespoon oil
Salt
1/2 cup flour
1/2 cup pastry flour
1/4 teaspoon vanilla extract
2 tablespoons sugar

- Beat eggs, milk, oil and dash salt in bowl. Add flour and pastry flour and mix well. Add vanilla and sugar and mix well.

- Pour 1/3 cup batter per cake onto greased skillet and cook over medium heat until golden brown, 3 to 4 minutes. Turn and cook until golden brown on other side, 2 to 3 minutes.

10 to 12 cakes. Each of 12 cakes: 109 calories; 72 mg sodium; 109 mg cholesterol; 5 grams fat; 12 grams carbohydrates; 5 grams protein; 0.02 gram fiber.

SOUR CREAM COFFEE CAKE

GIVEN HOW MANY REQUESTS we get for this recipe from the Los Angeles public schools every year, you'd think people only had good things to say about cafeteria food. Of course, if cafeterias still served homemade breads such as this, that might be true.

■ TOPPING

1/4 cup flour
3/4 cup brown sugar
1/4 teaspoon salt
1 cup chopped walnuts
1/4 cup (1/2 stick) butter

• Mix together flour, sugar, salt and walnuts. Add butter in small pieces. Rub in by hand until mixture is crumbly. Be careful not to over-mix.

■ CAKE

1 1/2 cups cake flour
1/2 cup all-purpose flour
1 teaspoon baking soda
1 teaspoon baking powder
1/2 cup (1 stick) butter
1 cup sugar
1 egg, slightly beaten
1 teaspoon vanilla extract
1 cup sour cream

• All ingredients should be at room temperature. Mix together cake and all-purpose flours, baking soda and baking powder in large bowl.

• In separate bowl, cream butter with sugar by beating mixture until fluffy and light. Add egg and vanilla and mix well. Add half flour mixture, mixing just until flour is blended. Blend in sour cream, then remaining flour mixture. Spread half batter lightly into 10-inch tube pan. Sprinkle with half Topping and spread with remaining batter.

• Sprinkle with remaining Topping. Bake at 350 degrees 40 to 45 minutes.

8 to 10 servings. Each of 10 servings: 415 calories; 253 mg sodium; 58 mg cholesterol; 22 grams fat; 52 grams carbohydrates; 5 grams protein; 0.61 gram fiber.

GORDITAS

GORDITAS ARE STUFFED FRIED CORN tortillas, but that basic description does not come close to doing them justice. This recipe, developed by longtime Food section contributor and novelist Michelle Huneven, is a perfect example—crisp on the outside, tender on the inside and preferably stuffed with delicious cheeses, salsas and meats.

4 pounds fresh masa, preferably masa refregada, masa molida, masa sin preparada
1/2 to 1 teaspoon salt
4 teaspoons baking powder
Water
1 to 2 tablespoons lard or corn oil
Corn oil, for frying

• Mix masa, salt and baking powder together with hands. Add just enough water and lard to make dough pliable. Continue kneading until dough begins to feel smooth.

• Pull off enough masa to form 1 smooth, 2-inch ball. Pat gently back and forth in your hands to form 4- to 5-inch cake about 1/2-inch thick.

• Cook on hot griddle, 2 minutes on each side. Set aside.

• Heat enough oil for frying to 375 degrees. Fry gorditas, 1 or 2 at a time, until they float, about 45 seconds. Remove and drain on paper towels. Split open each gordita with steak knife. (Opening should be wide enough for easy stuffing, but should not split apart.) Stuff with fillings of choice and serve with cotija cheese.

28 gordita shells. Each gordita, without filling: 245 calories; 105.7 mg sodium; 0.5 mg cholesterol; 3.43 grams fat; 4.86 grams carbohydrates; 6 grams protein; 0.96 grams fiber.

MAPLE BANANA NUT MUFFINS

TIMES TEST KITCHEN INTERN Janet McCracken came up with these muffins while researching a story on real maple syrup. They also can be made using only maple products for sweetening. Brown or granulated sugar may be substituted for maple sugar.

■ STREUSEL TOPPING

1/4 cup (1/2 stick) butter, melted
1 cup chopped walnuts
1/2 cup maple or brown sugar, packed
2 tablespoons flour

• Combine butter, walnuts, maple sugar and flour. Set aside.

■ MAPLE GLAZE

6 tablespoons powdered sugar, sifted
2 tablespoons grade B maple syrup

• Whisk sugar into syrup until smooth.

■ MUFFINS

1/2 cup (1 stick) butter, softened
1/3 cup maple or brown sugar, packed
1 egg
1/3 cup grade B maple syrup
1 cup all-purpose flour
1/2 cup whole-wheat flour
1/2 teaspoon salt
1 teaspoon baking soda
1 teaspoon baking powder
1 over-ripe banana, mashed
1/2 cup sour cream

• Beat butter and sugar until light and creamy. Mix in egg, then gradually add syrup.

• Sift together all-purpose flour, whole-wheat flour, salt, baking soda and baking powder. Add to butter mixture, mixing just until incorporated. Combine banana and sour cream and fold into batter.

• Spoon into 12-cup muffin tin lined with paper liners. Sprinkle Streusel Topping evenly on top of each muffin. Bake at 375 degrees until toothpick inserted in center comes out clean, 18 to 20 minutes. Cool slightly, then drizzle with Maple Glaze.

1 dozen muffins. Each muffin: 348 calories; 267 mg sodium; 53 mg cholesterol; 20 grams fat; 40 grams carbohydrates; 4 grams protein; 0.64 gram fiber.

VIRGINIA HAM BISCUITS

FEW PEOPLE KNOW AS MUCH about home baking as Marion Cunningham. After all, in addition to being our longtime columnist, she's the author of the "Fannie Farmer Baking Book." So when she says these biscuits are special, you had better believe it.

2 cups flour, plus more for kneading
1/2 teaspoon salt
2 teaspoons baking powder
1/2 teaspoon baking soda
1/2 cup shortening
2/3 cups buttermilk
1 cup finely chopped or ground ham

• Combine flour, salt, baking powder and baking soda in mixing bowl. Stir together with fork. Drop shortening into dry ingredients. Using pastry blender, 2 knives or fingertips, work shortening into dry ingredients until mixture is in irregular crumbs resembling soft bread crumbs. Add buttermilk and ham and stir with fork just until dough forms rough mass.

• Turn dough out onto smooth, lightly floured surface. Knead 12 to 14 times. Pat into 8x8 1/2-inch-square baking pan. Use knife to cut dough into 2-inch squares. Place biscuits in baking pans or on sheet (with biscuits touching for light and fluffy or at least 1 inch apart for darker and crisper). Bake at 425 degrees until golden, 15 to 20 minutes. Serve hot.

About 15 (2 inch) biscuits. Each biscuit: 156 calories; 266 mg sodium; 5 mg cholesterol; 8 grams fat; 12 grams carbohydrates; 4 grams protein; 0.05 gram fiber.

ZUCCHINI BREAD

CALIFORNIANS BEING GREAT GARDENERS, there's always a need for one more zucchini bread recipe. This one comes from Marmalade Café in Sherman Oaks.

3 eggs
1 1/4 cups oil
3 tablespoons butter, melted, plus more for greasing
1 1/2 cups sugar
1 teaspoon vanilla extract
2 cups unpeeled, grated zucchini
2 cups flour
2 teaspoons baking soda
2 teaspoons baking powder
1 teaspoon salt
1 teaspoon cinnamon
1 teaspoon ground cloves
1 cup chopped walnuts

• Beat eggs, oil, butter, sugar and vanilla until light and thick. Fold in grated zucchini.

• Sift together flour, baking soda, baking powder, salt, cinnamon and cloves in separate bowl. Fold into egg mixture. Fold in nuts. Pour batter into greased 9x5-inch loaf pan. Bake at 375 degrees until center of bread springs back when touched, about 1 hour 15 minutes. Cool on rack. Slice to serve.

8 to 10 servings. Each of 10 servings: 574 calories; 377 mg sodium; 73 mg cholesterol; 41 grams fat; 51 grams carbohydrates; 6 grams protein; 0.76 gram fiber.

MOIST MINIATURE
CORN *and* SOUR CHERRY LOAVES

CORN AND CHERRIES? It might sound unlikely, but frequent food section contributor Marcy Goldman made a believer out of us. Crunchy on the outside, airy and moist on the inside, these quick breads are outstanding. The sour cherries are interesting, but this recipe works well without them too. The loaves' deep corn flavor is exceptional.

3/4 cup oil
1 1/2 cups sugar
3 eggs
1 cup water
1 teaspoon vanilla extract
1/4 teaspoon lemon extract or lemon oil
1 teaspoon salt
2 1/2 teaspoons baking powder
1/2 teaspoon baking soda
1 1/2 cups flour
1 cup stone-ground cornmeal
1 cup sour cherries, well drained and dried, cut in half
Butter for greasing or nonstick cooking spray

• Mix together oil and sugar. Blend in eggs, then add water, vanilla and lemon extract. Combine salt, baking powder, baking soda, flour and cornmeal, then fold dry ingredients into wet. Stir in cherries. Batter will be thin.

• Pour batter into 10 generously greased (1 1/2x3- to 4-inch) mini loaf pans lined with paper muffin caps flattened to fit bottom of loaf pans. (You can also use 12 greased muffin cups lined with paper cups.) Bake at 400 degrees 10 minutes, then reduce heat to 350 degrees and bake until edges are lightly browned and tops are just firm (may have a crack down center) and spring back when touched, 16 to 20 minutes.

10 mini-loaves. Each loaf: 397 calories; 366 mg sodium; 64 mg cholesterol; 19 grams fat; 55 grams carbohydrates; 5 grams protein; 0.31 gram fiber.

MONASTERY PUMPKIN BREAD

A MONASTERY IN HOLLYWOOD? It might sound unlikely, but there certainly is one—the Monastery of the Angels—and it is famous for its homemade breads and candies, such as this great pumpkin bread.

3 1/2 cups flour
3 cups sugar
2 teaspoons baking soda
1 teaspoon cinnamon
1 teaspoon nutmeg
1 1/2 teaspoons salt
4 eggs, beaten
1 cup oil
2/3 cup water
2 cups mashed, cooked pumpkin
Walnut halves

- Sift together flour, sugar, baking soda, cinnamon, nutmeg and salt.
- Combine eggs, oil, water and pumpkin and mix well. Stir into dry ingredients. Turn into 3 greased 8x4-inch loaf pans and top with few walnut halves. Bake at 350 degrees until wood pick inserted in center comes out clean, 1 hour. Cool before slicing. (Tastes best slightly warm, spread with butter.)

Makes 3 loaves or 18 to 20 servings. Each of 20 servings: 325 calories; 249 mg sodium; 42 mg cholesterol; 14 grams fat; 48 grams carbohydrates; 4 grams protein; 0.64 gram fiber.

OLIVE BREAD

SOMETIMES IT'S FUN TO MAKE a side dish the most flavorful part of a meal, shifting the focus from the meat or fish that's being grilled. This bread from Test Kitchen cook Mayi Brady is both crunchy and chewy, salty and slightly sweet since it's made from packaged frozen bread dough. It's not for the timid—the flavors are quite strong—yet would complement a simple grilled chicken breast or fish filet. If ricotta salata (a hard, Parmesan-like version of ricotta cheese) is too salty, you can substitute a milder goat cheese.

1 (1-pound) loaf frozen bread dough, thawed

2 tablespoons cornmeal

3/4 cup Kalamata olives, pitted and coarsely chopped

1/4 cup freshly grated Parmesan cheese

2 cloves garlic, finely minced

1/4 cup thinly sliced sage leaves

1/2 cup walnut pieces

1 tablespoon butter

1/4 teaspoon salt

2 tablespoons shaved ricotta salata or goat cheese

• Cut thawed bread dough in half. Roll or stretch dough into 2 rectangles that measure about 12x9 inches each. Place on 2 baking sheets that have been sprinkled with 1 tablespoon cornmeal each.

• Sprinkle each half with olives, Parmesan, garlic and sage. Bake at 450 degrees until bread is golden brown, 10 to 12 minutes.

• As bread bakes, toast walnut pieces in small saucepan with butter and salt.

• When bread is done, top with walnut pieces and ricotta salata.

2 large breads, about 8 to 10 servings. Each of 8 servings: 271 calories; 758 mg sodium; 8 mg cholesterol; 40 grams fat; 33 grams carbohydrates; 8 grams protein; 0.79 gram fiber.

ORANGE MUFFINS

THESE DELICATELY SWEET MUFFINS with a fresh scent of orange come from Michelle Huneven, a novelist who is a frequent contributor to the Times Food section.

2 cups flour
1/2 teaspoon salt
1/4 cup sugar
1 teaspoon baking soda
1 teaspoon baking powder
1 cup freshly squeezed orange juice
2 eggs, beaten
1/4 cup (1/2 stick) melted butter
2 tablespoons orange zest, chopped
Raw sugar

• Sift together flour, salt, sugar, baking soda and baking powder in mixing bowl. Set aside. Beat together orange juice, eggs, melted butter and orange zest in separate bowl. Pour wet ingredients into sifted dry ingredients. Combine with few swift strokes. Do not worry about lumps.

• Fill cups of well-greased muffin tins 3/4 full. Sprinkle tops with raw sugar. Bake at 400 degrees until cracked on top, 20 to 25 minutes.

12 muffins. Each muffin: 142 calories; 184 mg sodium; 46 mg cholesterol; 5 grams fat; 21 grams carbohydrates; 3 grams protein; 0.08 gram fiber.

PERSIMMON BREAD

REALLY RIPE PERSIMMONS are one of those fruits that are practically unknown outside of California. They are so fragile that they simply don't ship well. Popular in farmers markets during the late summer and early fall, persimmons make an exceptionally moist quick bread.

2 cups flour
2 teaspoons ground cinnamon
2 teaspoons baking soda
1/2 teaspoon salt
1 1/4 cups sugar
1/2 cup raisins
1/2 cup chopped nuts
2 eggs
3/4 cup oil
2 cups pureed ripe persimmon pulp
1 teaspoon lemon juice

• Combine flour, cinnamon, baking soda, salt and sugar. Stir in raisins and nuts. Set aside.

• Beat eggs with oil. Add persimmon pulp and lemon juice. Add flour mixture. Mix until just blended.

• Turn into 2 greased 8x4-inch loaf pans and bake at 350 degrees (325 degrees for glass pans) until wood pick inserted in center comes out clean, 1 hour. Bread will not have high volume.

2 loaves of 8 servings each. Each serving: 289 calories; 84 mg sodium; 27 mg cholesterol; 14 grams fat; 41 grams carbohydrates; 3 grams protein; 0.57 gram fiber.

RASPBERRY BRAN MUFFINS

GETTING FIBER FROM BRAN is certainly no punishment with these moist, delicious muffins from longtime columnist Abby Mandel.

1/2 cup hot water
1 1/2 cups bran cereal (not bran flakes)
1 cup buttermilk, shaken well
1 egg
1/4 cup oil
2 tablespoons molasses
7 teaspoons raspberry preserves
2/3 cup raspberries

• Combine flour, sugar, baking soda, cinnamon and salt in large bowl. Set aside.

• Put hot water and cereal in bowl; stir until moistened. Add buttermilk, egg, oil and molasses. Stir well. Add to dry ingredients. Stir well. (Can be baked immediately or refrigerated as long as 1 week. Stir before using.)

• Spoon batter into muffin tins that have been greased or lined with paper cups until about 7/8 full. Put 1/2 teaspoon preserves in center of each. Sprinkle each with about 5 to 6 berries, slightly pressing them into batter.

• Bake at 400 degrees until toothpick inserted into center comes out clean, about 18 minutes. Let rest in pans 5 minutes. Serve warm.

14 muffins. Each muffin: 162 calories; 116 mg sodium; 16 mg cholesterol; 5 grams fat; 29 grams carbohydrates; 3 grams protein; 0.76 gram fiber.

RHUBARB BREAD

TERRIE SNELL DROVE TO HOLLYWOOD from Libertyville, Ill. in her rebuilt '78 Buick to pursue an acting career. Though she's been luckier than most at finding work (she was in "Home Alone" and a couple episodes of TV's "ER"), she is at heart a Midwesterner who makes apple butter from the fruit of her own apple trees. Her rhubarb bread is not to be believed.

1992

---

1 1/2 cups brown sugar, packed
2/3 cup oil
1 egg
1 cup buttermilk
1 teaspoon salt
1 teaspoon baking soda
1 teaspoon vanilla extract
2 1/2 cups flour
2 cups diced rhubarb
1/2 cup chopped nuts
1 tablespoon butter, softened
1/4 cup granulated sugar

• Combine brown sugar and oil in bowl. Stir well until smooth. Stir in egg, buttermilk, salt, baking soda, vanilla and flour. Blend until moist. Fold in rhubarb and nuts. Turn batter into 2 greased (8x4 inch) loaf pans.

• Combine butter and granulated sugar until crumbly. Sprinkle over batter.

• Bake at 350 degrees until wood pick inserted in center comes out dry, 50 to 55 minutes. Turn out onto racks. Cool before slicing.

---

10 servings. Each serving: 456 calories; 292 mg sodium; 25 mg cholesterol; 21 grams fat; 65 grams carbohydrates; 6 grams protein; 0 fiber.

RAISED WAFFLES

OF ALL THE RECIPES longtime columnist and cookbook author Marion Cunningham has written, this might be the most famous. Waffles don't get any better than this. The recipe does take some planning, but if you make the batter the night before, you can add the eggs and baking soda in the morning and be ready to go.

1/2 cup warm water
1 package yeast
2 cups milk
1/2 cup (1 stick) butter, melted
1 teaspoon salt
1 teaspoon sugar
2 cups flour
2 eggs
1/4 teaspoon baking soda

• Put water in large mixing bowl (batter will double in volume) and sprinkle in yeast. When dissolved, about 5 minutes, add milk, butter, salt, sugar and flour, and use hand mixer or electric beater to beat until smooth and blended.

• Cover bowl with plastic wrap and let stand overnight at room temperature. (Batter will keep several days if refrigerated.)

• Just before cooking waffles, beat in eggs and add baking soda, stirring until well mixed. Batter will be very thin. Pour 1/2 to 3/4 cup batter into very hot waffle iron. Bake waffles until golden and crisp to touch. Serve with butter and syrup of choice.

8 waffles. Each waffle: 260 calories; 459 mg sodium; 89 mg cholesterol; 14 grams fat; 26 grams carbohydrates; 7 grams protein; 0.09 gram fiber.

PUNJABI CORN BREAD
(*Makki Ki Roti*)

TRADITIONAL ROTIS ARE wonderfully fatty, but this version, from Hari Alipuria of Rosemead's Chameli restaurant, has been lightened. In this case, that hasn't hurt the flavor one little bit.

1994

3 cups water
3 cups yellow cornmeal
Butter

• Place water in large saucepan and bring to boil. While boiling, add cornmeal. Stir to make soft dough.

• Turn out onto board and cool slightly. Knead mixture thoroughly, occasionally picking dough up and slapping down hard on surface. Form mixture into 9 balls. With moistened hand, pat each ball into flat circle about 1/4-inch thick. Re-wet hand occasionally.

• Place bread on ungreased griddle over medium heat. Cook until bread is browned on bottom and slips about easily on griddle. If using gas range, place cooked bread directly over flame for few moments to brown. Place on plate and brush with stick of butter. Cook remaining breads as directed and stack on plate so top of each roti butters bottom side of roti above.

9 roti. Each roti: 414 calories; 882 mg sodium; 10 mg cholesterol; 24 grams fat; 46 grams carbohydrates; 8 grams protein; 2 grams fiber.

GEORGIAN CHEESE BREAD
(*Khachapuri*)

THIS RECIPE WAS CONTRIBUTED BY staff writer Charles Perry, who calls it the world's most elaborate melted cheese sandwich. Khachapuri is a traditional dish of the Republic of Georgia; it involves a certain amount of trouble, but not nearly as much as people will assume. The recipe is adapted from the Time-Life book "Russian Cooking."

■ BREAD

2 packages dry yeast
Sugar
1 1/4 cups lukewarm milk
Flour
2 teaspoons salt
1/2 cup (1 stick) butter, softened

• Sprinkle yeast and 1/2 teaspoon sugar over milk in small, shallow bowl. Cover with plastic wrap and place in warm place until yeast blooms and mixture nearly doubles in volume, 5 to 10 minutes.

• Combine 4 1/2 cups flour, 1 tablespoon sugar and salt in large mixing bowl. Make well in flour mixture and add milk-yeast mixture and softened butter. Beat vigorously with large spoon until smooth. Form into ball and place on lightly floured surface. Knead hard 10 minutes, adding more flour or water as needed to create medium stiff dough.

• When dough is smooth and elastic, place in large, lightly buttered bowl. Cover with plastic wrap and kitchen towel and let rise in warm, draft-free place, such as unlit oven with pilot light on, until doubled in bulk and dough springs back slowly when gently poked with finger, 45 minutes to 1 hour. Punch dough down and let rise until again doubled, 30 to 40 minutes.

■ CHEESE FILLING

1 pound Muenster cheese, shredded
2 tablespoons butter, softened
1 egg, beaten

• In large mixing bowl, combine cheese, butter and egg. Knead vigorously until texture is uniform. Shape into thick round cake 8 to 7 1/2 inches in diameter.

• Punch dough down and roll out on lightly floured surface into circle about 22 inches in diameter. If rolling surface is too small, divide dough in half and roll into 2 half-circles 22x11 inches.

CONTINUED ☛

- Roll dough up on rolling pin and unroll carefully over buttered 9-inch cake or spring-form pan so that it is centered, with edges overlapping more or less evenly on all sides. If using 2 half-circles of dough, form 1-inch seam to make whole circle and moisten thoroughly to seal. Carefully press center of dough down to bottom of pan.
- Place Cheese Filling on dough and bring up edges of dough over filling, forming thick, fabric-like folds. Moisten edges at top and seal.
- Let stand 10 to 15 minutes. Bake at 375 degrees in center of oven, on foil in case filling leaks, until golden brown, 50 minutes to 1 hour.
- Cool 1 to 2 hours before serving.

12 to 16 servings. Each of 16 servings: 423 calories; 744 mg sodium; 83 mg cholesterol; 23 grams fat; 39 grams carbohydrates; 16 grams protein; 0 fiber.

OATMEAL-COCONUT MUFFINS

THESE MUFFINS COME FROM The Winery, a little shop near the popular Southern California ski resort Mammoth Mountain.

1 cup oatmeal
1 cup buttermilk
1 cup flour
1/2 teaspoon salt
1/2 teaspoon baking soda
1 1/2 teaspoons baking powder
1/2 cup melted shortening or oil
1/2 cup brown sugar, packed
1 egg
3/4 cup shredded coconut
Strawberry preserves

- Combine oats and buttermilk in bowl. Let soak at least 30 minutes.
- Sift flour with salt, baking soda and baking powder.
- Blend together melted shortening, brown sugar, egg and coconut, then add to oatmeal mixture. Blend well. Stir in dry ingredients, mixing only enough to moisten. Spoon into greased muffin tins. Using small teaspoon, place preserves in center of each muffin and cover with dab of dough.
- Bake at 400 degrees until top is cracked, 20 minutes.

1 dozen muffins. Each muffin: 237 calories; 197 mg sodium; 18 mg cholesterol; 13 grams fat; 29 grams carbohydrates; 3 grams protein; 0.30 gram fiber.

BUTTER-DIPPED CLOVERLEAF ROLLS

BAKER AND FREQUENT CONTRIBUTOR Marcy Goldman developed this recipe for the classic dinner roll. Dipped chunks or balls of dough are tucked into a mini-loaf pan or regular muffin pans. They bake into a buttery-crusted roll, reminiscent of a croissant in taste but with the velvety crumb of a traditional rich white bread roll. Buttermilk makes these extra tender. This dough can also be used to make Parkerhouse or fan rolls.

1 teaspoon sugar
2 tablespoons dry yeast
1/4 cup warm water
1 1/4 cups buttermilk, warmed in microwave 1 minute
1/4 cup (1/2 stick) butter, softened, cut into small chunks, plus more for greasing
1/4 cup sugar
2 teaspoons salt
3 to 4 cups bread flour
1/2 cup butter, melted

• In large bowl, sprinkle sugar and yeast over warm water and stir briefly. Let stand, allowing yeast to swell, 2 to 3 minutes. Stir in buttermilk, butter chunks, sugar, salt and most of flour. Knead to make soft dough, adding more flour as required, until smooth and elastic, 8 to 10 minutes.

• Place in lightly greased bowl and cover. Allow to rise until double in bulk, about 45 minutes, or refrigerate at least 8 hours or overnight. (If refrigerating, allow dough to warm up before proceeding, 2 to 3 hours).

• Divide dough into 12 portions. Cut each portion into 3 chunks and dip in melted butter. (For more traditional looking rolls, form chunks into small balls by rolling dough between hands.) Place 3 balls or chunks into each well of 12-cup muffin tin. Drizzle any leftover melted butter over rolls. Cover lightly with plastic (slipping entire baking sheet into a large, trash bag works well) and allow to rise until double in bulk, 30 to 40 minutes.

• Bake at 375 degrees 10 minutes; reduce heat to 350 degrees and bake until lightly browned, another 15 to 20 minutes.

Variation: Add 1 tablespoon finely crushed garlic and 2 tablespoons minced fresh parsley to melted butter. Proceed as above.

1 dozen rolls. Each roll: 266 calories; 540 mg sodium; 32 mg cholesterol; 12 grams fat; 32 grams carbohydrates; 7 grams protein; 0.10 gram fiber.

POPPY SEED BREAD STICKS

BREAD DOESN'T GET MUCH EASIER than these sticks, which are based on frozen bread dough. But with the addition of forceful seasonings like poppy seeds and sea salt, no one will ever know you didn't make them from scratch.

Flour
1 (1-pound) package frozen bread dough, thawed
1 tablespoon butter, melted
2 tablespoon poppy seeds
2 teaspoons coarse sea salt

• Sprinkle work board with flour and roll thawed bread dough out to 18x12-inch rectangle. Brush dough with melted butter, then top with poppy seeds and salt.

• Cut dough into 12 strips, each about 1 1/2 inches wide. Twist dough 3 or 4 times and transfer to greased baking sheet. Immediately, without allowing to rise, bake at 375 degrees until browned, 12 to 14 minutes.

4 servings. Each serving: 337 calories; 1,859 mg sodium; 8 mg cholesterol; 62 grams fat; 57 grams carbohydrates; 10 grams protein; 0.14 gram fiber.

THIRTEEN

Assorted Sweets

ANGEL FOOD CANDY
(*Honeycomb Candy*)

1998

C.L. UNDERWOOD OF MAYWOOD sent us this recipe for Angel Food Candy, also called Honeycomb Candy, which is coated with chocolate. Many tasters in The Times Test Kitchen had made similar candies before. But this is a great version of the candy, which has an airy crunchiness, in part due to the use of baking soda. Semisweet or bittersweet chocolate is recommended to balance the sweetness of the candy underneath.

1 cup sugar
1 cup dark corn syrup
1 tablespoon vinegar
1 tablespoon baking soda
Butter, for greasing
2 pounds semisweet or bittersweet chocolate

• Cook sugar, corn syrup and vinegar in heavy saucepan over medium heat, stirring constantly until sugar dissolves, 3 to 4 minutes. Stop stirring and bring candy to boil. Continue cooking without stirring until candy reaches hard-crack stage (300 to 310 degrees on candy thermometer), about 10 minutes.

• Remove candy from heat and quickly stir in baking soda. Pour into greased 13x9-inch baking pan but do not spread (candy won't fill pan). Let candy cool.

• Melt chocolate in top of double boiler over simmering water and set aside to cool.

• Break hardened candy into chunks and dip into melted chocolate. Place on wax paper until firm, about 30 minutes, or refrigerate. Store in airtight container.

2 1/2 pounds. Each serving: 313 calories; 20 mg sodium; 0 cholesterol; 16 grams fat; 48 grams carbohydrates; 2 grams protein; 0.45 gram fiber.

APRICOT-ALMOND CLAFOUTIS

1995

A CLAFOUTIS IS SOMETHING between a cake and a custard. Food Editor Russ Parsons tried dozens of recipes before settling on this basic mixture of milk, cream, eggs and flour. You can add whatever fruit you like to it after that.

Sugar
3 eggs
3/4 cup whipping cream
3/4 cup milk
1/2 teaspoon almond extract
1/2 cup flour
About 8 apricots, cut in half and pitted
Butter, for greasing
1/3 cup slivered almonds

• Place 1/4 cup sugar, eggs, cream, milk and almond extract in blender or food processor and blend until smooth. Sift flour over mixture and pulse just to mix. Set batter aside to stand 10 minutes.

• Arrange apricots, cut-side down, in heavily greased and sugared 9-inch glass pie plate. When batter has rested, pour batter over apricots. Sprinkle with almonds and 1 to 2 tablespoons sugar.

• Bake at 400 degrees until puffed and brown, about 45 minutes. Serve immediately.

6 to 8 servings. Each of 8 servings: 217 calories; 44 mg sodium; 107 mg cholesterol; 13 grams fat; 23 grams carbohydrates; 6 grams protein; 0.51 gram fiber.

CHOCOLATE PATE

NAPA VALLEY CHEF GREG COLE of Celadon restaurant makes this dessert, which is essentially a slab of soft, luxurious chocolate with raspberry sauce, simple to make but completely irresistible to chocolate lovers.

1 pound bittersweet chocolate, chopped
3/4 cup Zinfandel or other red wine
1/4 cup whipping cream

• Combine chocolate, wine and cream in top of stainless steel double boiler and cook over simmering water over medium heat, stirring frequently, until chocolate melts and mixture is just smooth. (It's important that chocolate not get too warm.) Remove from heat and mix well with balloon whisk.

• Depending on how deep you want the pate, pour into 1 (8x4-inch) or 2 (5x2 1/2-inch) loaf pans lined with parchment or wax paper and refrigerate overnight. Before serving, unmold and slice with knife dipped in hot water.

■ BERRY SAUCE

2 pints fresh berries, such as raspberries
1/2 cup sugar

• Puree berries and sugar in blender until smooth. Serve with Chocolate Pate.

8 servings. Each serving: 389 calories; 6 mg sodium; 10 mg cholesterol; 26 grams fat; 47 grams carbohydrates; 5 grams protein; 2.87 grams fiber.

FLAN

FLAN IS THE CLASSIC DESSERT of Mexican restaurants in Southern California. This one, from the landmark El Cholo restaurant, benefits from the addition of a small amount of cream of coconut, which adds a subtle distinction.

1988

2 (14-ounce) cans sweetened condensed milk
2 cups milk
1/2 cup cream of coconut
1/2 cup corn syrup
1 teaspoon vanilla extract
6 eggs
1 cup sugar

• Place sweetened condensed milk, milk, cream of coconut, corn syrup, vanilla and eggs in blender container. Blend thoroughly, or whisk vigorously with wire whip to blend well.

• Melt sugar in heavy skillet over low heat, stirring occasionally to keep caramel from scorching. Add few drops of water a little at a time, stirring until caramel is of spreading consistency.

• Distribute caramel evenly among 8 (4 1/2- to 5-ounce) custard cups, tilting cups to spread caramel evenly. Or spread in 13x9-inch rectangular baking pan. Pour flan into caramel-lined cups or pan and place in shallow baking pan with 1/4-inch hot water.

• Cover with foil and bake cups at 350 degrees until firm, 50 minutes, or baking pan, 1 hour. When cool, place in refrigerator about 1 hour.

• To serve, run knife around outer edges of cups or pan and invert on serving platter.

8 servings. Each serving: 560 calories; 229 mg sodium; 198 mg cholesterol; 14 grams fat; 98 grams carbohydrates; 15 grams protein; 0.04 gram fiber.

CREME BRULEE

1990

OF ALL THE CREME BRULEES in Southern California, nobody's was better than the one Michel Richard made at his Citrus restaurant. If you use a 13x9-inch baking dish, individual servings may be cut out with cookie cutter for scalloped effect, if desired.

10 eggs, separated
3/4 cup granulated sugar
3/4 cup milk
2 1/4 cups whipping cream
1 tablespoon vanilla extract
1/4 cup brown sugar, packed

• Mix egg yolks and 1/2 cup sugar until well combined and sugar has dissolved. Add milk, whipping cream and vanilla and mix well.

• Place 1 (13x9-inch) glass baking dish or 6 (5-inch) fluted glass flan dishes in baking pan. Pour creme brulee mixture into baking dish or fill flan dishes 3/4 full with mixture.

• Place in oven and fill baking pan with hot water up 3/4 sides of dishes. Bake at 350 degrees until knife inserted near center comes out clean, 30 to 40 minutes. Remove dishes from hot water bath and set aside to cool.

• Combine remaining 1/4 cup granulated and brown sugars. Sprinkle top of each serving evenly with combined sugars.

• Caramelize sugars with torch. If torch is not available, place creme brulee in refrigerator until chilled. When ready to serve, place sugar-coated creme in preheated boiler 5 minutes to brown, being careful not to scorch.

6 servings. Each serving: 581 calories; 157 mg sodium; 480 mg cholesterol; 42 grams fat; 39 grams carbohydrates; 13 grams protein; 0 fiber.

CHOCOLATE CREME BRULEE

THIS VERSION OF creme brulee from Joachim Splichal's Pinot restaurants is a twist on the favorite dessert.

4 cups whipping cream
2 cups milk
1 cup granulated sugar
1 vanilla bean
10 egg yolks
9 ounces fine-quality dark sweet chocolate (such as Valhrona Majari), melted
Raw sugar

• Combine cream, milk, 1/2 cup granulated sugar and vanilla bean in saucepan. Bring to boil over medium heat. Mix yolks (save egg white for another use) with remaining 1/2 cup sugar. Add 1/2 cup milk mixture to egg mixture to temper. Then pour egg mixture into remaining milk mixture and stir. Add melted chocolate and stir to mix. Strain.

• Pour into 8 (1-cup) ramekins. Place ramekins in another pan filled halfway with water and bake at 275 degrees 45 minutes.

• Refrigerate until set. Sprinkle with raw sugar. Place ramekins under broiler until sugar melts.

8 servings. Each serving: 667 calories; 137 mg sodium; 510 mg cholesterol; 54 grams fat; 39 grams carbohydrates; 9 grams protein; 0 fiber.

GRAPEFRUIT ICE

Ices, granitas and sorbets are perfect desserts not only in the heat of summer, but in winter too, when the weight of heavy holiday meals can become great. This one by Test Kitchen Director Donna Deane not only tastes great, it also has a beautiful pink hue. The amount of sugar will vary according to the sweetness of the grapefruit—some people love it without any sugar. The ice is best when served slightly slushy.

2 cups pink grapefruit juice (about 3 grapefruit)
1/4 cup sugar
1 tablespoon Grand Marnier
1 tablespoon lime juice

• Combine grapefruit juice, sugar, Grand Marnier and lime juice. Freeze in ice cream freezer according to manufacturer's directions. Spoon into chilled glass dishes, cover and freeze until serving time.

4 servings. Each serving: 105 calories; 1 mg sodium; 0 cholesterol; 0 fat; 24 grams carbohydrates; 1 gram protein; 0 fiber.

PEARS BRAISED IN CREAM

1994

We usually associate braising with meats, but Mayi Brady, a recipe tester in the Times Test Kitchen, gave us this dessert braise. Gentler than most braises, the pears bake in butter for the first half of the cooking, then bake in cream for the second half. This allows the characteristic deep flavors and melting textures of a true braise to emerge.

1 1/2 tablespoons butter
1 tablespoon granulated sugar
1 tablespoon brown sugar, packed
4 firm pears, peeled, cored and halved
3/4 cup whipping cream

• Rub bottom of 8x6-inch oval baking dish with 1 tablespoon butter. Sprinkle both sugars evenly over bottom of dish. Place pears, cut-side-down, in dish and dot with remaining butter.

• Bake at 350 degrees 20 minutes. Pour cream into dish and tilt dish back and forth several times to mix with butter-sugar mixture. Bake another 15 minutes or until pears are tender when pierced with sharp knife. Serve warm.

4 servings. Each serving: 312 calories; 62 mg sodium; 73 mg cholesterol; 22 grams fat; 32 grams carbohydrates; 2 grams protein; 2.33 grams fiber.

INDIAN RICE PUDDING WITH
TAMARILLO SAUCE

Thanks to the boom in home cooking, supermarkets now stock a wide variety of fruits and vegetables that only a decade ago we might have found only in reference works. The addition of a tamarillo fruit sauce adds another dimension to this rice pudding by former Staff Writer Joan Drake.

1989

■ RICE PUDDING

4 cups half-and-half or milk
1/2 cup basmati rice
1/4 teaspoon salt
1/2 teaspoon crushed cardamom seeds
1/4 cup sugar
1 teaspoon vanilla extract
1/4 cup plumped golden raisins
1/2 cup shredded coconut
Chopped pistachios

• Combine half-and-half, rice, salt, cardamom and sugar in large saucepan. Bring to boil. Reduce heat, cover and simmer 30 to 40 minutes, until rice is tender.

• Stir in vanilla, raisins, coconut and 2 tablespoons chopped pistachios. Chill.

■ TAMARILLO SAUCE

3 tamarillos
1/4 cup sugar
1/4 cup water

• Cover tamarillos with boiling water and let stand 1 to 2 minutes. Plunge into cold water, then remove, peel and chop.

• Place tamarillo pulp in small saucepan with sugar and water. Bring to boil. Reduce heat and simmer until fruit is very soft, 15 to 20 minutes.

• Press fruit through strainer to remove seeds. Chill sauce. Makes about 1/2 cup.

• Serve pudding topped with Tamarillo Sauce and additional chopped pistachios.

4 to 6 servings. Each of 6 servings: 275 calories; 202 mg sodium; 12 mg cholesterol; 7 grams fat; 46 grams carbohydrates; 7 grams protein; 0.37 gram fiber.

BRIOCHE PUDDING

It seems that every time we turn around, someone is asking for another variation on bread pudding. This one from McCormick & Schmick restaurants is one of our favorites. Brioche is a rich, eggy French bread that is almost a pastry. If you can't find it, you can substitute Jewish challah.

---

3 to 4 (4-inch) brioche
6 egg yolks
1 teaspoon vanilla extract
1/2 cup sugar
3 cups whipping cream
6 tablespoons semisweet chocolate chips

• Cut brioche into 1/2-inch-thick crouton-size squares (you'll need about 40.) Toast in 350-degree oven 10 minutes. Set aside.

• Beat together egg yolks, vanilla and sugar in bowl.

• Scald cream in medium saucepan over medium heat. Pour 1 cup cream into egg mixture to temper, then return cream and egg mixture to saucepan. Cook over medium-low heat, stirring, until slightly thickened, about 3 to 4 minutes.

• Place 1 tablespoon chocolate chips and 6 or 7 croutons in each of 6 (6-ounce) ramekins.
• Pour custard over croutons and chocolate. Immerse croutons completely in custard. Place cups in baking pan filled halfway with hot water. Bake at 350 degrees until pudding is set, about 40 minutes.

---

6 servings. Each serving: 674 calories; 165 mg sodium; 437 mg cholesterol; 57 grams fat; 29 grams carbohydrates; 7 grams protein; 0 fiber.

MICROWAVE PEANUT BRITTLE

MAKING CANDY CAN BE DIFFICULT. Usually you have to monitor the temperature of sugar syrups or temper chocolate, but not with this recipe from reader Sharon Herdina of La Verne. What's truly remarkable is that it makes some of the best-tasting peanut brittle we've had. Cooking times will vary depending on your microwave. After the first 4 minutes of cooking, keep an eye on the brittle and judge it by its color, not microwave time.

1 cup sugar
1/2 cup light corn syrup
1 cup salted cocktail peanuts
1 tablespoon butter, plus more for greasing
1 teaspoon vanilla extract
1 teaspoon baking soda

• Stir together sugar and corn syrup in 2-quart glass casserole. Microwave on high 4 minutes until boiling. Stir well. Add peanuts and microwave on high until golden, 3 to 4 more minutes. Don't overcook; watch the color. Add butter and vanilla, blending well. Microwave on high 30 seconds to 1 minute 30 seconds. Peanuts will be lightly browned and syrup very hot. Add baking soda and stir until light and foamy.

• Quickly pour mixture onto greased baking sheet, spreading somewhat with rubber spatula. Cool completely, about 30 minutes to 1 hour. Brittle will harden fast. When cool, break into pieces and store in air-tight container.

8 servings. Each serving: 270 calories; 117 mg sodium; 4 mg cholesterol; 10 grams fat; 44 grams carbohydrates; 5 grams protein; 0.96 gram fiber.

OLD-FASHIONED STRAWBERRY SHORTCAKE

MOST OF THE STRAWBERRIES sold in the United States are grown in California. It's a fair bet that a good percentage of them wind up on shortcakes. This shortcake from Larry Forgione of New York's An American Place is the best we've ever had. The addition of the mashed egg yolks makes the biscuits richer without making them dense.

■ SHORTCAKE

2 cups flour, plus more for kneading
1/4 cup plus 1 tablespoon sugar
1 tablespoon plus 1/2 teaspoon baking powder
6 tablespoons butter, chilled and cut into small pieces
3/4 cup whipping cream
2 hard-boiled egg yolks, mashed
2 tablespoons melted butter

• Sift flour, 1/4 cup sugar and baking powder into bowl. Add chilled butter pieces. Using your fingertips, work butter quickly and lightly into flour until mixture is consistency of very fine crumbs of sand. Add cream and egg yolks and stir with fork until dough just comes together.

• Turn dough out onto floured work surface and knead briefly, just until smooth dough forms. Do not overwork. Pat or roll out dough to 3/4-inch thickness. Using floured 2 1/2- or 3-inch cookie cutter, cut out 4 rounds of dough. Gather up dough scraps, reroll and cut out 2 more rounds.

• Put rounds on lightly greased baking sheet. Brush with melted butter and sprinkle with remaining tablespoon sugar. Bake on middle rack of oven at 375 degrees until biscuits are golden brown and firm to the touch, 12 to 15 minutes.

• Transfer biscuits to cooling rack and cool 2 to 3 minutes.

■ FILLING AND ASSEMBLY

3 pints strawberries, washed, hulled and halved or quartered (depending on size)
2 tablespoons sugar
1 cup whipping cream
Toss strawberries and sugar together in bowl.
Whip cream several minutes until soft peaks form. Cover and refrigerate.

• Carefully split biscuits in half and set tops aside. Place bottom halves on dessert plates and heap strawberries onto them. Generously spoon whipped cream over strawberries and replace biscuit tops. Serve immediately with any remaining whipped cream on side.

6 servings. Each serving: 642 calories; 421 mg sodium; 208 mg cholesterol; 44 grams fat; 57 grams carbohydrates; 8 grams protein; 0.96 gram fiber.

PICKLED LEMON CHEESECAKE

WHAT CAN YOU DO with a pickled lemon? When pressed, staff writer Charles Perry came up with a number of dishes beyond the usual Middle Eastern stews. While this was one of the more unusual, it was also one of the best.

1995

To pickle a lemon or a lime, first wash and scrub it with water (there's often a thin layer of wax or other preservative on the peel). Make two cuts at right angles to each other from one end almost to the other, leaving enough uncut so that the fruit can be opened without falling apart, about 1/2 inch. Next, generously salt the exposed flesh, using at least 3 tablespoons per pound of lemons. Put the salted fruit in a big, clean jar and cover with fresh lemon juice or water. Lemon juice gives a better flavor, but resist the temptation to use bottled lemon juice, which gives an unpleasant metallic quality. Put on the lid and leave the jar at room temperature for four or five weeks. Pickled lemons should keep about one year in brine; they also freeze well.

■ PASTA FROLLA

3/4 cup flour

3 tablespoons sugar

3 tablespoons butter, at room temperature

1 egg

• Combine flour and sugar in mixing bowl. Cut butter into flour mixture until crumbly. Mix with egg. Knead just until mixture can be formed into ball. Cover with plastic wrap. Let stand 30 minutes at room temperature. Roll out pasta frolla and line 8-inch springform pan with dough.

■ CHEESECAKE

1 pound ricotta

1 cup sugar

3 eggs

2 pickled lemons, or 3 pickled limes, seeded and diced

3 tablespoons flour

• While dough is resting, combine ricotta, sugar and eggs in mixing bowl. Add diced lemons. Stir in flour and mix well.

• Pour in ricotta mixture. Bake at 375 degrees until slightly set in center, about 40 minutes. Remove from oven. Let stand 30 minutes before slicing or removing from pan. When cool, refrigerate.

8 servings. Each serving: 457 calories; 166 mg sodium; 195 mg cholesterol; 19 grams fat; 60 grams carbohydrates; 15 grams protein; 0.05 gram fiber.

SCOTCH-CARAMEL ICE CREAM

1994

A COUPLE OF TASTERS called this recipe by Campanile's Nancy Silverton the best ice cream they had ever eaten. It's not too icky sweet, yet it's got a luscious flavor and texture that makes it difficult to put down.

1 pound sugar
1 vanilla bean
1 1/2 cups Scotch
4 cups milk
4 cups whipping cream
16 egg yolks

• Place sugar, vanilla bean and Scotch in large pot and cook until dark caramel color. Add milk and cream and bring to boil. Remove from heat. Let stand 30 minutes. Bring mixture again to boil and pour over egg yolks while whisking. Strain through fine mesh strainer into bowl. Whisk to release heat until cool. Chill.

• Freeze in ice cream maker according to manufacturer's instructions.

1/2 gallon. Each 1/2 cup: 456 calories; 64 mg sodium; 360 mg cholesterol; 32 grams fat; 32 grams carbohydrates; 8 grams protein; 0 fiber.

WILD BLUEBERRY BUCKLE

A BUCKLE IS AN OLD-FASHIONED dessert, kin to cobblers, slumps and pandowdys. In effect, it is an upside-down cake with the fruit in the middle. "To make a buckle," Staff Writer Charles Perry wrote, "you mix fruit (usually berries) into the pudding dough and bake it, usually with a streusel topping. The result is like a rich, fruity coffee cake. In some recipes, the fruit is arranged on top of the dough and sinks into it while baking. There's no persuasive explanation for the name 'buckle,' though maybe people thought it looked as if it were buckling when the fruit sank."

1996

■ BUCKLE

3/4 cup sugar
1/4 cup shortening
1 egg
2 cups flour
1/2 teaspoon salt
2 teaspoons baking powder
1/2 cup milk
2 cups blueberries

• Cream sugar and shortening by beating until fluffy, then beat in egg.
• Sift together flour, salt and baking powder. Add to shortening alternately with milk. Blend in blueberries and pour into buttered and floured 8x6-inch oval baking dish.

■ STREUSEL

1/2 cup sugar
1/2 teaspoon cinnamon
1/3 cup flour
1/4 cup (1/2 stick) butter
• Mix sugar, cinnamon, flour and butter and sprinkle over top of buckle. Bake at 375 degrees until top is browned, about 45 minutes.

6 to 8 servings. Each of 8 servings: 388 calories; 330 mg sodium; 43 mg cholesterol; 14 grams fat; 63 grams carbohydrates; 5 grams protein; 0.57 gram fiber.

FOURTEEN

Miscellaneous

RED PEPPER SAUCE

1987

FOR YEARS, ALICE'S RESTAURANT, located at the base of the Malibu Pier, was known throughout Southern California for being one of the few beachfront dining places where the food was as good as the view. This versatile sauce can be used on seafood, pork, poultry or pasta.

3 tablespoons olive oil
1 tablespoon minced garlic
1 tablespoon minced shallots
2 large red bell peppers, seeded and diced
1 tablespoon tomato paste
1 teaspoon minced fresh thyme or 1/2 teaspoon dried thyme
1/2 cup dry white wine
1 cup chicken stock
1 cup whipping cream
Salt

• Heat oil in large saucepan. Add garlic and shallots and saute until shallots are translucent. Add peppers, tomato paste and thyme. Cook 2 minutes, stirring constantly. Add wine. Bring to boil. Boil 1 minute, then add chicken stock. Bring to boil. Continue to boil until sauce is reduced by 1/2. Add whipping cream.

• Bring to gentle simmer until reduced again by 1/2. Remove from heat and puree in blender. Strain through fine strainer. Season to taste with salt. Serve as desired.

2 1/2 cups sauce. Each tablespoon: 34 calories; 30 mg sodium; 8 mg cholesterol; 3 grams fat; 1 gram carbohydrates; 0 protein; 0.03 gram fiber.

CHRISTMAS
BREAD *and* BUTTER PICKLES

TEST KITCHEN INTERN Gordon McKnight adapted this recipe from the 1951 edition of "Joy of Cooking" by Irma S. Rombauer and Marion Rombauer Becker. The combination of green and red in these pickles will remind you of Christmas. Process them in 12-ounce jars and give as gifts. The red bell peppers (green or yellow work fine too) add a bit of sharpness to a smooth and sweet pickle that has been modestly tempered by using both brown and white sugars.

About 4 pounds pickling cucumbers, cut into 1/4-inch-thick slices
6 to 8 onions (3 to 3 1/2 pounds), cut into 1/4-inch-thick slices
4 red bell peppers, cut in 3/4-inch dice
1/2 cup coarse salt
5 cups white wine vinegar
3 cups granulated sugar
2 cups brown sugar, lightly packed
1 1/2 teaspoons turmeric
1 teaspoon ground allspice
2 tablespoons mustard seeds
1 teaspoon ground cloves
1 (1-inch) stick cinnamon

• Place cucumbers, onions and peppers in large bowl. Top with salt and cover with weighted lid. Refrigerate 3 hours. (This softens vegetables so they can absorb syrup.) Place vegetables in colander and thoroughly rinse off salt.

• Combine vinegar, granulated and brown sugars, turmeric, allspice, mustard seeds, cloves and cinnamon in large stockpot and bring to boil over medium-high heat. Slowly add vegetables with very little stirring. Heat to scalding point, but do not boil, 5 to 7 minutes.

• Divide vegetables among 6 (12-ounce) jars, cover with liquid, leaving 1/2-inch head space. Remove air bubbles by sliding a nonmetallic spatula down side of jar and press gently on the food to release any trapped air. Close with two-piece caps. Can according to instructions.

Makes about 6 (12-ounce) jars. Each of 30 servings: 40 calories; 239 mg sodium; 0 cholesterol; 0 fat; 9 grams carbohydrates; 1 gram protein; 0.67 gram fiber.

CRANBERRY-ORANGE RELISH

SEVERAL YEARS AGO WE CHALLENGED a couple of Test Kitchen interns, Rommel Delos Santos and Andy Broder, to come up with a California-influenced Thanksgiving dinner menu. This combination of cranberries and oranges was not unexpected, but the lift this recipe gets from the red onion and cilantro certainly was.

1 (3/4-pound) package cranberries
1 cup sugar
1 cup water
6 oranges, peeled and cut in sections
1/2 red onion, thinly sliced
1/3 cup cilantro, coarsely chopped
2 1/2 tablespoons olive oil
2 tablespoons white vinegar
Salt, pepper

• Bring cranberries, sugar and water to boil in saucepan and simmer 15 minutes until cranberries are cooked to thick sauce. Transfer to bowl to cool. When cooled, add oranges, onion, cilantro, oil, vinegar and salt and pepper to taste. Mix well. Chill until ready to serve.

4 cups. Each 1/4-cup serving: 104 calories, 19 mg sodium, 0 cholesterol, 2 grams fat, 22 grams carbohydrates, 1 gram protein, 0.47 gram fiber.

CUCUMBER KIMCHI
(*Oi Sobaegi Kimchi*)

1999

UNLESS YOU'RE KOREAN, you may never have thought about making your own kimchi. But it's not difficult, as this recipe by writer Cecilia Hae-Jin Lee demonstrates, and the results can be spectacular. Buchu, or wild leeks, can be found in Korean markets.

1/2 gallon plus 1/3 cup water
3/4 cup plus 1 tablespoon salt
20 Asian pickling cucumbers
1 head garlic, cloves separated and peeled
1 onion, cut into 1/2-inch dice
1 bunch green onions, sliced into 1/2-inch lengths
1 bunch Korean buchu, cut into 1/2-inch pieces
1/2 cup Korean ground chile
1 teaspoon sugar plus 1 teaspoon, optional

• Mix 1/2 gallon water with 3/4 cup salt, stirring for salt to dissolve. Soak cucumbers in salt water about 30 minutes. (Be careful not to soak too long.) Remove cucumbers and rinse. Cut about 1/4 inch from each end of cucumbers. Cut cucumbers in half in middle, not lengthwise.

• Hold cucumber facing circular middle. Cut in half lengthwise, leaving about 1/2 inch at end uncut. Cut in half lengthwise again, perpendicular to your first cut, leaving the end uncut. You should have 4 semi-equal parts of cucumber, cut but still attached. Repeat with remaining cucumbers.

• Place garlic in a food processor or blender and mince. Combine onion, green onions, buchu, garlic, ground chile, 1 tablespoon salt and 1 teaspoon optional sugar in large bowl. (If mixing with your hands, be sure to wear rubber gloves to avoid chile burn.)

• Set 3 (1-quart) jars on work surface. Using your fingers, separate cucumber quarters and stuff mix into cucumbers. Divide evenly among jars, pressing cucumbers down firmly into jars. Stir 1 teaspoon sugar into 1/3 cup water until sugar is completely dissolved. Pour sugar water over cucumbers.

• Let sit 1 day before serving. Cucumber kimchi ferments very quickly.

• Refrigerate after opening.

3 quarts. Each 1/4 cup: 10 calories; 0 sodium; 0 cholesterol; 0 fat; 2 grams carbohydrates; 0 protein; 0.45 gram fiber.

FRESH PLUM SAUCE

SPICY PLUM SAUCE is to Chinese roast duck what mustard is to ham in American cooking. And just as with mustard, few people would ever consider making their own from scratch. But this recipe by John Sharpe, chef-owner of the Newport Beach restaurant Aysia 101, is convincingly better than store-bought plum sauce. It is quite nice with grilled foods, such as shrimp or pork.

1 pound red plums, quartered
1 cup sugar
1 (2-inch) piece ginger root, sliced into 4 pieces
2 tablespoons vinegar
Salt
Cold water

• Place plums, sugar, ginger root, vinegar and pinch of salt in nonreactive pan. Cook over low heat until thick and syrupy, about 1 hour.

• Cool at room temperature about 45 minutes.

• Puree in food processor. Thin with a little cold water if sauce is too thick. Serve as dipping sauce.

1 1/2 cups. Each tablespoon: 42 calories; 10 mg sodium; 0 cholesterol; 0 fat; 11 grams carbohydrates; 0 protein; 0.11 gram fiber.

SALSA

SALSA IS THE KETCHUP of Southern California. Each cook has his or her own version. But we especially like this recipe from reader Laura Vera for the smokiness lent by the sauteed chiles de arbol. You can make this with as few as 6 chiles de arbol, depending on heat desired.

1 teaspoon oil
13 dried chiles de arbol
1 1/2 large tomatoes, peeled
1/4 onion, diced
1 clove garlic
1/2 teaspoon salt

• Heat oil in small skillet and saute chiles few minutes. Place in blender with tomatoes, onion, garlic and salt. Puree.

2 cups. Each tablespoon: 14 calories; 51 mg sodium; 0 cholesterol; 0 fat; 3 grams carbohydrates; 1 gram protein; 0.97 gram fiber.

CILANTRO-MINT CHUTNEY

WRITER MIRA ADVANI contributed this delicious chutney for a story on Diwali, India's festival of lights.

1 bunch cilantro, leaves only
1/2 bunch mint, leaves only
2 serrano chiles, seeded
1 small onion, diced
2 cloves garlic
Juice of 2 lemons
Salt

• Chop cilantro, mint, chiles, onion and garlic in food processor or blender. Add lemon juice. Process until finely ground. Season to taste with salt.

1 cup. Each tablespoon: 6 calories; 19 mg sodium; 0 cholesterol; 0 fat; 1 gram carbohydrates; 0 protein; 0.11 gram fiber.

MOM PARSONS' CRANBERRIES

We first published this old family recipe from Food Editor Russ Parsons before Thanksgiving in 1992. It has become an annual ritual in the food section. Every October, we start taking calls from readers who ask whether we plan to run it again. We always do.

1 1/2 cups sugar
3/4 cup water
3 cloves
3 allspice berries
2 (3-inch) cinnamon sticks
1 (12-ounce) bag fresh cranberries
Grated zest of 1 orange

• Bring sugar, water, cloves, allspice and cinnamon sticks to boil in 4-quart saucepan. Cook, stirring, until syrup is clear, about 3 minutes. Add cranberries and cook just until they begin to pop, about 5 minutes.

• Remove from heat, add grated orange zest and cool. Refrigerate 1 to 3 days before serving. Remove cloves, allspice and cinnamon sticks before serving.

2 1/2 cups relish. Each 1/4-cup serving: 132 calories; 1 mg sodium; 0 cholesterol; 0 fat; 35 grams carbohydrates; 0 protein; 0.41 gram fiber.

SESAME-THYME DIP
(*Za'tar Bi-Zait*)

THIS RECIPE FROM STAFF WRITER Charles Perry should appeal to people who like to dip their bread in olive oil. The ideal thyme for it is the Middle Eastern variety called za'-tar, which has a wild, resinous aroma. It is rarely sold by itself in Middle Eastern markets, but is usually mixed with the sour purple spice sumac (a mixture which itself is confusingly called za'tar)—or with toasted sesame seeds for this exact dip. However, many Lebanese prefer more sesame in the mix than the usual store brands have, and you can use any thyme.

1/4 cup sesame seeds
1/2 cup dried thyme leaves
1/2 teaspoon salt
1/2 cup plus 2 tablespoons extra virgin olive oil, or more to taste

• Toast sesame seeds in small dry skillet set over low heat, stirring a few times, until fragrant and light brown, 6 to 7 minutes. Set aside.

• Using mortar and pestle or spice grinder, grind thyme fine. Mix with sesame seeds and salt. Blend with olive oil.

• To serve, put small amount on plate and scoop up with bread.

3/4 cup. Each tablespoon: 120 calories; 99 mg sodium; 0 cholesterol; 13 grams fat; 2 grams carbohydrates; 1 gram protein; 0.40 gram fiber

SEVEN-LAYER MEXICAN DIP

IT'S HARD TO IMAGINE a Southern California cookbook without some kind of layered bean dip. They may not be trendy, but we'll bet most everyone has a bean dip recipe or two squirreled away. This one was developed by Test Kitchen Director Donna Deane and interns Jana Lieblich and Julianne Tantum.

1 (1-pound) can low-fat refried black beans
2 avocados
1 to 2 tablespoons lemon juice
1 (1 1/4-ounce) package taco seasoning
1 (8-ounce) carton sour cream
1/4 pound sharp Cheddar cheese, shredded
1/4 pound Monterey Jack cheese, shredded
1 cup chunky-style salsa
3 to 4 green onions, chopped
1 (4 1/4-ounce) can black olives, chopped

• Spread beans in bottom of 8-inch square glass baking dish.

• Mash avocados and mix with lemon juice. Spread on top of beans.

• Mix taco seasoning into sour cream and spread on top of avocado mixture. Sprinkle grated cheeses over sour cream. Spread salsa over cheese. Sprinkle green onions over salsa. Sprinkle olives over all. Bake at 350 degrees until hot and bubbly, 40 to 45 minutes.

6 1/2 cups. Each tablespoon: 31 calories; 94 mg sodium; 4 mg cholesterol; 2 grams fat; 2 grams carbohydrates; 1 gram protein; 0.40 grams fiber.

THE BIG AIOLI

AIOLI IS A PUNGENT, garlic-flavored mayonnaise-like mixture from the south of France. This version comes from chef Alain Giraud of Citrus and then Lavande restaurants. He recommends using it as the center of a big party buffet, garnished with the likes of hard-boiled eggs and lots of blanched vegetables, such as green beans, artichokes, cauliflower and potatoes. You can also serve it with plain cooked seafood, such as mussels and shrimp.

1 baking potato, peeled and diced
Saffron
Kosher salt
8 cloves garlic
4 egg yolks
2 cups extra-virgin olive oil
1 cup vegetable oil
Juice of 1 lemon

• All ingredients should be at room temperature. Cook potato in medium saucepan with water to cover, dash saffron and dash salt until very tender, about 15 minutes. Strain and pass through sieve or fine strainer. Keep warm.

• Halve garlic cloves and remove green parts. Crush garlic in mortar with dash salt until consistency of smooth paste. Add warm potato puree and mix. Add egg yolks and mix. Combine olive oil and vegetable oil and add slowly, drop at a time, whisking constantly, until consistency of thick mayonnaise. You may not need all of oil. Stir in lemon juice and salt to taste. Refrigerate until ready to serve.

• Place aioli in bowl in center of large tray and arrange garnishes on tray.

24 servings. Each serving: 332 calories; 12 mg sodium; 44 mg cholesterol; 34 grams fat; 2 grams carbohydrates; 1 gram protein; 0.04 gram fiber.

TZATZIKI

EVERY COUNTRY HAS ITS DIP and tzatziki is Greece's. Surprisingly, this recipe came from Los Angeles restaurateur Hans Rockenwagner, who is not Greek but German. Serve this light, zesty dish with bread, crackers or crudites.

1 cup plain nonfat yogurt
1/2 cucumber, peeled, seeded and grated
1 tablespoon minced dill
1 tablespoon minced mint
3 cloves garlic, minced
1 teaspoon salt
White pepper

• Combine yogurt, cucumber, dill, mint, garlic, salt and white pepper to taste. Chill 1 hour to allow flavors to blend.

1 1/4 cups. Each tablespoon: 7 calories; 126 mg sodium; 0 cholesterol; 0 fat; 1 gram carbohydrates; 1 gram protein; 0.05 gram fiber.

PESTO

1985

IN 1985, PESTO WAS something brand new. This recipe by longtime Southern California restaurateur Celestino Drago was the winning entry in the second annual Pesto Cookoff in Malibu. At the time, Drago was chef at the landmark Melrose Avenue Italian restaurant Chianti. Since, he has opened a half-dozen places of his own.

3/4 teaspoon coarse salt
1 ounce pine nuts
1 ounce garlic
3 ounces small basil leaves
3/4 ounce grated Pecorino cheese
1 1/4 ounces grated Parmigiano Reggiano cheese
1/2 cup extra-virgin olive oil

• Using marble mortar and wooden pestle, mash together salt, pine nuts and garlic. Blend in basil to make coarse paste. Gradually add cheeses and oil.

1 cup. Each tablespoon: 78 calories; 156 mg sodium; 2 mg cholesterol; 8 grams fat; 1 gram carbohydrates; 1 gram protein; 0.02 gram fiber.

INDEX

Note: Page numbers in **boldface** indicate one of the L.A. Times Best Recipes of the Year.

OTHER BOOKS FROM THE LOS ANGELES TIMES

LOW-FAT KITCHEN
by Donna Deane
     From the pages of the *Los Angeles Times* Food Section come more than 110 recipes that use fresh food flavor, not fat, to satisfy your taste buds. $20.45

SOS RECIPES 30 YEARS OF REQUESTS
by Rose Dosti
     This best-selling hard-cover book offers hundreds of tried-and-true recipes for all-time favorite dishes that literally range from soup to nuts. $19.45

DRAWING THE LINE
by Paul Conrad
     Two hundred drawings, spanning the period from the late 1960s to President Clinton's impeachment trial, from America's premier political cartoonist. $25.45

ETERNALLY YOURS
by Jack Smith
     Who can forget Jack Smith, the Los Angeles Times' columnist for nearly 40 years? When he died in 1996, we all lost a treasure. But at least his words survived. In this volume, Jack's widow, Denise, and his sons, Curt and Doug, have collected some of their favorite columns, including those that explain Jack's life as well as his death. $16.95

IMAGINING LOS ANGELES PHOTOGRAPHS OF A 20TH CENTURY CITY
     More than 175 photographs tell the story of Los Angeles' coming of age in the 20th Century. With a foreword by celebrated author Ray Bradbury. Hardcover. $28.95

CURBSIDE L.A. AN OFFBEAT GUIDE TO THE CITY OF ANGELS
by Cecilia Rasmussen
     Enjoy a truly eclectic tour of Los Angeles. Explore the L.A. you've not seen with enticing excursions into the city's peerless history and diversity. $19.45

DAY HIKERS' GUIDE TO SOUTHERN CALIFORNIA
by John McKinney
     Walks in Southern California, from the simply scenic to the challenging, as described by Los Angeles Times hiking columnist and author John McKinney. $16.45

52 WEEKS IN THE CALIFORNIA GARDEN
by Robert Smaus
     How to make the most of your garden by the foremost authority on gardening in Southern California. $17.45

HIGH EXPOSURE / HOLLYWOOD LIVES FOUND PHOTOS FROM THE ARCHIVES OF THE LOS ANGELES TIMES
by Amanda Parsons
     In this beautiful hardcover book you'll see photographs of Marilyn Monroe, Liz Taylor, Mae West, Jane Russell, Frank Sinatra, Rita Hayworth, Errol Flynn and scores more stars at the height, and sometimes the depth, of their Hollywood lives. $29.95

L.A. UNCONVENTIONAL
by Cecilia Rasmussen
   Where some people see roadblocks, others,
such as the men and women in this volume, see
possibility, opportunity and excitement. $30.95

LAST OF THE BEST
90 COLUMNS FROM THE 1990s BY
THE LATE JIM MURRAY
   The best of Jim's columns from the last
decade of his life are included in this paperback
volume compiled by Times Sports Editor Bill
Dwyre and featuring a foreword by Dodger legend Tommy Lasorda. $19.45

THE GREAT ONES
by Jim Murray
   The top men and women of the sports world
written about as only this late, great sports
columnist could. Foreword by Arnold Palmer.
$24.45

LAKER GLORY
THE 2000 NBA CHAMPIONS
   Relive the team's awe-inspiring 1999-2000
season. With eye-popping photos from the Los
Angeles Times. $18.95

To order, call (800) 246-4042 or
visit our web site at
http://www.latimes.com/bookstore